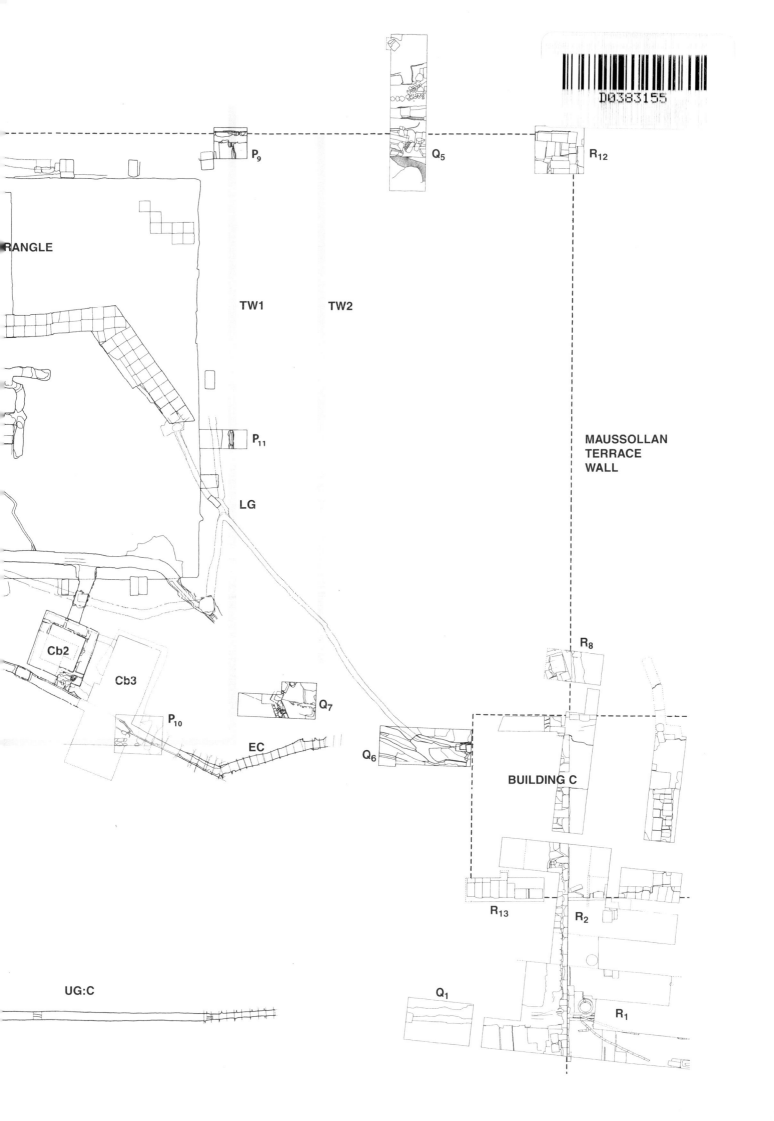

P_9

Q_5

R_12

RANGLE

TW1

TW2

MAUSSOLLAN
TERRACE
WALL

P_11

LG

R_8

Cb2

Cb3

Q_7

P_10

EC

Q_6

BUILDING C

R_13

R_2

UG:C

Q_1

R_1

Subterranean and pre-Maussollan structures on the site of the Maussolleion

The finds from the tomb chamber of Maussollos

THE MAUSSOLLEION AT HALIKARNASSOS

Reports of the Danish Archaeological Expedition to Bodrum

volume 6

SUBTERRANEAN AND PRE-MAUSSOLLAN STRUCTURES ON THE SITE OF THE MAUSSOLLEION

The finds from the tomb chamber of Maussollos

by Jan Zahle and Kjeld Kjeldsen

with contributions by Despina Ignatiadou and Vinnie Nørskov

Jutland Archaeological Society Publications XV:6, 2004

In Commission at Aarhus University Press

THE MAUSSOLLEION AT HALIKARNASSOS
Subterranean and pre-Maussollan structures
on the site of the Maussolleion

Jan Zahle & Kjeld Kjeldsen © 2004

ISBN 87-88415-16-3
ISSN 0107-2854

Pre-press: Narayana Press
Reproduction of plans: F. Henriksen's Eftf. A/S

Cover: Kristian Jeppesen
Linguistic revision: P.J. Crabb
Printed by: Narayana Press

Type: Baskerville 11/13,5
Paper: Arctic Silk, 130 g.

Published by
Jutland Archaeological Society
Moesgaard
DK-8270 Højbjerg

Distributed through
Aarhus University Press
Langelandsgade 177
DK-8200 Aarhus N

The publication of this book has been
supported by The Carlsberg Foundation

Contents

Preface

This volume reports on the work in 1972, 1973, 1974 and 1976 concerning the pre-Maussollan and subterranean structures in the close vicinity of the Maussolleion proper. Moreover, the remaining parts of the small finds from the tomb chamber of Maussollos are finally published.

Thanks to the excavations in 1857-1858 and 1865 by C.T. Newton and his collaborators, the existence of several chambers, walls and galleries was well known – as was also the inadequacy of the documentation of the structures in question. For good reason, therefore, the evidence has hardly entered into the debate on the history of the site or on Carian archaeology.

Prof. Kristian Jeppesen generously assigned the investigation of these remains to Jan Zahle. Architect Kjeld Kjeldsen was responsible for the architectural recording. The work was initiated in 1972 concurrently with completion of the re-emptying of the Maussolleion cutting – the Quadrangle. In order to complete the task of excavation and of recording more than 300 m of subterranean galleries, we were assisted by our collaborators, the archaeologist Poul Pedersen and the architect Henrik Hoffmeyer. Several of our Turkish workmen proved invaluable. Especially Naci Özdağlı deserves to be mentioned.

Important new evidence on the site proper has already been published in the 1st and 4th volumes of this series concerning both features in the ground and strata that have survived the spoliation by the Hospitallers, and Newton's investigation – and depredation. His 'Western Staircase', in fact, turned out to belong to the well-defined tomb of Maussollos, as he believed, but was not able to prove. This structure, therefore, forms no part of this volume (see Flemming Højlund and Kristian Jeppesen in *The Maussolleion at Halikarnassos* 1, 1981 and 4, 2000), although it is discussed in connection with the subterranean

drain, the Lower Gallery that surrounds the Quadrangle. This, however, is presented in the present volume, because it was – for the similarity of the features – studied together with the other subterranean galleries, the aqueduct and corridors. Other structures, as well, may be Maussollan, but were in 1972 rather expected to be pre-Maussollan. At least they formed no part of the Maussolleion building proper.

During the work in the early 1970s the great importance of the pottery finds was also realized. Not only were several contexts excavated in layers firmly dated *ante quem* the building of the Maussolleion c. 350 BC, but also exquisite small finds from the burial of Maussollos were carefully excavated in a small, well-defined, albeit disturbed area.

In 1982 and 1986 the present authors worked in Bodrum on the finds, and the work with regard to the main bulk of pottery has now been completed by John Lund, Vinnie Nørskov and Leif Erik Vaag in the volume *The Maussolleion at Halikarnassos* 7, 2002. In the present volume are treated the remaining small finds: the highly important, albeit very fragmented remains of glass, bone, pottery and alabaster from the burial of Maussollos.

Unfortunately, also the work on the pre-Maussollan structures has taken too long. This is partly due to other obligations, but there is also a scholarly reason. Although much new evidence turned up during the excavation, it also became clear that much, perhaps crucial evidence was lost forever because of the previous spoliations. The evidence and the 'network' of relative chronologies of structures appeared to be contradictory. And this lack of consistency and thereby of meaning could not – despite several essays over the years – be changed and solved, and was felt like a prohibition.

But fortunately, the situation has improved

considerably after all evidence from Newton's and our own investigations has finally been scrutinized and worked through with a view to publication. Certain arguments, though, depend more on careful reading of texts than on archaeological evidence. Certain uncertainties remain, and some of them could perhaps be removed by means of supplementary soundings.

Besides the reasons enumerated above, a major reason for 'loose ends' in the conclusion – we believe – lies in the fact that the Hecatomnid planning of the site appears to have been changed within a few decades. A fairly modest adjustment of pre-existing structures seems to have evolved into a huge tomb-building enterprise on an immense terrace. Our methods of the 1970s could not overcome the damage from several spoliations, and we could hardly find evidence to distinguish between phases separated by even only a few years.

Our foremost thanks go to the Carlsberg Foundation that has funded our work throughout, including recent supplementary studies in the British Museum, the Department of Greek and Roman Antiquities, and in the Archaeological Museum in Bodrum. We are most grateful to Dr. Brian Cook, Dr. Ian Jenkins and Dr. Neil Adams for generous help. The Turkish Antiquities Department and the director of Bodrum Museum, Dr. Oğuz Alpösen, has furthered our work throughout.

During the writing of the book we profited from many conversations – sometimes heated! – with Vinnie Nørskov, Leif Erik Vaag, John Lund, and Poul Pedersen, author of *The Maussolleion at Halikarnassos* 3, 1991 and since the 1970s deeply concerned with the archaeology of Halikarnassos. The publication of this volume will hardly constitute the final word on the crucial years, 375-350 BC, at the Maussolleion site.

Last but not least we wish to thank Prof. Kristian Jeppesen for his confidence and his interest in our work. This final volume on the excavations, which he initiated in 1966 after many years of work and thinking on the Maussolleion, is certainly an appropriate tribute for his 80th birthday, December 2004.

1. The site of the Maussolleion and its study with regard to pre-Maussollan remains Status quo 1970

The excavation of the Maussolleion site by Charles Thomas Newton (1816-1894) and his assistant, Robert Murdoch Smith (1835-1900), lasted about one year, from 27th December 1856 until February 1858. Lieutenant Murdoch Smith of the Royal Engineers headed a small contingent of English sappers, two of whom, Corporal Benjamin L. Spackman and Lance-Corporal J. H. MacCartney, acted as photographers. Corporal William Jenkins was "Stonekeeper and general Superintendant" or "usbaschi" of the up to c. 130 Turkish workmen who were employed at the same time. From 28th August 1857 the architect Richard Popplewell Pullan (1825-1888) joined the expedition. During the excavation period they managed to explore the Maussolleion foundation cutting – the Quadrangle – together with the subterranean galleries and pre-Maussollan structures on its west, east and south sides. Moreover, they established the course of the peribolos wall of the huge Maussolleion terrace on two sides, to the north and east.

Unfortunately, logistic obstacles and Newton's major interest in museum pieces resulted in the failure to have the area of the Maussolleion laid bare at the same time. The inhabitants only reluctantly sold their houses (four in the Quadrangle proper, and eight in its immediate neighbourhood) – or they refused – so huge amounts of soil had to be temporarily placed, which rendered impossible a comprehensive view of the site. Compare Newton: *the expense of the excavation was very great; for their being no convenient manner of disposing of the earth and rubble as it was dug out, it had to be piled up in mounds, which interfered with a proper survey of the ground.*[1] Consequently, progress was sometimes made by means of sinking pits and driving mines – most often, but not always – followed by clearance.

Not least, however, the excavation strategy adopted by Newton contributed to the deficiencies in the recording of the site. Already in the months before starting at the Maussolleion, Newton had decided how to excavate: *The mode of excavating which Mr. Newton has found most economical is to dig a trench to a certain depth and carry this forward always throwing the earth behind thereby covering the part already dug.*[2] By this means the prime objective of the fieldwork, to secure sculptures for the British Museum, could be obtained. Fortunately, however, the strategy, so common in the period, did not preclude many useful topographical and stratigraphical observations, as will be shown below.

Because a considerable part of the area surrounding the Quadrangle could not be excavated in 1857-1858, Newton had arranged a supplementary campaign in Bodrum with the dual purpose of finding more sculptures from the Maussolleion and of determining the size of the Maussolleion terrace. G.M. Alfred Biliotti, together with Auguste Salzmann (1824-1872), conducted excavations there between 1st March and 2nd September 1865. Biliotti's diary shows him to be an experienced excavator, who throughout notes stratigraphy in relation to finds and structures.

The documentation of the fieldwork in 1857 and 1865 consists of diaries and contemporary letters and reports, as well as the prompt publications and accounts in 1862 and 1865:

- Murdoch Smith, R. 1856-58, *Diary* Wednesday *8th, October 1856 – March 1858*, unpublished manuscript, owned by H.M. Harvey-Jamieson, Edinburgh.
- Murdoch Smith, R. 1856-59, *Letters no. 43-80 to Sir John Burgoyne, et al., Nov. 26/1856 – May 11/1859*, manuscript, owned by H.M. Harvey-Jamieson, Edinburgh. Partially published in W.K. Dickson, *The Life of Major-General Sir*

Robert Murdoch Smith, Edinburgh & London 1901: 23-117.

- Newton, C.T. 1858, *Papers respecting the Excavations at Budrum 1-16*, pp. 52, Dec. 1856 – Dec. 1857, London.
- Towsey, Captain, *Narrative of the Expedition by Sir Charles Thomas Newton to Asia Minor in 1856-57*, MS pp. 135. in the library of the Department of Greek and Roman Antiquities, British Museum.
- Newton, C.T. 1859, *Further Papers respecting the Excavations at Budrum and Cnidus 1-17*, pp. 101, Dec. 1857 – July 1859, London.
- Biliotti, G.M.A. 1865, *Diary of the Excavations on the Site of the Mausoleum*, manuscript in the British Museum. Published by P. Pedersen 1991,1: 118-173.
- Newton, C.T. 1862, *A History of Discoveries at Halicarnassus, Cnidus and Branchidae*, London: Ch. IV-V, p. 86-156, Pl. I-XV, LX on the site and selected finds. (Ch. VI-VIII with pl. XVI-XXXI deals with the reconstruction of the Maussolleion.)
- Pullan, R.P., *Drawings and Plans of Discoveries at Halicarnassus etc. 1856-1859*, British Library, ref. no. *Additional Ms 31,980*. Pullan's original drawings and watercolours as well as photographs from the excavations. Most of the latter, as well as a few others, are kept also in the Department of Greek and Roman Antiquities, British Museum.
- Newton, C.T. 1865, *Travels and Discoveries in the Levant*, Vol. 2, London: 57-146.

The character of the written information varies according to the purpose – diaries, semi-official letters, official reports, etc. As part of his work, Murdoch Smith executed both plans and sections of the Quadrangle (Figs. 1.2.1, 3 and Pl.1) (including the galleries) that were used in *P, FP, HD* and *TD*. Only a few weeks after his arrival, Pullan started surveying the subterranean structures, and he also produced several watercolours (Plates 2-12).

Newton had many photographs made in Bodrum, Knidos, and Didyma, as well as during several excursions, and his extensive use of this kind of documentation was progressive for the time.[3] Their purpose varies. Some record the single finds, some were meant to convey general impressions of the sites during the work (Fig. 1.2.2), and some show landscapes around the places of the discoveries. Newton used the new medium for his almost monthly official reports home and also for the publications. Murdoch Smith often includes photographs in his letters to Sir John Burgoyne, and most of the existing photographs in the BM can be identified from his careful descriptions. However, not all photographs were mentioned, and more photographs were taken than seem to be preserved.

For our purpose, however, it is disappointing that only one single photograph documents the pre-Maussollan structures, Fig. 4.1.1. In his *Papers* and *Further Papers* Newton sent tracings from drawings by Pullan to convey an impression of these important monuments. Together with several photographs, they were engraved for the publication in 1862.

An overview of the preserved pictorial documentation from the British investigations of the site and the pre-Maussollan structures is given in the table, p. 23-28. The exact dating of several of the drawings contributes to the reconstruction of the course of the excavation.

1.1. Dictionary of structures, terminology, abbreviations

The dictionary partly conforms with that adopted in the previous volumes of the Danish Halicarnassus excavation, partly specifies several more terms, together with their abbreviations. The latter are specified on the plans of the site, Fly-leaf, Figs. 3.1.1 and 6.0.1.

- *The Quadrangle* The foundation cutting of the Maussolleion, measuring roughly 32.5 m N-S and 38.5 m E-W.
- *The tomb of Maussollos* **MauTb** The western staircase, landing, corridor and chamber cut at right-angles to the west side of the Quadrangle. Højlund 1981: 25, published the recent excavation in the staircase. Jeppesen 2000: 37, published the tomb structure proper.

Along the four sides of the Quadrangle are situated altogether:
- *18 pillars* **P1-P18** Published by Jeppesen 2000: 45, 52 with Fig. 6.1.

10

Three subterranean structures partly overlap the south line of the Quadrangle. They are referred to as 'chambers', despite their more complex character and the fact that the third was more an open courtyard. They are roughly parallel to one another and differently oriented than the Quadrangle:

- *Chamber 1* **Cb1** The structure comprises a staircase of 18 steps, a landing and a chamber. From the lower steps of the staircase a doorway opened into the aqueduct, UG:B1 (see below), and through the
- *Main Corridor* **MC** one could reach the two following structures. Through a shaft there was access from above.
- *Chamber 2* **Cb2** Subterranean chamber with a doorway from the Main Corridor and access to the UG:B2.
- *Chamber 3* **Cb3** An open space or courtyard with an entrance from the south and communicating with the Main Corridor and the
- *East Corridor* **EC** through which there was access to Cb3 from an unknown point to the east.

A terrace ashlar wall, facing east and south, runs along the east and south sides of the Quadrangle.
- **TW1e** on the east side, about 2.75 m from the Quadrangle.
- **TW1s** on the south side, about 13.60 m from the Quadrangle.

Newton also established the existence of another terrace wall c. 7 m to the east of TW1e:
- **TW2** This was not re-excavated as a part of the recent studies.

Newton and Murdoch Smith investigated what they believed to be three different subterranean galleries (aqueducts, corridors): the Lower Gallery, the Upper Gallery and the Short Gallery. The first two designations have for the sake of convenience been retained for two structures. The Short Gallery, however, forms a part of the Upper Gallery, and the term is now obsolete. Moreover, parts of Newton's Upper Gallery are here treated in connection with the three subterranean structures which they served as corridors. The designation 'gallery' will be used as a generic term for them all.

- *The Lower Gallery* **LG** is a flat-bottomed drain with 1) a central, ashlar-built axis with a subterranean outlet in the SE, and 2) subterranean branches encircling the Quadrangle and joining the axis. The narrow, built channels within the Quadrangle were by Newton appropriately termed "The Marble Drain" and "The Rag-Stone Drain". Jeppesen 2000: 88, studies The Marble Drain. 10 shafts gave access to the gallery: **L1-L10**. The sequence is that given in Jeppesen & Zahle 1975: 69 Ill. 1, which so to say follows the two courses of the water from the highest point in the NW either towards the east or towards the south that converge close to Shaft L10 on the east side of the Quadrangle.
- *The Upper Gallery* **UG** is an aqueduct that runs from the NW towards the SE and divides into two branches, one of which conducted water to the chambers **Cb1** and **Cb2**, the other to a place east of the Maussolleion terrace. The Upper Gallery was also served by shafts, of which we encountered three, **U6-U8**. Newton ascertained another five shafts, **U1-U5**, and Biliotti one more, **U9**.

1. **UG:A** The tributary branch in the NW ending at Shaft U6.
2. **UG:B1** The course between U6 and the west parapet of Cb1, with an opening into its staircase and landing.
3. **UG:B2** The continuation around Cb1 and towards the SE corner of the Quadrangle, where it continues in a SE direction. The part east of Cb1 was termed "Short Gallery" by Newton. His gallery "F" connects the gallery with Chamber 2 (Cb2).
4. **UG:C** The course from Shaft U6 towards the SE ending in line with the eastern wall of the Maussolleion terrace.

- *The peribolos wall* delimits the huge Maussolleion terrace measuring 242.5 m east-west by c. 105.8 m north-south. Newton established the north and east walls situated only 3.6 m and 32 m respectively from the Quadrangle. The situation of the south and west walls was first established by Jeppesen in 1966-1967. The south wall is situated 69 m from the Quadrangle. P. Pedersen published this structure in *MH* 3,1-2, 1991.

11

The excavation trenches are named from their position in the general grid system of the excavation, cf. *MH* 1, pl. I, and *MH* 3, pl. I. The trenches P_{10}, P_{11}, Q_6 and Q_7 were dug with regard to the structures discussed in this volume. Reference will be made to other trenches dug during the investigation of the peribolos wall 1966-1972. These were published by P. Pedersen in *MH* 3,1-2, 1991.

Finally it appears useful to state the geological terms established by J. Gifford in *MH* 4, 2000: 144, and used by Jeppesen in the same volume. The two first constitute the bedrock of the area.

- *Claystone* is yellowish in colour and highly fractured. This is termed "yellowish andesite" by Pedersen 1991.
- *Sandstone* is a tuffaceous, sedimentary and friable sandstone. This is termed "soft, andesitic lava" or "whitish andesite" by Pedersen 1991. It was quarried (also) in the Maussolleion area and was used in the foundation of the peribolos wall, in the MauTb for the parapet walls and the sealing of the animal offerings, and for the pillars.

The sandstone (Gifford, *op.cit.*: 148, layers 3-4) forms a horizontal stratum upon the claystone (Gifford, *op.cit.*, layer 1, 2a-b), however, at varying levels created by vertical faults. The surface of the claystone is exposed in the whole central and NW part of the Quadrangle, including the chamber, corridor and part of the landing of Maussollos' tomb, as well as south of its parapet wall. The horizontal joints between the two stones are often seen in the galleries, e.g. Figs. 3.1.3 and 3.1.5. A vertical fault is well documented in the wall between Chamber 2 and Chamber 3, Fig. 5.3.3 and Figs. 5.3.7-8.

- *Green Andesite* A porphyritic hornblende andesite quarried in the western part of the Bodrum peninsula. Newton termed this stone "green ragstone". It was used for the foundation of the Maussolleion proper as well as for certain features in the Lower Gallery.
- *Grey Andesite* A porphyritic hornblende andesite probably quarried in the Bodrum peninsula. See Pedersen 1991,1: 193 n. 13 for a petrographic analysis. It was used for the terrace wall TW1 and possibly also for the euthynteria of the peribolos wall.

1.2. The progress of the British excavation 1857-1858, 1865

A brief outline of the course of the excavations appears useful for two reasons: to introduce the reader to the British work and the results, because these are indispensable for our understanding of certain of the structures, finds and layers under discussion; and to investigate the reliability of Newton's and Murdoch Smith's information and measured drawings and of Biliotti's excavation diary with regard to understanding the site before and contemporaneous with the building of the Maussolleion. For this reason the plan and sections of the Quadrangle, made by Murdoch Smith and published by Newton in *HD* pl. III-IV, and V, and in *TD* pl. 2 and 3 (here Fig. 1.2.1 and Pl. 1, cf. also Fig. 1.2.3), will be analysed and compared with the recent plan produced under ideal circumstances from 1970 onwards by the Danish team, Fig. 1.2.4.

Essential for the exposé are Murdoch Smith's diary and letters, Newton's reports, *Papers* 1858 and *Further Papers* 1859, as well as the dates of measured drawings, watercolours and photographs.

The course of the excavation is briefly characterized by Jeppesen & Zahle 1975: 67-68, and outlined in some detail by Jenkins 1992: 176-183 and Cook 1997 (see below). It has recently been studied with regard to certain aspects:

- The finding-places of sculptures: Waywell 1978: 1-13, 241-244.
- The finds in the Western Staircase: Højlund 1981: 25, 43, and passim.
- The Maussolleion peribolos and terrace wall and adjoining structures: Pedersen 1991: passim.
- The Maussolleion terrace surface: Pedersen 1991,1: 79.
- The finding-places of sculptures: Jeppesen 2002: 11-18.

Work on the site started 27th December (Towsey, however, 29th) 1856 near the SW corner of the Quadrangle where *the rock formed a kind of wall nearly running North and South.* From there they moved south and before 10th January found the entrance to the subterranean aqueduct "Upper

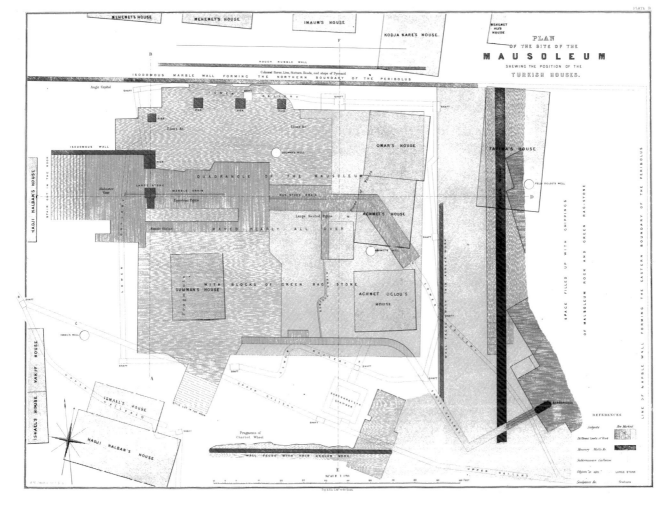

PLATE IV

Fig. 1.2.1. Murdoch Smith's plan of the Maussolleion site showing the position of the houses that were demolished. The position of the sections A-B, C-D and E-F in Pl. 1 is also shown. January 1858. From *HD* 1862, pl. IV.

Gallery" (UG:B1), which together with parts of the Branches UG:A and C was explored and found to be almost empty. By means of mines they proceeded north, finding a flight of steps (The Western Staircase), that was uncovered between 27th February and 13th March. Still in February, they penetrated into the Main Corridor and found the Subterranean Tomb (Cb2), which was emptied through the hole in its ceiling.

During the first two months of 1857 Murdoch Smith also finished both the plan of the Roman villa and the recording and partial removal of the mosaics found there, and he directed the excavations at Ross' platform (the Temple of Mars). He moreover made several short trips in the surrounding area and was absent during three excursions May 10-18, July 11-30, August 28 – September 8.

Between 13th March and 16th April the excavation proceeded north and east, and both the NW and the SE corners of the Quadrangle were found. A house in its SE part was demolished (23rd March). And already 16th April Murdoch Smith notes in his diary: *Filling in at the Mausoleum the central area being all dug. Laying down N. and E. sides of the excavations.* This information is confirmed in *Letter* 55 of June 22 to Sir John Burgoyne, in which Murdoch Smith relates: *We have finished the whole of the interior,* and in an explanatory text to a photograph of the NW angle he notes:

No. 3 is a view of the N.W. angle. One of the piers is seen just behind where Mr. Newton is standing. The flight of steps [Western Staircase] *which I mentioned in a former letter, but which had been covered up by the time this view was taken, was immediately in front of*

13

Fig. 1.2.2. North side of the Quadrangle. To the right Omar's house with an arch on its north side, beyond, Kodja Kare's house. Murdoch Smith, *Letter* 55, 1857.06.22, Photo no. 1. By courtesy of the Trustees of the British Museum.

the small house, part of which is seen on the left of the picture. Jeppesen 2000: 40 Fig. 4.2, publishes the photograph in question.

In the same letter Murdoch Smith describes another photograph, Fig. 1.2.2:
No. 1 is a view of the N.E. part of the site of the Mausoleum. The first of a line of piers that seems to have been the northern boundary of the building is seen near the middle of the picture. The house on the right [Omar's house], *the archway and the tall dark house next to it have now been pulled down and the excavations carried on past them. The white house on the left has been bought, and will be taken down to-morrow, as we now dug up to its foundations.* The photograph can be dated to some time before May 23, when Murdoch Smith in his diary notes the finding of a fine piece of frieze under Omar's house.

Also the published photographs from the excavation give the overall impression of chaotic and inadequate working conditions. On the engravings *HD* pl. VIII the two sappers besides the 'plug-block' in the landing in the Western Staircase stand in a hole surrounded by steep soil faces.[4] *HD* Pl. XI (below) shows part of the north side of the Quadrangle and the houses beyond.[5] The area is only partially emptied, and just the main features are discernible. See also the photograph first published by Jeppesen 2000: 40, Fig. 4.1, showing the NW corner of the Quadrangle and part of the north parapet of the Western Staircase. It is not surprising that important structures or their precise relation to one another escaped the notice of Murdoch Smith, when he put together the patches of measured

14

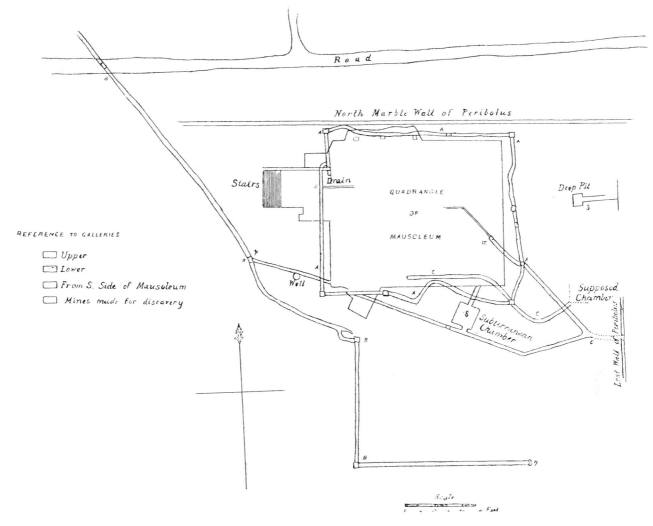

Fig. 1.2.3. Sketch plan of the Maussolleion site by Murdoch Smith appended to *P15*, 30th Sept. 1857.

evidence to establish the final plan and sections (in January 1858 and possibly later).

From July onwards the work was moved to the east and south sides of the Quadrangle, but in between also to the north with the main objective of establishing the course of the peribolos wall. However, about 20th August the clearing of the Lower Gallery was initiated, and before the end of September this, together with the Upper Gallery, was laid down. As a part of this work, the gallery running in a SE direction from the SE corner of the Quadrangle (UG:B2) was investigated through mining (*P15*: 48), Fig. 1.2.3. Where it opened into a rectangular cutting a sarcophagus (*soros*) was found: *When first entering this cutting through the gallery, I imagined that I had discovered another sepulchral chamber. In con-*

sequence of the great depth of soil about it, much time and labour were required to clear this spot out, when the supposed chamber proved to be a rectangular cutting in the quarry. (*FP2*: 7)

On 10th September Murdoch Smith stated in his diary: *Found a staircase at SW corner of Mausoleum leading down to the pavement.* This information is surprising, because already by the end of February, the Main Corridor starting from this point had been entered, but only now was the area (partially) investigated. More surprising, indeed, is the laconic statement of 18th September: *Putting the SW corner into plan of Mausoleum.* The corner was reached during the very first days of the excavation. In September the terrace wall (TW1) south of the Quadrangle was found (the course east was found several months before).

15

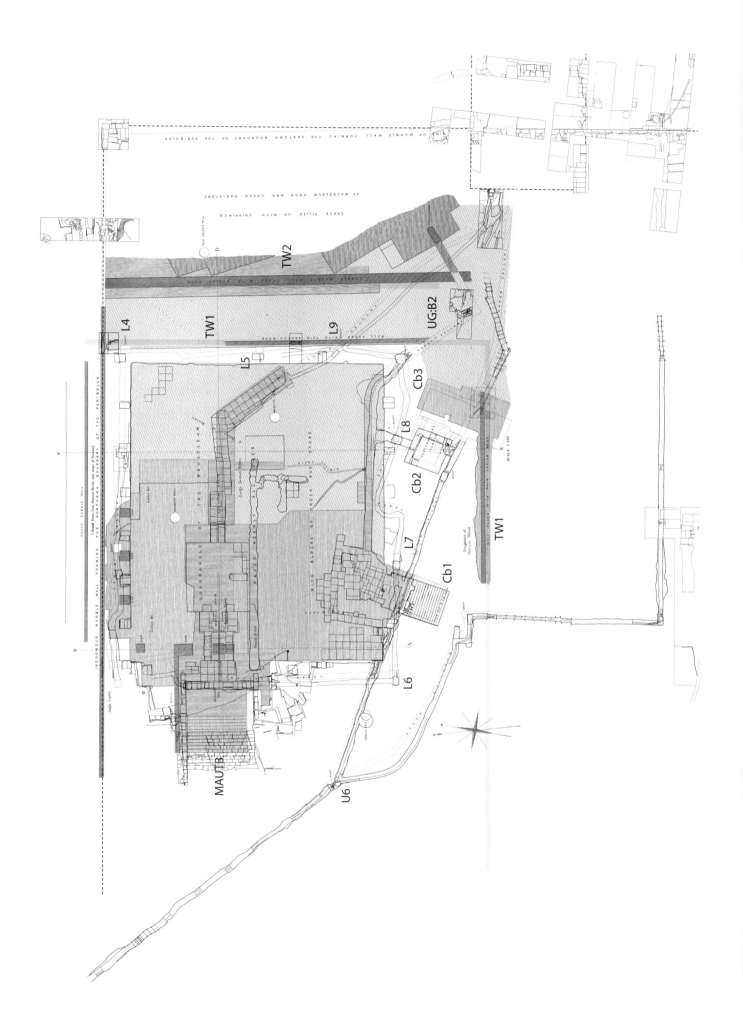

LINE OF MARBLE WALL FORMING THE EASTERN BOUNDARY OF THE PERIBOLUS

OF MAUSOLEUM ROCK AND GREEN RAG-STONE

SPACE FILLED UP WITH CHIPPINGS

TW2

COARSE MASSIVE WALL FACED WITH REGULAR WORK

TW1

L4

L5

L9

UG:B2

WALL FACED WITH REGULAR WORK

Cb3

L8

Cb2

L7

Cb1

TW1

SCALE 1:320

WALL FACED WITH TWO REGULAR WORK

Fragments of Chariot Wheel

THE MAUSOLEUM

QUADRANGLE OF

PAVED NEARLY

WITH BLOCKS OF GREEN RAG STONE

MAUT:B

U6

L6

ISODOMOUS MARBLE WALL FORMING THE NORTHERN BOUNDARY OF THE PERIBOLUS

ROUGH RUBBLE WALL

Angle Capital

Very important was the discovery, by mining, of the east peribolos wall.[6]

The message from 1st December (*Letter* 64) is revealing of the situation by then: *We are brought almost to a stand still by the obstinacy of the proprietors of the surrounding houses and fields. On this account we are reduced to the necessity of searching their property by mining, ... Along the East and South sides where we are now at work.* In the diary of 9th January 1858 it is stated: *Digging as usual at Mausoleum. Reduced the force to 70.*

The dated (and datable) photographs, measured drawings and watercolours, a list of which is given in the table, p. 23-28, confirm the chronology of the excavation, outlined here.

The consequences of the careless or random work for the reliability of *the plan* of the site are grave, as appears clearly from Fig. 1.2.4, where Murdoch Smith's and Jeppesen's plans are superposed. The true relation between the various structures or clusters of structures, which were measured one by one, is most often faulty, but to varying degrees. Obviously Murdoch Smith neglected to relate the detached measured drawings to common ground points of control.

- The sizes of the Quadrangle conform, as is already noted in Jeppesen & Zahle 1975: 75 n. 31: "Newton measured (see *HD*: 95) 108 × 127 feet = 32.92 × 38.71 metres; we measured in different places 32.50-32.75 m by 38.15-38.40 metres, respectively."
- The position of the Western Staircase and landing is, as noted by Jeppesen 1976: 47 and Højlund 1981: 43, wrong. The length of the MauTb (staircase, landing, *stomion*, and chamber) matches perfectly, but it is displaced towards the east (the staircase also towards the north) together with the NW part of the Quadrangle. The area was, as demonstrated above, measured before the rest of the Quad-

rangle, and it was already buried when the general plan was finished in January 1858. Also, the quite wrong relation of the Western staircase to the SW corner of the Quadrangle is remarkable. The staircase was discovered in the very early stage of the excavation (in February 1857) proceeding from the corner; but, as noted by Murdoch Smith, the SW corner was first measured in September.

- Moreover, even if the overall length of MauTb is correct, neither the corridor nor the west and south sides of the tomb chamber were noticed, cf. Jeppesen 1976: 48.
- The Southern Staircase, Cb1, is displaced towards the east in relation to the SW corner of the Quadrangle, and its angle to the south side of the Quadrangle is slightly tilted towards ENE. The lower, inner part of the structure was not revealed.
- The Shafts U6, L6, L7, L8, and the structures Cb2 and Cb3 are situated almost correctly in relation to one another and to the south border of the Quadrangle, but not to the SW and SE corners.
- The position of the terrace wall, TW1e, c. 2.75 m east of the Quadrangle, as well as of Shaft L9, is correct. However, the position of the Shafts L4, L5 and L10 is displaced towards the east. As a result the latter is shown as if it were situated below the terrace wall TW1.
- The position of the terrace wall, TW1s, c. 13.75 m south of the Quadrangle, and Cb2 and Cb3 is shown about 1 m too close to the Quadrangle, but fairly correctly in relation to the Shaft U7. Newton, though, states the correct distance (*HD*: 130-131).
- The distance between the line of the east border of the Quadrangle and the conjunction of the Lower Gallery and the East Corridor is correct, but the place is displaced several metres to the south. This may be bound up with the inaccurate notion of the bend in the East Corridor between our Trenches P_{10} and Q_6.
- Something also went wrong with the course of Newton's "Short Gallery" = UG:B2, SE of the Quadrangle. Our Trench Q_7 was intended for studying its course, but it did not turn up where it should according to the old plan.

◀ Fig.-1.2.4. Murdoch Smith's and Jeppesen's plans of the Quadrangle superposed on the same scale. The congruence between the NE, SE and SW corners determines the relation of the plans to each other. 1:500.

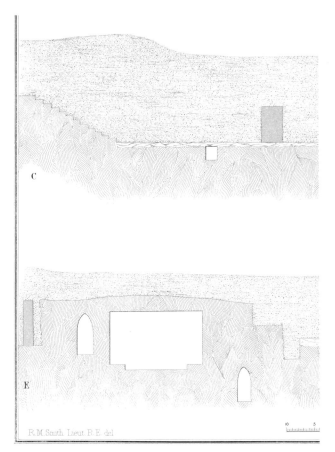

Fig. 1.2.5. Detail of Murdoch Smith's sections C-D and E-F. From *HD* 1862, pl. V.

Also between the drawings there are discrepancies. The course of the East Corridor bends to the right in *HD* pl. II, but to the left in pl. III-IV, our Fig. 1.2.1. Murdoch Smith made both plans. The edge of the rock just east of the terrace wall TW2 is on Murdoch Smith's plan shown with one re-entrant, whereas Pullan, Pl. 3, shows the edge more irregular and with two re-entrants.

The consequences of the excavation procedure for the reliability of Murdoch Smith's *three sections* do not appear too grave, except, of course, with regard to the displacement of the Tomb of Maussollos in the east-west section. However, when the sections – first published in *FP*16, 1859, Inclosure 2 – were prepared for publication in *HD*, both the west-east section, C-D, and the south-north section, E-F, were shortened by more than two cm, corresponding to c. 2.5 m on the site, compare Pl. 1 and Fig. 1.2.5.

The above observations fully confirm Newton's own assessment in *FP*16, 1859.04.12: 93-94 – which was not repeated in the official publication from 1862:

The views which I have had the honour to submit in this Report are the result of much study of the ground and of the plans, in which I have had the benefit of Lieutenant Smith's judgment on a number of points.

I could have wished to have been able to assert, more positively, conclusions which I have adopted as on the whole most probable; but it appeared both to Lieutenant Smith and myself, that the evidence before us up to this date would not justify a more confident tone. It is to be regretted that, from the delay and difficulty in obtaining the houses, we were compelled to explore the site of the Mausoleum by instalments, and to cover up the excavated parts as we went on, instead of laying bare the whole area continuously, and transporting the dug earth to a convenient distance.

For, though great care has been taken to record by plans, by delineation, and by photography, every fact which seemed worthy of observation, it is probable that, if the area of the excavation had been presented to the eye as a whole, and not in detached portions, we should have remarked significance and relation in many details, which, viewed in isolation, appeared meaningless or contradictory; and we might thus have been enabled to comprehend more fully the design of that monument which was the marvel of the ancient world, and of which, even after so much discovery, our knowledge is still so imperfect.

1.3. Newton's and Biliotti's stratigraphical observations

The reports and publications by Newton and Biliotti include several descriptions of the colour, the structure and the direction of different strata of earth, and this evidence is interpreted with common sense with regard to the dating of the small finds and the chronological relationship between different walls, etc. In general terms, the observations are confirmed by the new investigations, and they are instrumental for the understanding of the history of the site. It may be unfair to compare Newton's reports with Biliotti's diaries, but they make obvious that the latter was by far the more meticulous and experienced.

Regrettable and disquieting is the almost complete absence of stratigraphical observations in both diary and letters of Murdoch Smith, who together with Corporal Jenkins was in charge of the daily work. He notes if the earth is "loose and full of stones" or "compact and firm", and the following remark is very characteristic: *Along the East and South sides where we are now at work, the mines have to be driven through a mass of stones and rubble that in most places requires propping and framing and the heavy rains with which we are now frequently visited add to the difficulties.*[7] Murdoch Smith headed the sappers and viewed the strata professionally. On the other hand, he is very interested in geology and the character of the volcanic rock. In one letter he presents a description of both folds and faults of the bedrock together with two drawings of "stratified rock", and – in one of the galleries – a curious rock-like layer separating two layers of soft mould and formed by sedimentation.[8]

There are no drawings showing a soil stratigraphy in the entire written material from the British excavations.

The stratigraphical observations are listed below according to area:

- Western Staircase: *P5*: 12; *FP*16: 84-85; *HD*: 91, 140
- NW part of the Quadrangle: *HD*: 101-102
- Beyond the NE corner of the Quadrangle: *HD*: 117
- East of the Quadrangle: *P*13: 31; *FP*2: 7, *FP*16: 93; *HD*: 120-121, 123, 125; Biliotti 1865.03.25-27; 07.15-20.
- South of the Quadrangle: *HD*: 131, 134; Biliotti 1865.03.07-08; 04.01-03; 04.07-08; 04.18-20; 04.28-29; 06.02-03.
- Subterranean Galleries: *HD*: 153.
- Subterranean Chamber (Cb2): *HD*: 147.

All over the site both Newton and Biliotti first encountered a humus layer, between two and six feet deep, to which there are many references and appraisals throughout their notes and writings.

From one fine example, however, it appears that the careful descriptions do not necessarily testify to a careful excavation with any similarity to later archaeological practice. Three times

Newton describes the very first days of excavation on the Maussolleion site, and the role of stratigraphy markedly increases:

Therefore commenced excavations on this site, and after about two days' digging, came some very small fragments which had evidently been broken off from a frieze in high relief, similar to that removed from the Castle at Budrum, and presented to the British Museum by your Excellency some years ago. While I was engaged in this excavation, I took down, at the same time, an adjacent wall, composed almost entirely of large pieces of columns and fragments of marble. Among them, I discovered part of the body of a colossal lion exactly similar in style to those in the Castle, and on the same scale. Continuing the excavation and the examination of adjacent walls, I discovered part of a colossal arm, ···.[9]

I commenced operation in a field near the house of a Turk called Hadji Nalban. Here the soil was full of small fragments and splinters of the finest white marble, as if from the breaking-up of ancient sculpture. After digging for a day or two, I came to several small fragments broken off from a frieze in high relief. ··· This was enough to convince me that I was on the right track, ···[10]

After a few spadefuls had been thrown up, I examined the character of the soil. It was a loose black mould, full of small splinters of fine white marble and rubble. The whole appearance of this soil, and the absence of stratification in it, suggested the notion that it was a recent accumulation, such as might have taken place in the 400 years which have elapsed since the building of the castle of Budrum by the Knights.[11]

This wonderful improvement from text to text between 1857 and 1865 should be considered an afterthought, but is interesting all the same: it most probably reflects Newton's growing insight into archaeological excavation and its methods obtained both during his excavations and from colleagues back in England.

The most detailed – and reliable – stratigraphical discussions by Newton concern the area to the east of the Quadrangle, and they will for two reasons be quoted in full: 1) we excavated two trenches, Q$_6$ and Q$_7$, in the same area and were able to verify his observations, 2) his and Biliotti's observations and conclusions are indispensable for the correct understanding of the terrace walls TW1 and TW2, and they will be referred to later (see below, Ch. 2 & 4).

Newton proceeded eastwards from the terrace wall, TW1, the purpose of which was hard to define:

Advancing eastward from this line, I found that the native rock only appeared at a depth of from 20′ to 25′ (see the section C D, Plate V) [our Pl. 1]. *The upper surface of the soil was the black vegetable humus which covered the whole Quadrangle and platform around it. Below this, at the depth of from 6′ to 8′, was the same white soil which I had found over the staircase on the west, and between the north margin of the Quadrangle and the north peribolus wall. This soil composed of rubble, intermixed with large blocks of stone, was all apparently formed by the decomposed rock of the platform. Beyond the second wall on the east* [TW2, c. 10 m from the Quadrangle], *the vertical section of this lower soil presented a curious series of zigzag strata, such as would be formed by casting in rubble and soil from opposite directions.*

In these strata were veins of chippings of green stone. The occurrence of these veins seems for me a proof that the platform was artificially prolonged in an eastern direction from the place where the native rock failed, and that this prolongation took place at the time of the building of the Mausoleum. It might then have been accomplished in a very simple and economical manner by shooting into the deeper parts the rubble as it accumulated in levelling the site and dressing the stones for the Mausoleum.

It is specially to be observed that these zig-zag strata rose fully to the level of the rocky margin west of the trench, and such an artificial stratification proves that the wall [TW1] *was intentionally concealed at the time of the making of the platform, in the level of which it consequently does not mark a change.*

I am therefore inclined to think that this wall has no connection with the plan of the Mausoleum, and that it is anterior to it. What its purpose may have been, it is difficult to conjecture.[12]

Newton searched in vain for the eastern peribolos wall about 24 m east of the Quadrangle, where he had observed that the level of the land sinks abruptly about 8 feet. The excavation is described at length. Cf. Murdoch Smith's sketch map of 30th September 1857 (Fig. 1.2.3).[13]

At a depth of about 6 feet I found a layer of broken Hellenic pottery, below which was a layer of splinters of marble and green ragstone, intermixed with fragments of the freestone rock of the platform, by the decomposition of which the whole had been amalgamated into a concrete mass.

Cutting through this I found a mass of rubble composed of fragments of native rock, such as would accumulate near a spot where it had been quarried. I dug a pit in the rubble to the depth of 30 feet, when failing to discover the rocky bottom, and getting no trace of the eastern limit of the peribolus, I determined to postpone the further examination of this part ⋯.

From the peculiar stratification of the ground east of the deep trench, I am inclined to think that the higher level of the rocky platform has been artificially prolonged here by filling up a natural hollow with the fragments of native rock accumulated in the course of cutting out the Quadrangle of the Mausoleum, and the galleries and shafts round it; that upon the surface of this mass of rubble, were subsequently strewn the chippings of the marble and green ragstone employed in the building;[14]

The following observation by Newton on the find-spot of some terracottas confirms that excavation in this area was conducted with remarkable diligence: *On the level surface produced by these amalgamated chippings, we met with many fragments of pottery, among which were several small terracotta figures, beautifully modelled in the same style as the sculptures of the Mausoleum.* ⋯ *These were probably votive figures, brought to the tomb of Mausolus, and deposited within the sacred precinct of the peribolus.*[15] Most recently Burn & Higgins 2001: 187 have established their post-Maussollan dating, see below p. 164.

From 15th July 1865 Biliotti conducted excavations in the very same area, and his report complements Newton's, in as much as he proceeded from the east towards the west. As mentioned above, the diary is published *in extenso* by Pedersen 1991,1: 117-173.

From just outside the peribolos wall – c. on line with the SE corner of the Quadrangle – he dug a trench, 6 feet wide, towards the west. On the 19th he reaches the marked change in level, noted also by Newton:
We push our trench as far as the Western boundary of Hadji Imam's field, where the soil gradually rises to 7

feet above the average level. We find splinters of marble and of green stone showing the limit of the platform on which stood the Mausoleum.[16]

Thursday 20th. We deepen the trench towards the W. At 7 feet W. of the Peribolus wall the green stone, and other chippings form a perpendicular surface facing the E., regularly plane and parallel to the wall. The only way to explain this peculiar formation is to suppose that an inner wall had been erected there when the platform was levelled to prevent that too much strain should weigh on the outer or Peribolus wall, and that the chippings having agglomerated and become compact preserved the form they had acquired after the destruction of the wall by which they were originally supported. However, no traces of this supposed wall have been discovered as yet, ···[17]

This perpendicular surface of chippings, facing east, we encountered in Trench Q$_6$ (see below, p. 37 ff and the views Fig. 2.4.4-5). The surface was in all likelihood created when the Hospitallers looted the stones of the peribolos wall. There seems to be no reason to suppose an inner retaining wall as Biliotti does.

In Trenches Q$_7$ and Q$_6$ we encountered these chipping layers about 1.2-1.5 m below the present surface. Newton found the layers about 7 feet below the surface. Biliotti did not state the level, but at an earlier date (25th March) he excavated a spot slightly to the north and noted:

At about four feet from the surface we find a very hard and compact layer formed of chippings of marble. [27th] We cut through the marble layer and find under it a white sandy soil intermixed with fragments of stone, but as it was evident that this layer was formed with the chippings of the marbles cut at the time of the erection of the Mausoleum, and that no fragments connected with it could be discovered under this layer, we did not continue the excavations any further.[18]

Finally it appears useful to have a look at the situation to the south of the Quadrangle, where Biliotti excavated from March 1st 1865 onwards.

March 7th Tuesday. For about 3 feet from the surface the soil is black, & intermixed with fragments of coarse pottery & tiles.

March 8th Wednesday. At one foot deeper we come on a hard layer a kind of Cement of a grey colour, under which the soil is whitish. The deeper we proceed the more we find fragments of coarse pottery & tiles &

splinters of rock, but meet with no marble fragments of any description. ···[19]

April 28th & 29th Friday & Saturday. ··· In general we have not proceeded much deeper than the Artificial platform raised at the time of the erection of the Mausoleum, as it is evident that no fragments of sculpture belonging to this edifice can be discovered under it. This artificial platform is easily distinguished being formed of the pieces cut from the rocky platform when it was levelled, and of other rough stones intermixed with a whittish sandy soil. It is met usually at 6 feet deep, but we cut through it in several places, and attained 12, 15 and as much as 18 feet deep.[20]

June 2nd & 3rd Friday & Saturday. ··· The black humus is not thicker than 3 feet, and before reaching the white soil under it we meet a thin layer of greenish colour formed, no doubt of the splinters and dust of the green stone slabs thrown there at the time of the erection of the Mausoleum to level the platform.[21]

In conclusion, it can be said that the stratigraphical observations by Newton and more consistently by Biliotti are very useful, and below we shall benefit from their careful descriptions, both of the soil and of features of the bedrock and the walls. One is certainly inclined to endorse Brian F. Cook's gentle remark on matters from the incipient days of archaeology: *In general Newton's field technique, with his failure to keep detailed records of the finds, leaves much to be desired.*[22] Already in 1862, though, J. Fergusson did put the point bluntly: *The truth of the matter seems to be that Lieutenant Smith's business there was to take charge of the Sappers and Miners under his command; Mr. Newton was only anxious to procure specimens of sculpture for the National Museum; ··· Many points that might then have been easily cleared up must now, therefore, be left in doubt, unless some one will take the trouble of doing over again what has been so carelessly done once.*[23] He is harsh, but as we have seen above p. 18, Newton himself would agree in the criticism,[24] and the quality of the almost contemporaneous work of Biliotti shows what could have been achieved. Surprising is the recent attempt by Ian Jenkins to credit Murdoch Smith 'for his important part in the success of the expedition to Halicarnassus'.[25] Murdoch Smith, R.E., should not be blamed for Newton's strategy and decisions. The responsibility was his.

1.4. A sketch of the topography of the site at the time of the building of the Maussolleion

It appears useful at this point to summarize our knowledge of the features of the surroundings of the Quadrangle before and in the period when the Maussolleion was built, in order to contribute to a proper overview during the following chapters. The documentation, which combines the new evidence and results with the British results of the 19th Century, will show up piecemeal, cf. the Front and the Back Leaf:

The Maussolleion proper is situated on the lower slope of Göktepe on a kind of platform or plateau, bordered by ravines on the east and south, while the ground to the west is fairly even.

The level of the bedrock around the Quadrangle now ranges between 9.65-10.00 m a.s.l. to the west, 9.85-8.90 m to the south, and 8.9-9.6 m to the east and in the eastern half of the north side. The evidence of the well-preserved top-opening of the shaft in the Main Corridor and the top edge of the southern staircase, being pre-Maussollan, demonstrates that this was also the ancient level. We may reckon that the situation was identical also on the four sides of the Quadrangle, although a certain levelling cannot be excluded.

The situation within the Quadrangle, of course, will remain partly unknown, because the ground was prepared for the huge weight of the tomb building. At present the level of the bedrock varies from 8.60 m a.s.l. in the NE corner to 4.78 m a.s.l. at the bottom of the tomb chamber of Maussollos. Some of the surfaces are with certainty or great probability pre-Maussollan, others were certainly cut down.

In the NW part of the Quadrangle the pre-Maussollan situation is preserved in a marked depression, level 6.78 m a.s.l., which has a certain extension towards the north, where it is spanned by the built foundation for the peribolos wall running east-west 3.5 m north of the Quadrangle. Both in this depression and in the area to the

north and south of the Western Staircase there is ample evidence for quarrying. Its east limit is well defined by a vertical cutting beyond which the level is 1.82 m higher up.

The southern part of the site destined for the cutting of the Quadrangle contained both the pre-Maussollan chamber, Cb1, and the aqueduct, UG:B, which certainly were subterranean, with floor levels down to 5.55 m a.s.l. Probably, the original upper surface matched the level along the south margin. We have no means to establish how far north this level extended, but a fair guess could be that it covered the area to the south of a line from pillar P17 (on the west side) to between pillars P5 and P6 (on the north side). The shape and exact position of the transition down to the lower level in the NW part of the Quadrangle can only be conjectured. The sides may have been in a 'quarry state', as outside the Quadrangle to the west.

The bedrock on the east side of the Quadrangle terraces down in two broad steps parallel to the Quadrangle, the first of which was separated from it by a regularly cut ridge or 'bench'. On the south side there was one, at least partly, regular, vertical edge, also parallel to the Maussolleion. Beyond and below the vertical steps, faced by walls (TW1 and TW2), there are depressions or ravines partly formed by quarrying, that reach c. 4.5-2.5 m a.s.l., but a kind of salient or projecting corner of the bedrock plateau towards the SE separates the ravines towards the east and south from each other. This salience was exploited for the easternmost course of the aqueduct, UG:B2, the East Corridor and for the subterranean outlet of the Lower Gallery.

The aqueduct, UG:C, crosses the ravine immediately to the south of the Quadrangle in a built section of about 11 m in length before it re-enters another salience of the rock (surface c. 9.40 m a.s.l.). Then, about 34 m east of the Shaft U8, the gallery once more had to be built in order to cross another depression. Further on it was conducted on an ashlar-built substructure, 5.5 m high, as far as the line of the Maussollan East Terrace Wall. At this point the level of the bedrock reaches only 2.8 m and 2.65 m a.s.l.

Table. Synopsis of the preserved pictorial documentation (Photographs, measured drawings, watercolours) from the British investigations of the Maussolleion 1857, 1858, 1865..

Date	Mentioned	Identification	Type	Artist	British Museum	British Library	Repro 1858-65	Repro 1950-	Fig. Pl.	Remarks
1857.02.03	Murdoch Smith, *Letter* 45	Section of built part of UG:C between U7 and U8	Sketch	R. Murdoch Smith			Dickson 1901: 38			
1857.04.03 before	*P6*: 14. – FP16: 84 photo no. 1?	Western Staircase, scaffolding with seated sapper	Photograph	B. Spackman	"Western Staircase."	Folio 6, no. 6	*HD* Pl. VI,1			Cf. Murdoch Smith, *Letter* 68, 1858.01.30 no. 15
1857.04.03 before	*P6*: 14. – FP16: 84 photo no. 1?	Plug block with two sappers, view west	Photograph	B. Spackman	"1290 Part of Large Stone of North West Staircase, Mausoleum."	Folio 7, no. 8 (together with other photo from same position with one sapper)	*HD* Pl. VIII,1	*MH* 1: 44 Fig. 40. – Feyler 1987: 1038, Fig. 5. – *MH* 4: 64 Fig. 10.5		Obs. two photos, cf. also Murdoch Smith, *Letter* 68, 1858.01.30 no. 14
1857.04.03 before	*P6*: 14. – FP16: 84 photo no. 1?	Western Staircase, detail of steps	Photograph	B. Spackman	"1271 Western Staircase, Mausoleum"			*MH* 4: 39 Fig. 3.3		Cf. Murdoch Smith, *Letter* 68, 1858.01.30 no. 15
1857.04.03 before	*P6*: 14. – FP16: 84 photo no. 1?	View of Western Staircase, southern half unexcavated, to right north parapet, sapper standing on top of staircase	Photograph	B. Spackman	"1287 View of North West Staircase, Mausoleum"			*MH* 1: 48 Fig. 53. – *MH* 4: 39 Fig. 3.2		Cf. photo HD: 92
1857.06 before	FP16: 85 photo no. 3	Plug block with two sappers, view east	Photograph	B. Spackman	"1283 Part of Large Stone of North West Staircase. Mausoleum"	Folio 8, no. 10	*HD* Pl. VIII,2	*MH* 1: 44 Fig. 41. – *MH* 4: 65 Fig. 10.6		Cf. also Murdoch Smith, *Letter* 68, 1858.01.30 nos. 16-18

Date	Mentioned	Identification	Type	Artist	British Museum	British Library	Repro 1858-65	Repro 1950-	Fig. Pl.	Remarks
1857.06 before	FP 16: 85 photo nos. 5-7?	North side of Quadrangle. In foreground NE corner of landing in MauTb, pillars behind	Photograph	B. Spackman	"Excavation, North side, Mausoleum."	Folio 166 rev., nos. 320-321; Folio 167, nos. 322-323		*MH* 4: 40 Fig. 4.1		
1857.06 before	Murdoch Smith, *Letter* 55, 1857.06.22 no. 1. FP 16: 85 photo nos. 5-7?	North side of Quadrangle. To right Omar's house with arch on its north side, through which access to Maus. Site. Beyond, Kodja Kare's house and a third house	Photograph	B. Spackman	"[1]270" "Excavation below Imaum's Field. North side. Mausoleum."	Folio 10 rev., no. 14			1.2.2	Carefully described by Murdoch Smith, cf. also Murdoch Smith, *Letter* 68, 1858.01.30 nos. 16-18
1857.06 before	Murdoch Smith, *Letter* 55, 1857.06.22 no. 2. FP 16: 85 photo nos. 5-7?	North side of Quadrangle	Photograph	B. Spackman	"[1]282 View of Piers. North side of Mausoleum"	Folio 10, no. 13	*HD* Pl. XI,2	*MH* 4: 42 Fig. 4.3. – *MH* 5: 10 Fig. 1.1		Carefully described by Murdoch Smith, cf. also Murdoch Smith, *Letter* 68, 1858.01.30 nos. 16-18
1857.06 before	Murdoch Smith, *Letter* 55, 1857.06.22 no. 3	NW angle of Quadrangle. View west	Photograph	B. Spackman	"1248 Excavation of North West angle, Mausoleum"	Folio 169 rev. nos. 329-330; Folio 170 no. 331		*MH* 4: 41 Fig. 4.2		Carefully described by Murdoch Smith. With Mr. Newton. Part of small house seen to left, cf. also Murdoch Smith, *Letter* 68, 1858.01.30 nos. 16-18
1857.06 before	Murdoch Smith, *Letter* 55, 1857.06.22 no. 4. *P*9: 22 (list of five photos)	Peribolos wall with standing sapper	Photograph	B. Spackman	Written in pencil "Cpt. Jenkins, RE."	Folio 6 no. 7	*HD* Pl. VI,2	*MH* 3.1: 24 Fig. 23. – Cook 1997: 12, Fig. 10		Carefully described by Murdoch Smith. "The figure standing by the wall is Corporal Jenkins,"

Date	Mentioned	Identification	Type	Artist	British Museum	British Library	Repro 1858-65	Repro 1950-	Fig. Pl.	Remarks
1857.06 before	Murdoch Smith, Letter 55, 1857.06.22 no. 5	Pyramid steps with one seated and one standing man	Photograph	B. Spackman	Written with pencil (left) "Lt. Smith" (right) "presumably Newton"		HD Pl. XI,1	MH 3,1: 25 Fig. 24. – Cook 1997: 12 Fig. 6. – MH 5: 10 Fig. 1.1		Carefully described by Murdoch Smith. With Murdoch Smith and Newton: Murdoch Smith, Letter 68, 1858.01.30 no. 20
1857.06 before	Murdoch Smith, Letter 55, 1857.06.22 nos. 15-18, 23-24. P9: 21-22 (06.12)	Slabs of Amazon frieze	Photographs	B. Spackman		Folio 9, nos. 11-12	Cf. HE Pl. IX,1-2; X,1-2			
1857.06 before	Murdoch Smith, Letter 55, 1857.06.22 nos. 19-22. P9: 22 no. 3. (06.12)	Finds of sculpture, incl. head of "Maussollos"	Photographs	B. Spackman			Cf. HE opposite p. 104			
1857.09.17		Sections, etc. Cb1	Measured drawing	R.P. Pullan		Folio 14, no. 23 "Sep. 17 1857"	HD Pl. XIII,5		Pl. 7	
1857.09.22	P 15: 48	6 sections, LG & UG	Measured drawing	R.P. Pullan		Folio 14, no. 22 "Sep 22 1857"	HD Pl. XIII,4			
1857.09.30 before	P 15: 47; P 16: 52, Inclosure 1	"Rough Sketch of Galleries at the Mausoleum"	Measured drawing, coloured	R. Murdoch Smith			P16, Inclosure 1	MH 3,1: 73 Fig. 80	1.2.3	Murdoch Smith, Diary 57.10.05 "Made rough sketch of galleries for Lord Clarendon."
1857.10 possibly		Turk standing in Main Corridor	Watercolour	R.P. Pullan		Folio 13, no. 21	HD Pl. XIII,3		Pl. 8	
1857.10 possibly		Section of door to Cb2	Measured drawing	R.P. Pullan		Folio 13, no. 21	HD Pl. XIII,2		Pl. 8	

Date	Mentioned	Identification	Type	Artist	British Museum	British Library	Repro 1858-65	Repro 1950-	Fig. Pl.	Remarks
1857.10.10		Cb3 view towards west	Watercolour	R.P. Pullan		Folio 16, no. 27 "Second Sepulchral Chamber R.P. Pullan Oct 10 1857"	*HD* Pl. XIV,2		pl. 12	
1857.10.12		Plan & section of Cb3	Measured drawing	R.P. Pullan		Folio 13 no. 20 "Oct. 12 1857"	*HD* Pl. XIII,1		Pl. 10	
1857.10.12		Cb3 view towards north	Watercolour	R.P. Pullan		Folio 15, no. 25 "2. Sepulchral Chamber Oct 12 1857"	*HD* Pl. XIV,3		Pl. 11	
1857.12.10 before	*P* 16: 49, Inclosure 2	"Tracing of Termination of South Gallery of the Mausoleum." Section in UG:C of wall with four pipes	Measured drawing	R.P. Pullan?			*P* 16: 52		6.3.13	Wrongly referred to as a photograph
1857/ 1858.02		TW1 and vertical cutting in bedrock	Photograph	B. Spackman	"[1]280 Excavation. East side, Mausoleum"	Folio 165, no 316; Folio 166 nos. 318-19			4.1.1	
1857 / 1858?		Two faience beads discovered in the soil of the platform	Drawing				*HD* 274, Figs.			
1858.01		View of TW1s with 8 courses	Watercolour	R.P. Pullan		Folio 11, no. 15 "Jan 1858"	*HD* Pl. XII,1		Pl. 2	
1858.01		Cb2 view SE	Watercolour	R.P. Pullan		Folio 15, no. 24	*HD* Pl. XIV,1		Pl. 9	
1858.01	*FP* 16, April 12 1859, Inclosure 1	Plan of the site of the Mausoleum	Measured drawing, coloured	R. Murdoch Smith		Folio 3-4 "R.M. Smith Lieut. R.E. January 1858"	*HD* Pl. III. – TD Pl. 2	*AJA* 1975 pl. 63 Fig. 1b; p. 69 ill. 1. – *MH* 1: 24 Fig. 2	1.2	

Date	Mentioned	Identification	Type	Artist	British Museum	British Library	Repro 1858-65	Repro 1950-	Fig. Pl.	Remarks
1858.01	*FP* 2: 6	View of Sarcophagus south	Watercolour	R.P. Pullan		Folio 11, no. 16 "View of Sarcophagus towards the South R.P. Pullan _an 1858"	*HD* Pl. XII,3		Pl. 6	Newton sends tracings from drawings by Pullan
1858.01	*FP* 2: 6	View of TW2 and sarcophagus looking north	Watercolour	R.P. Pullan		Folio 12, no. 17 "View of Eastern Wall and Sarcophagus looking north"	*HD* Pl. XII,2		Pl. 5	Newton sends tracings from drawings by Pullan
1858.01	*FP* 2: 6	View of TW2 looking north	Watercolour	R.P. Pullan		Folio 12, no. 18 "View of Wall East Side looking North"	*HD* Pl. XII,4		Pl. 3	Newton sends tracings from drawings by Pullan
1858.01	*FP* 2: 6	View of TW2 looking south	Watercolour	R.P. Pullan		Folio 17, no. 28 "Jan 1858"	*HD* Pl. XIV,4		Pl. 4	Newton sends tracings from drawings by Pullan
1858.01?	Cf. *FP* 16, April 12 1859, Inclosure 1	Plan of the site of the Mausoleum showing the position of the Turkish houses	Measured drawing, coloured	R. Murdoch Smith			*HD* Pl. IV	*MH* 3,1: 43 Fig. 58		
1858.01 possibly	*FP* 16, April 12 1859, Inclosure 2	Three sections of the site of the Mausoleum	Measured drawing, coloured	R. Murdoch Smith		Folio 5	*HD* Pl. V. – *TD* Pl. 3	*MH* 3,1: 42 Fig. 57 (North part of sections A-B and E-F)	1.2.5	
1858.02 before	*FP* 2: 7	Head vase and dagger	Watercolour	R.P. Pullan		Folio 18, no. 19 "(11 ½ inch long)"	*HD* 124. – *TD* 204		7.3.3.3	Newton sends tracings from drawings by Pullan
1858.05	*FP* 16, April 12 1859, Inclosure 3	Plan of the Mausoleum area incl. part of harbour	Measured drawing, coloured	R. Murdoch Smith		Folio 2 "R.M. Smith Lt. R.E. May 1858"	*HD* Pl. II (with certain changes in signatures)	Jeppesen 1968: 32 Fig. 2		

Date	Mentioned	Identification	Type	Artist	British Museum	British Library	Repro 1858-65	Repro 1950-	Fig, Pl.	Remarks
1859.04.12 before	FP 16: 91	Section. Built upper part of UG:C between U7 and U8	Drawing	R.P. Pullan						
1865.03.31	Diary	Plan of area of the Mausoleum with houses	Drawing	A. Biliotti				MH 3,1: 123		
1865.04.20	Diary	Section. Cut and built part of UG: C between U7 and U8 and, above, andesite ashlar	Drawing	A. Biliotti				MH 3,1: 127	6.3.5	
1865.08.16	Diary	Plan of Hadji Imam's property	Drawing	A. Biliotti				MH 3,1: 151		
1865.08.16	Letter to Panizzi	Plan of Maussolleion area and the properties to the east and south	Drawing	A. Biliotti				Ashmole 1950: 6 Fig. 1. – Jeppesen 1968: 34 Fig. 3. – MH 3,1: 173		

2. The trenches excavated 1972-1976

The major part of the task during the re-excavation of the Maussolleion was to bring to light what was already seen in 1857-1858 and 1865 by means of emptying the Quadrangle and related structures. Besides the opportunity to study in depth the many overlooked architectural features, both finds and pockets of undisturbed strata and substantial structures were chosen for special study. Important results concerning the tomb proper of Maussollos and the peribolos wall have already been brought in the previous volumes of the Maussolleion publication.

For the purpose of studying the pre-Maussollan remains, five trenches were decided upon, and also Newton's Southern Staircase (our Chamber 1, Cb1) and its immediate surroundings turned out to be a promising place for supplementary excavation.

The terrace wall TW1 was investigated in Trenches P_9, P_{10} and P_{11}, the East Corridor in Trenches P_{10} and Q_6, and the easternmost chamber or courtyard, Cb3, to the south of the Quad-rangle, in Trench P_{10}. Trench Q_7 was scheduled for the branch of the Upper Gallery (UG:B2) termed "Short Gallery" by Newton – but it did not turn up where we expected. Both this trench, however, and also Q_6 produced valuable information on the Maussollan fill of the terrace between the Quadrangle and the East Terrace Wall.

Below, the evidence from the trenches will be documented in some detail. The results will be used and placed in context in the following chapters on the individual structures as well as in the final Chapter 8. The task is to explore the combined evidence from the British and the recent excavations in order to understand the history of the site before c. 350 BC.

A further, minor excavation was carried out in the Maussollan fill behind the north parapet of the Western Staircase, M_2. The structure is firmly dated to the time of the Maussolleion, for which reason the sounding is reported on below in Ch. 3 in connection with the contemporaneous Lower Gallery.

2.1. Trench P$_9$:
Terrace Wall 1, east

Date of excavation: 1974, September.
Dimension: 2.5 m × 2.5 m.
Subject: The terrace wall TW1 east and its relation to the North peribolos wall.
Documentation: Plan, elevations and section W-E of wall.
Publication: Pedersen 1991,1: 18, 83; 1991,2: 57-58 Trench 25. Plan (Fig. 243), section W-E of wall (Fig. 245), photo (Fig. 247).

In the trench is preserved a part of the east-west course of the Maussollan peribolos wall and at right-angles to this a single block of the terrace wall TW1 towards the south. The latter rests in a 1.2 m wide wall bedding at 8.6 m a.s.l., limited to the west by the bedrock, which forms a kind of bench, about 0.9 m high and c. 2 m wide along the east side of the Quadrangle (see below). The vertical side of the 'bench' turns 90° towards the west and most likely forms a c. 3 m wide bench along the north side of the Quadrangle. As appears from section E1 in Jeppesen 2000, the level of the bench towards the west is irregular (9.6 - 8.4 - 9.04 - 9.6 m a.s.l.). About 21 m from the NE corner of the Quadrangle, the peribolos wall is again visible, resting on the bedrock at level. c. 8.92 m a.s.l.[26] The vertical north side of the 'bench' may run all the way between this point and our Trench P$_9$.

Two courses of the foundation for the euthynteria of the peribolos wall are preserved, but in a repaired state of the Roman period. Mortar is used in the gaps of the limestone blocks in the north façade, on the top of the wall in its whole width, and between the more irregularly laid blocks towards the south.

The single block of grey andesite, 0.30 m high, 0.47 m long and 0.31 m deep, lies at right-angles to the wall. Its face towards the east is rusticated, at both short ends and on the top surface is an anathyrosis. The east side of the wall bedding, c. 0.3 m high, is situated only 0.20 m from the wall. The lower course in the wall, therefore, was hardly visible from the east, being partly hidden by the rock.

Pedersen ascertained that the block lies *in situ* and must have been present when the repair on the peribolos wall was carried out. He moreover states that "contact with the north wall could be observed".[27] Due to the circumstances, however, we have no evidence for its relation to the original peribolos wall. The anathyrosis might testify to a continuation towards the north, but we have no evidence to decide whether it abutted on the peribolos wall or whether an earlier continuation further north was interrupted by the erection of the peribolos. Also the regular cutting of the angle of the bench is ambiguous. The two walls might be contemporaneous, but the north-south line of the bedrock could originally have continued further north.

On top of the 'bench', in the SW corner of the trench, was disclosed a part of a capstone in green andesite of Shaft L4 of the Lower Gallery. Its top level is at 9.64 m a.s.l.

2.2. Trench P₁₁: Terrace Wall 1, east

Date of excavation: 1974.09.09-13.
Dimension: 1.5 m × 2.5 m.
Subject: The terrace wall TW1 east and the terrain east of the Quadrangle.
Documentation: Plan, section, elevation (Fig. 2.2.1). Photos 2.2.2-3.
Mentioned: Pedersen 1991,1: 84 with Fig. 88.

Three courses in a single row are preserved of the same wall, TW1, as in trench P₉. The level of the wall bedding is 7.76 m a.s.l. Again on the west, but at a distance of about 0.65 m, the bedrock rises vertically to level 9.25 m. Towards the east, however, the level rises only c. 8 cm.

The andesite stone, identical with the one in Trench P₉, is greyish brown, micaceous, and with black and white particles, and occasionally with a yellow to greenish nuance. The face is rusticated and on all four sides is an anathyrosis – also on the top level. The supporting surface, however, is narrow, so the wall must have been built in connection with the gradual filling of the gap between the rock and the wall. The length of the stones varies considerably, 1.02 m / 0.54 m

/ 0.30 m / 0.80 m, as does the height of the courses of 0.34 m (top course) and 0.38 m (the other two), but the thickness 0.30 m is uniform. The top surface is at level 8.84 m a.s.l., conforming fairly well to the top level of the single ashlar in Trench P₉. The slight discrepancy between the trenches, however, with regard to the height of the ashlars, only 0.30 m in Trench P₉, should not be neglected, and the top level differs by 6 cm. Most likely, however, the ashlar in P₉ belongs to the same string course as the top block in Trench P₁₁.

The soil between rock and wall was homogeneous whitish to brown with chips of green andesite and marble and of various types of pottery. It must be Newton "Schutt", as in a large area east of the Quadrangle which was emptied in 1857. Newton first believed the space between the bedrock and the wall to be a drain, cf. Fig. 4.1.1, but later he correctly understood the wall as a terrace revetment wall.[28] In the hope of finding evidence for dating, preserved spots of whitish fill wedged in between the ashlar blocks on the back side of the wall were studied. It contained exclusively some small pottery fragments of reddish local ware and many chips and bits of the same stone as the wall and thus differed from the main fill in the trench. In comparison with the situation be-

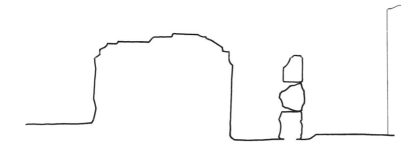
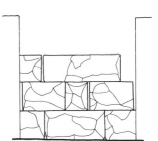

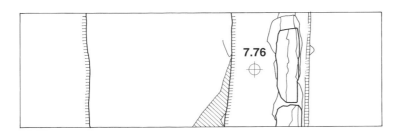

Fig. 2.2.1. Plan and sections in Trench P₁₁ with the terrace wall TW1e, the easternmost part of the Quadrangle and the 1.8 m wide bedrock ridge or "bench" in between. 1:50.

hind the north parapet in the Western Staircase, MauTb (below, p. 67), where the characteristic Maussollan fill with green andesite and marble chips in great quantity had penetrated every hollow space in the back wall, its absence in TW1 is remarkable. The original fill along the wall most likely is earlier than the building of the Maussolleion. And so is the wall.

Fig. 2.2.2. The east façade of the terrace wall TW1e in Trench P$_{11}$. View SW. 1974. Cf. Pedersen 1991,1, Fig. 88.

Fig. 2.2.3. The inner side of the terrace wall TW1e in Trench P$_{11}$. View east. 1974.

2.3. Trench P$_{10}$: Terrace Wall 1, south, Chamber 3 and East$_9$ Corridor

Date of excavation: 1974.09.09-10.15; 1976.08.25-28.
Dimension: 3.1 m × 3.9 m.
Subject: The terrace wall TW1 south of the Quadrangle, the East Corridor, the chamber or courtyard, Cb3.

Documentation: Plan top level (Fig. 2.3.1). Plan bottom level (Fig. 5.4.1 and 5.5.1). Views A-A and B-B (Fig. 2.3.2-3). Section C-C, corridor and ceiling, view west (Fig. 5.5.2). Photos 2.3.4-5.

Newton had the area completely excavated, so the soil was characteristic Newton "Schutt" right from the ground level of c. 9.40 m a.s.l. and down to c. 7.60 m. The topsoil (0.40 m) consisted of whitish to brown soil, the rest being of the same

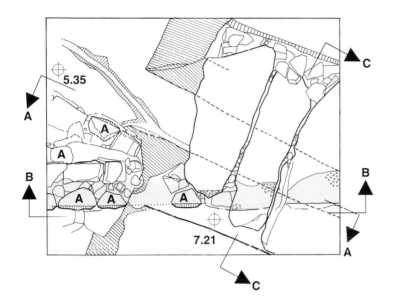

Fig. 2.3.1. Plan of Trench P$_{10}$ showing the limestone ceiling slabs of the East Corridor, the remains of TW1s and the wall intersecting the chamber Cb3. 1:50.

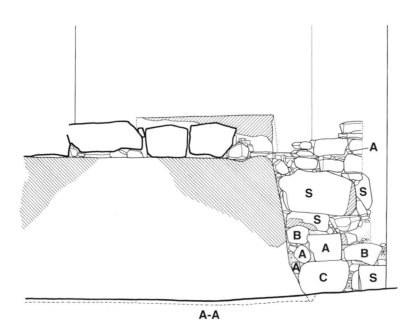

A-A

Fig. 2.3.2. Trench P$_{10}$. Section and view A-A showing the south side of the East Corridor (with section of ceiling blocks) and view of the combined transverse wall in Cb3 and foundation of the terrace wall TW1. 1:50.

33

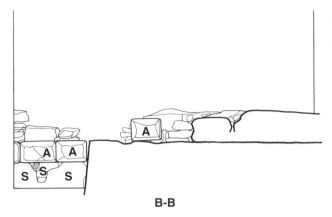

B-B

Fig. 2.3.3. View B-B of terrace wall TW1 in Trench P_{10} from the south. 1:50.

Fig. 2.3.4. TW1s crossing Cb3 in Trench P_{10}. View south. 1974.

Fig. 2.3.5. The ceiling blocks of the East Corridor and the terrace wall TW1s in Trench P_{10}. View west. 1974.

colours but mixed up with a great number of stones of bedrock.

The trench revealed what we searched for: the area along the east side of Chamber 3, where the East Corridor opens into the chamber and where the terrace wall TW1 crosses the ceiling of the corridor and continues across the chamber on a built foundation. Newton and Murdoch Smith situated both this structure and the subterranean chamber, Cb2, about one metre to the east of its real position in relation to the SE corner of the Quadrangle and Shaft L9.

The eastern two-thirds of the trench revealed 2½ limestone-ceiling blocks of the East Corridor situated in a ledge, c. 7.21 m a.s.l. Both to the north and south the bedrock rises to a higher level, 8.45 m and 7.80 m a.s.l. respectively. In the SW corner and at about the same level lie a few ashlars of the east-west course of the terrace wall TW1 built as a double wall. The foundation of this wall appears to be built together with the lower, transverse wall that according to Newton formed part of the corridor that connected the East Corridor with the Main Corridor across the chamber. In the NW corner of the trench, at level c. 5.30 m a.s.l., appears a small part of both the floor of Chamber 3 and of its east side.

Chamber 3

Newton had the structure completely emptied and both Murdoch Smith and – in fair detail – Pullan recorded Cb3 in measured drawings and watercolours (see below, Ch. 5.4). Therefore we did not proceed further, even if only about 1½ m² of the floor of the chamber – at level 5.3 m a.s.l. – was revealed together with two small parts of its east side.

The east side of the chamber is cut in the bedrock and appeared in two places (claystone): one of c. 1 m length just north of the opening into the East Corridor. The measurable height of the eroded and oblique side is 2.0 m, rising 1 m more to about 8.30 m a.s.l., slightly to the east. A second stretch of the side is seen to the south of the corridor, and only its upper part was revealed in a length of c. 1.7 m, having the top-level at 7.80 m a.s.l. It follows the orientation of the first section.

In the floor of the East Corridor (5.30 m a.s.l) and in its continuation into Chamber 3 is a narrow groove or channel, 14 cm wide and 10 cm deep. Towards the west it divides into two, one part turning south around the corner underneath the wall, the other crossing from the south side of the corridor in the direction of the north side of the opening into the Main Corridor. This conforms well to the fact that the channel in the Main Corridor (see p. 92, Fig. 5.2.2) runs along the north side. The 'southern' branch of the channel was blocked up by the building of the wall, which therefore obviously is the younger of the two.

In the floor of the chamber in line with the north side in the East and Main Corridors, there are no traces of a wall that according to Newton would form the north side of the corridor, which at some time connected the corridors on both sides of the chamber and destroyed its original purpose.

The combined transverse wall in Chamber 3 and foundation of the terrace wall, TW1.

The lines of the wall on the floor of the chamber and the double wall TW1 run NW and W respectively, and on different levels. They form a wedge-shaped, thick alignment of walls, that prolonged would be almost 2 m wide in the western side of the chamber. According to Newton's plan Fig. 1.2.1 and section Pl. 1, the foundation throughout rests on the floor of the Chamber 3, about 5.30 m a.s.l., and this applies also for the foundation for the terrace wall in its continuation towards the west.

Only two courses in a height of about 0.80 m are preserved of the lower wall Fig. 2.3.2. It is somewhat irregular and consists of various types of stones: greyish andesite (A), a variant of this but with a greenish tint (B), a reddish andesite (C), and sandstone (S). The situation behind and above this wall is quite different. Up to the level 6.96 m, the wall is built as an irregular and rough foundation in sandstone for the wall, TW1.

Only a single ashlar course of TW1 in greyish andesite (stone A) is preserved, the top side of which is flush with the bedrock to the east, Fig. 2.3.1 and 3. The two completely excavated ashlars measure respectively 0.48 m and 0.40 m in length, 0.30 m in thickness, and 0.31 in height. The wall, however, is a double wall, about 0.60 m thick, and the north side consists of rectangular limestone ashlars of various sizes, Fig. 2.3.4-5. Two views of the back wall figure in Pullan's watercolours, Pl. 11-12, and it also appears in his section Pl. 10. The same stone was also used for the ceiling blocks of the East Corridor (see below).

It should be noted that there is a single piece of green andesite in the upper wall and that the fill both in the upper and lower wall included many chips of the stone (A) and also a few of marble and of green andesite. Their distribution at the time of excavation was explained in the following way: "No conclusive evidence for considering the wall to be contemporaneous with the Maussolleion, but the possibility cannot be excluded." As in Trench P_{11}, this conclusion was based on a comparison with the situation behind the north parapet in the Western Staircase, MauTb, where the characteristic Maussollan fill with green andesite and marble chips in great quantity had penetrated every hollow space in the back wall (see below, p. 67).

The ceiling of the East Corridor and the continuation of TW1 towards the east

In the trench two complete ceiling limestone slabs and part of a third are visible. From below, inside the corridor, two more slabs in the same material are visible, Fig. 5.5.1. The continuation of the corridor further east, however, has ceiling blocks in the local, soft sandstone. The five limestone slabs are situated exactly on the line of the continuation of the terrace wall, where it spans the corridor. Moreover, their top surface has been levelled with a pickaxe or pointed chisel in a strip, c. 40 cm in width, in order to make possible the placing of the wall (so already Newton). The narrow preparation shows that the wall was continued not as a double wall but only in one line of blocks (as in Trenches P_9 and P_{11}).

Fig. 2.3.1.4 and Fig. 5.5.2 show how the ceiling slabs are placed in a ledge. Also on this ledge one single ashlar block of the terrace wall is preserved facing south. Its top surface lies at level 7.54 m, slightly lower than the bottom level of the continuation to the east.

Altogether, two courses of TW1 are documented in the trench, as well as the bottom level of a third. The height of both ashlar courses is 0.31 cm, spanning from 6.92 m to 7.54 m a.s.l. If the next course was similar, we reach about 7.85 m, a little higher than the bottom level, 7.76 m, in trench P_{11} which is situated 25 m towards the north. Most probably the (not preserved) third course in P_{10} belongs to the same string course as the bottom course in Trench P_{11}. It should be noted that the ashlar in the second course in P_{10} is placed in a ledge and was hidden behind the bedrock to the south.

2.4. Trench Q₆: The outlet of Lower Gallery and East Corridor

Date of excavation: 1976.08.09-10.14.
Dimension: 3 m × 4 m, later extended 3.6 m eastwards, and in the SW corner.
Subject: The junction of Lower Gallery and East Corridor, the 'propylon', Building C, the ground to the south east of the Quadrangle.
Documentation: Plan (Fig. 2.4.1), west elevation (Fig. 2.4.2), north elevation (Fig. 2.4.4), south elevation (Fig. 2.4.5), sections A-A and B-B (Fig. 2.4.6), east elevation (Fig. 2.4.3). Photos 2.4.7-10.
Mentioned: Pedersen 1991,1: 64-65, Fig. 73, the north elevation (combined with mirror image of south section of Trench R₁₄, cf. Pedersen 1991,2: 35), and the east elevation. The plan is shown on his pl. II = his Fig. 72.

The level of the surface in the NW corner is 9.64 m a.s.l., in the SW corner 9.56 m, in the NE corner 8.80 m a.s.l., and in the SE corner 8.59 m a.s.l.

The soil profiles north and south show the same marked difference between the west and the east end. Below the topsoil and the characteristic Newton fill layer of 1 m's thickness and in about the middle of the trench there is a sharp, almost vertical division between the intact Maussollan fill layers (7-10) to the west and the recent fill of layer 3 to the east. This consisted of debris and of sedimentary gravel and soil, obviously accumulated over some time. The steep side of Maussollan fill is the one referred to by both Newton and explicitly Biliotti (see above, p. 20). In all likelihood it indicates the western edge of the ditch cut by the Hospitallers in their systematic search for ashlars – at this point from the foundations of the proposed propylon, Building C, of the Maussolleion terrace.[29]

Newton and also Murdoch Smith describe how they reached the area of Trench Q₆:

Newton: *At the point of convergence of the upper and lower galleries, ε, we have lost, for the present, all trace of both galleries; but digging onward to the east, on their supposed track, we made a discovery of great interest. ···, we came upon the lowest course of the eastern wall of the peribolus.*[30]

Murdoch Smith: *We have made another important discovery this month by mining. By this means we have found the wall of the peribolus on the east side. ··· We are now mining right and left along this eastern wall from the point where we discovered it.*[31]

The stratification in the East Corridor confirms the above statements, see Fig. 2.4.2, west elevation. The layers 12, 14-17 are sedimentary and of varying composition. Only layer 13 is different, being a part of the compact ceiling, layer 7, that

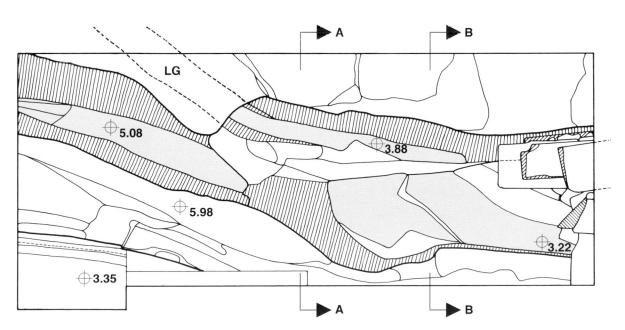

Fig. 2.4.1. Trench Q₆ Plan. 1:50.

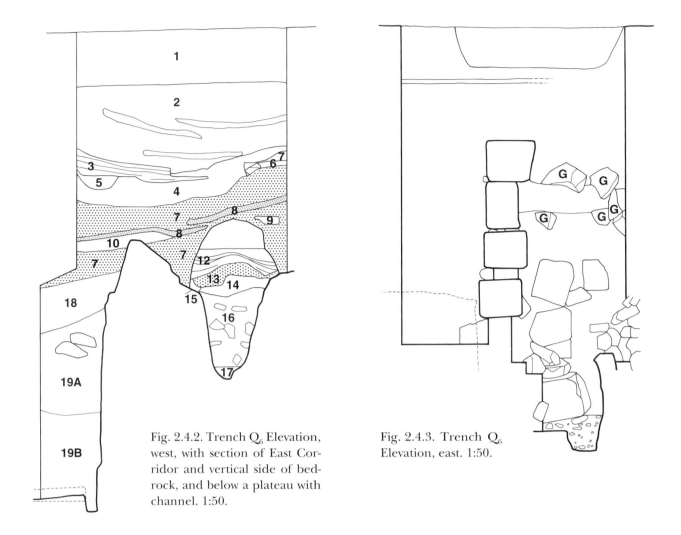

Fig. 2.4.2. Trench Q₆ Elevation, west, with section of East Corridor and vertical side of bedrock, and below a plateau with channel. 1:50.

Fig. 2.4.3. Trench Q₆ Elevation, east. 1:50.

Fig. 2.4.4. Trench Q₆ Elevation, north. 1:50.

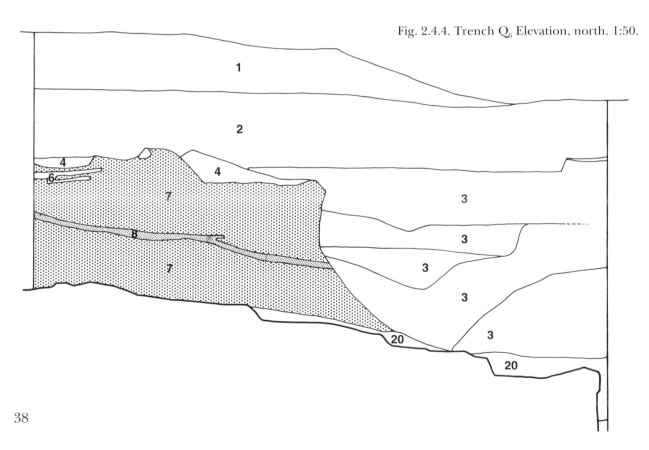

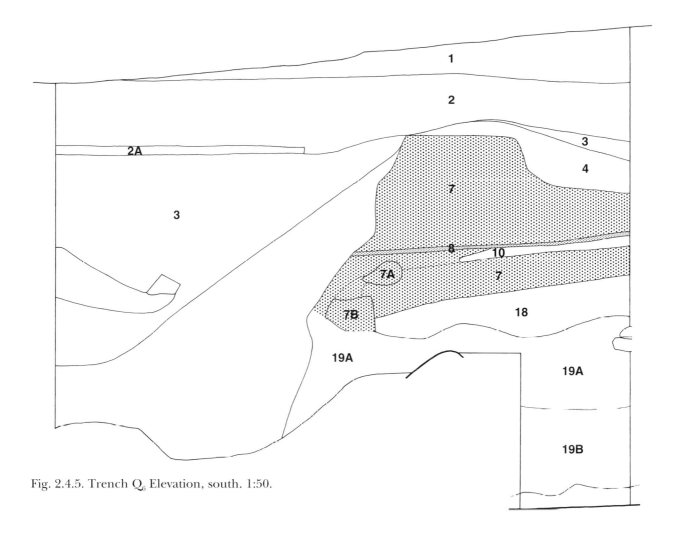

Fig. 2.4.5. Trench Q_6 Elevation, south. 1:50.

Fig. 2.4.6. Trench Q_6 Sections A-A, and B-B. 1:50.

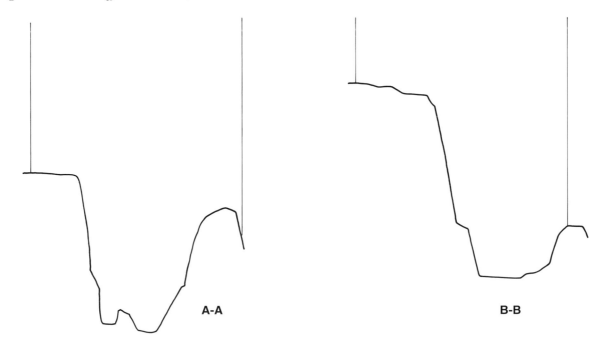

Fig. 2.4.7. Bottom in SW corner of Trench Q₆ with water-channel. 1976

Fig. 2.4.8. Western part of Trench Q₆ at the end of the excavation. 1976.

has fallen down at some point. There are no ceiling blocks preserved, and the British sappers had to explore the corridor towards the east through Maussollan fill. After having explored further east and the lucky discovery of the eastern peribolos wall, the British removed the upper layers in what corresponds to the eastern part of the trench and also further east. The same peculiar procedure of arrival through mining followed by excavation from above was used elsewhere, e.g. in the Western Staircase (MauTb) and in the area of the eastern end of UG:B2 and the *soros*, cf. Pl. 5-6, and Ch. 1 above.

The evidence from the East Corridor in Trench Q₇ allows an important conclusion on its state in the 4th Century BC. Originally the corridor was cut as an open ditch and was roofed by ceiling blocks, just as in its course only about 4 m to the west (see below, p. 109) and as in the east end of UG:B2, as is documented by Newton (see below, p. 134). When the British sappers worked

their way through, there were no ceiling blocks in this part, and they can have been removed only before the waste from the building of the Maussolleion filled the whole area. By that time then, at least the eastern part of the corridor was of no use and was partly pillaged and filled up.

Description of the strata in the elevations Figs. 2.4.2.4-5:

1. Surface layer from recent levelling of the area.
2. Sedimentary, light brown with few finds. 2A Fine-washed and compact.
3. Partly sedimentary, dark brown layers, 3A with lumps and chips of green andesite, sandstone and marble. Mixed pottery, *i.a.* Turkish glazed ware. In the easternmost part of the trench – as shown in the east elevation Fig. 2.4.3 – there was a heavy concentration of both regular ashlars and fractions, in sandstone and also green andesite.

Fig. 2.4.9. Eastern side of Trench Q_6. 1976.

Fig. 2.4.10. Eastern part and bottom of Trench Q_6. 1976.

4. Whitish-brown layer with pieces of white andesite.
5. Like 3, but lighter.
6. Sedimentary, gravel-containing layer with a few fragments of blue limestone and greyish andesite.
7. Thick layer of white and grey, decomposed rock. With chips of green andesite and with pockets of green andesite (layer 8), bluish marble (layer 9) and lumps of sandstone and claystone (layer 10). Finds of iron slags and a little charcoal. This layer with a top level of c. 8.15 m a.s.l. is the typical Maussollan fill so often encountered and described by the British. The same layer was also ascertained during the Danish excavations in Trench R_{12}, just inside the NE corner of the foundation of the peribolos wall.[32]
8. Layer of green andesite chips and dust.
9. Layer of blue limestone chips and pieces, some with chisel-marks.

10. Lumps of sand- and claystone with pieces of green andesite.
11. Rose-coloured layer mainly consisting of decomposed white andesite, pottery fragments, and chips of green andesite.
12. Sedimentary, light brown soil and fine gravel. This layer accumulated upon layer 13 that, in fact, is a part of layer 7 fallen from above.
13. As 7, but fallen down from top / ceiling of corridor.
14. Sedimentary, light brown gravel and fine gravel.
15. Brown layer with bits of charcoal.
16. Sedimentary, whitish and light-brown gravel mixed with stones of varying sizes. Close to the bottom of level 5.20 m a.s.l. a Turkish glazed sherd was found.
17. Sedimentary, dense brown soil.
18. Yellowish, loose layer of white and green andesite pieces. Few white marble pieces and some pottery, *i.a.* a black glazed cup-kan-

tharos[33] and four red-figure sherds showing parts of a satyr and maenad.[34]

19. Brownish, loose soil with fragments of green, sand- and claystone as well as of chips of green andesite, white marble, blue limestone, as well as pottery. B is slightly more compact than A. In the bottom of the channel was found a fragment of a terracotta figure, left side of draped female body, the back hollow.[35]

20. Reddish, decomposed rock with some pottery and chips of green andesite.

All along the north side of the trench the bedrock is preserved in a ledge, up to 1 m wide, and sloping and stepping down towards the east from 6.46 m to 5.29 m, and even less than 5.03 m a.s.l. in the very eastern end. The situation along the south side of the trench at first seemed to be similar, but in fact the south section runs almost on the edge of a vertical cutting in the bedrock that is only documented in the SW corner of the trench.

In the west section of the trench, Fig. 2.4.2, the East Corridor is clearly seen with its oblique sides and the somewhat corrupted top of the bedrock on both sides where the ceiling blocks originally rested (see for a discussion of the evidence, below, Ch. 5.5). The bedrock forms a kind of narrow ridge, vertically cut on its south side down to an uneven horizontal surface in level 3.46 / 3.35 / 3.41 m a.s.l., Fig. 2.4.7. Only an area of 1.40 m × 0.70 m was revealed. Along the foot of the 3 m high side runs a narrow channel, 12 cm wide and 20 cm deep. On top of the vertical side is preserved a ledge, 0.12-0.14 m wide, above which the bedrock is cut obliquely and fairly smooth. Otherwise, however, the original features of the main part of the bedrock between the East Gallery and the vertical cutting have been destroyed. This destruction took place before the area was buried to form the huge Maussolleion terrace. The 'central ridge', however, continues right to the east end of the trench, cf. the south section Fig. 2.4.5, where its top level is at 4.45 m a.s.l. It is fair to assume that the vertical cutting continued east in a straight line. Both in the sections A-a and B-b, Figs. 2.4.6, and in the east elevation Fig. 2.4.3 the beginning of the vertical line is conspicuous.

The central part of the trench in its full length is extremely complicated. The bedrock is cut to receive both the East Corridor and the Lower Gallery and varies in level from 6.46 m to 3.19 m a.s.l. Moreover, parts of the structures in its eastern part have been utterly destroyed both in the 4th Century BC and in the 16th Century by the Hospitallers.

From the west, the cutting of the East Corridor is clearly seen, with a fairly narrow flat bottom, 0.32 m to 0.45 m wide, at level 5.08-5.02 m a.s.l. (the first 55 cm narrower – corrupted?). About 2.50 m from the west side of the trench the bottom and north side is cut off obliquely. It declines sharply to the NE about 1 m down to the bottom of the Lower Gallery that debouches from the north at this point, bottom level 3.98 m a.s.l. The two courses, however, did not meet directly. The bottom line of the Lower Gallery turns in a more easterly direction, almost parallel to the East Corridor, but first its south side, then its bottom, fade away and through an almost vertical and very smooth side end in the lowest central part of the trench, level about 3.25-3.09 m a.s.l., into which also the main part of the East Corridor opens after a fall of c. 1.75 m. The north side of the Lower Gallery, however, continues right to the east end of the trench. The sides and bottom of the East Corridor at its original level appear destroyed, whereas the Lower Gallery rather fades away and connects to the bottom at the east end of the trench.

The extreme east termination of the trench appears flat-bottomed (3.47 m a.s.l.) with a kind of channel, almost 0.26 m wide and 0.20 m deep, along the south side. To the south is preserved a 1.2 m high (top level 4.45 m) and slightly curved side reminiscent of the hewn side of the Lower Gallery. Unfortunately, the north side could not be investigated at bottom level for safety reasons, so the exact extension of the flat bottom is not known. 0.45 m is clearly seen, and to judge from the almost vertical side of the bedrock ledge above to the north, it could be as wide as 1 m. With a fair degree of certainty, the bottom was formed as an altogether c. 1.2 m wide cutting with almost vertical sides and a channel along its south side. The top level of the north side, however, is c. 1 m higher than in the south side, and if there ever was a ceiling, no traces are preserved.

Both the function and continuation to the east of this fairly well defined 'ditch' with a channel are enigmatic. It bears no resemblance to the East Corridor or to the Lower Gallery. And where did it lead to? Pedersen has presented the results of the excavations in 1966-1967 in the area just to the east of our trench.[36] Trench R$_7$ lies 7 m to the east and at right-angles to Trench Q$_6$. The level of the bedrock in R$_7$ is about 4.25 m a.s.l., about 0.75 m above the bottom of the 'ditch' and only 20 cm lower than the bedrock on its south side. There are, however, no traces of a channel to either side of this elevation, where the level reaches only 2.60 m.

Newton believed that both galleries emptied themselves into a reservoir further east, but gave no details whatsoever.[37] The existence of such a reservoir was not verified during the Danish excavations.[38] In the south and east walls of 'Building D', however, short stretches of three water pipes (in Trenches S$_2$ (3.24 m a.s.l.), T$_2$ and T$_1$) were documented.[39] Neither their dating – Hellenistic / Roman? – nor their architectural context is known.

Perhaps the congruence of levels between the channel in the east end of the trench Q$_6$ (3.22 m a.s.l.) and the one in the bottom of its SW corner (3.19 m a.s.l.) is more than a coincidence, even if the latter certainly is pre-Maussollan. On this line of thought, the channels could meet just beyond the limits of trench Q$_6$. However, neither origin nor destination of the latter channel is known. The investigation in Trench Q$_6$ certainly was rewarding in many respects, but it also has posed many questions that can hardly be answered without further excavation. Two problems remain unsolved:

1. What was the function of the East Corridor? And to where did it lead towards the east?
2. What was meant to happen with the water issuing through the outlet of the Lower Gallery?

2.5. Trench Q₇: The terrace of the Maussolleion

Date of excavation: 1976.08.30-09.28.
Dimension: 6.5 m × 3 m (west) / 2 m (east).
Subject: The Upper Gallery B2 and the ground to the east and south of the Quadrangle. To follow the stratigraphy towards the west on line with the north side in Trench Q₆.
Documentation: Plan (Fig. 2.5.1), south elevation (Fig. 2.5.2), east elevation, partial (Fig. 2.5.3). Photos Figs. 2.5.4-6.
Mentioned: Pedersen 1991,1: 79 with Fig. 82: the south elevation; the plan is shown on his pl. II = Fig. 72.

The trench measured first 3.00 m × 3.00 m. Newton's "Short Gallery", where it turns 90° was expected to turn up south of its centre, cf. Fig. 1.2.4, but did not appear. Therefore the trench was extended 3.5 m towards the west to the line of TW1e, but only 2 m in width due to several sandstone ashlars in the lower part of layer 2.

The level of the surface in the NW corner is 10.10 m a.s.l., in the SW 10.00 m a.s.l., in the NE corner 10.00 m a.s.l. and in the SE corner 9.88 m a.s.l.

The two upper layers are first a recent surface layer, and second a characteristic, mixed Newton "Schutt" layer. Layer 4, and probably also the thin layer 3, are fine intact Maussollan layers running the whole length of the trench except in its western extremity, where they are cut almost vertically in a line only c. 0.8 m from the assumed line of TW1e. This is the edge of Biliotti's excavations, when he searched in vain for the angle of the terrace wall TW1 (see below, p. 74). Layer 4 slopes from west to east (8.84 m-8.42 m a.s.l.), and perhaps it reappears as the thin layer 8 at level 6.84 m a.s.l. (in Trench Q6) that is embedded in the thick, whitish Maussollan layer 7.

Altogether, the original Maussollan fill with its dated finds of pottery, etc., has been studied in depth for the length of about 11 m in the two trenches. These are the layers, so often referred to by Newton and Biliotti, that they found everywhere 3-6 feet below the surface. The gentle slope from west to east demonstrates – if there should be any doubt about the origin – that the fill was thrown in this direction from a work site to the west. Remarkable is the fact that the top level of the layer is identical to the top level of the terrace wall TW1 in Trench P₁₁ (8.84 m a.s.l.), and to the bedrock along the SE corner of the Quadrangle (8.90 m a.s.l.).

Description of the strata in the south and the east elevations:

1. Surface layer from recent levelling of the area.
2. Brownish to whitish layer with pottery, 2B also with chips of marble and green andesite and 2C with a large content of decomposed sandstone. In the lower part, several ashlars of sandstone (cf. plan), one measuring 35.5 × 90 × 52 cm, and green andesite, one measuring 30 × 97 × 70 cm.
3. Layer with a large quantity of decomposed sandstone.
4. Layer with a large quantity of bits and chips of green andesite besides some bits of lead, in 4B also with several fragments of roof tiles, some of which with antefixes having a floral ornament.[40]
5. As 4.
6. Yellowish layer containing small fragments of sandstone. In 6A also green andesite and – at the western end – a large amount of marble chips.
7. Whitish to rose-coloured layer of partly decomposed whitish sandstone and rubble in the same material. Also some chips of marble and green andesite.
8. As 4.
9. Grey to yellowish layer with a few pieces of sandstone and many chips of green andesite. In the east part of the trench, c. 7.25 m a.s.l., were found a handle in local ware,[41] a red-figure sherd with meander decoration and a black-glazed neck piece.[42]
10. Firm yellow-brown layer (claystone) with large fragments of whitish sandstone. Finds of pottery, local burnished ware, black-glaze, a thin body fragment and a nozzle of a lamp, a few tiles, several fragments of pipes (in both ends of trench).

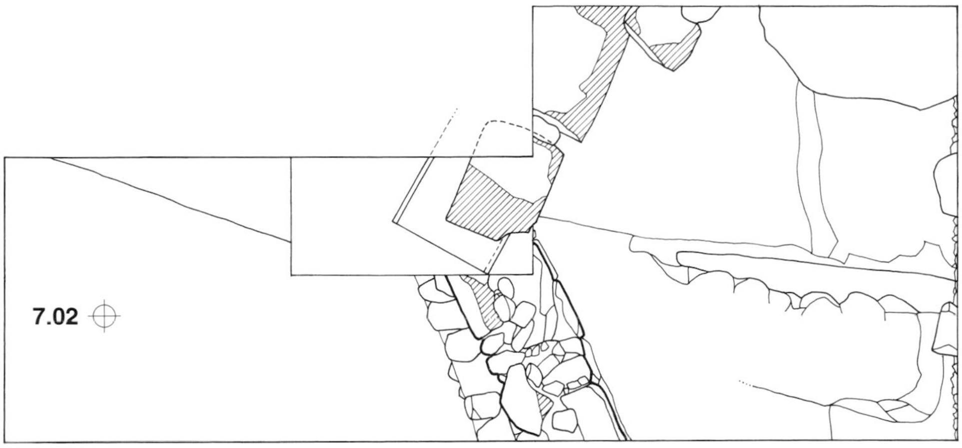

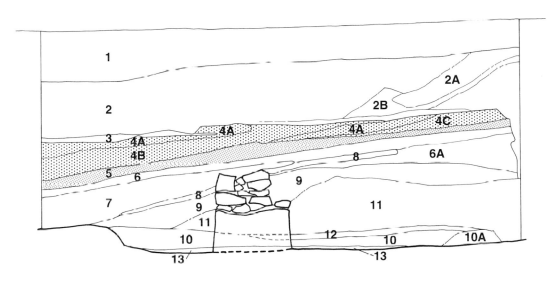

Fig. 2.5.1. Trench Q₇ Plan. 1:50.

7.02

Fig. 2.5.2. Trench Q₇ Section, south, with the rubble wall and with the soil profile after its removal. 1:50.

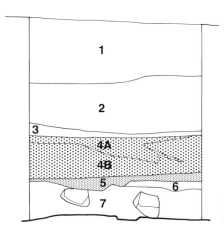

Fig. 2.5.3. Trench Q₇ Section, east. 1:50.

Fig. 2.5.4. Trench Q₇ View east. 1976.

11. As 9, but with only occasional chips of green andesite.
12. Layer of decomposed claystone. Part of 10.
13. Sedimentary brownish gravel.

A roughly built double wall crosses the trench obliquely in a SE direction. It is c. 0.55 m high, 0.75 m wide (1 m wide including the ledge along the west side), and consists of pieces of sandstone and claystone, among which are many green andesite chippings and pieces, as well as one in marble. A study of the soil profile to the south shows that the wall can have been built only in the course of the filling up of the area. It lies on layer 11 at about 7.55 m a.s.l., and in neither layer 9 nor 8 is there any trace of a foundation cutting. Layer 7, moreover, runs uninterrupted over the wall that was never higher and can have been hidden only very soon after its construction. Its purpose is hard to imagine. Biliotti discovered two rough walls in the Maussollan fill (10 feet below the surface) south of the Maussolleion.[43] One, 2-3 feet high, ran north-south more or less on top of the northern part of UG: C south of Shaft U7. Another ran at right-angles to this one (24 feet south of the ashlar wall TW1) and extended about 25 feet. Biliotti offered no explanation for these rubble walls, and the one in Trench Q₇ does not bring us closer to an explanation.

The floor of the trench is somewhat irregular, and conspicuous is the vertical fault-set line between claystone to the north and sandstone to the south. Within the Quadrangle itself J.A. Gifford noted a similar fault set.[44]

Contrary to our expectations, Newton's "Short Gallery" (UG:B2) did not show up where it should be according to the plan of Murdoch Smith. A grave error has occurred, probably due to the fact that the aqueduct was explored by tunnelling. The aqueduct running from the SE corner of the Quadrangle should show up in the trench. Because its ceiling height close to the Quadrangle is 7.92 m a.s.l., nearly one metre higher than the level of the bedrock in the trench (6.86 m to 7.02 m a.s.l.), the gallery should have appeared as an open ditch, as in its well-known termination to the east, cf. Pl. 5-6.

Fig. 2.5.5. Oblique rubble wall in Trench Q$_7$. View west. 1976.

Fig. 2.5.6. Detail of south profile in Trench Q$_7$ with fragments of roof tiles in the Maussolleion fill strata. 1976.

2.6. The excavation in the staircase of Chamber 1

Date of excavation: 1972.05.13-; 1972.06.14-07.05; 1973.08.06; 1973.08.23.
Dimension: 4.7 m × 4.5 m.
Subject: Soil block in the staircase leading down to Chamber 1 not excavated by Newton.
Documentation: North elevation (Fig. 2.6.3). East section A-A (Fig. 2.6.4). Photos 2.6.1-2, 5. Cf. Newton, *FP*16 (1859.04.12.): 86; *HD*: 127-28, Pl. XIII = Pl. 7, with plan, sections A-B and C-D, plan at C enlarged, and view of eastern part of staircase towards south.

Newton mentions the southern staircase twice, using more or less the same wording, and he states in both places: *A rubble wall crossed the lowest step obliquely.* On Pullan's measured drawing, Pl. 7, this wall appears in plan, section and even in a curious view from below in connection with the careful recording of certain architectural features of the pre-Maussollan structure. Apparently, a part of the rubble was allowed to remain in the centre of the staircase, and excavation was undertaken only along the parapets of the staircase and in its upper part. Newton does not present any stratigraphical observations.

During the excavation in 1972, the "rubble wall" turned up again, and being, at least partly, undisturbed by Newton, it was duly excavated. It consists of irregular and carelessly laid stones and originally spanned the whole width, 4.7 m, of the staircase. On both sides, recent dark soil documented the excavation by Newton, where he cut through both the "rubble wall" and the thick Maussollan layers 4 and 5 below, see Fig. 2.6.4. In all likelihood the Maussollan layers originally also covered the built corridor and what was left of the landing of Cb1 to the south of the Maussolleion podium proper (see below, p. 51).

Fig. 2.6.1. The staircase of Cb1 partly excavated. View south. The rubble wall rests on top of a thick layer of undisturbed 4th Century BC fill and on the ashlar-built transverse corridor crossing the staircase. 1972.

Fig. 2.6.2. View of the opening from Cb1 into the Main Corridor and of the walls of the transverse corridor in the landing. Above the south wall the lower part of the fill of the unexcavated staircase. View SE. 1972.

1. Topsoil (humus) mixed with pieces and splinters of sandstone, green andesite, marble and pottery. Of pottery various types, black-glaze, local burnished ware, 'terra sigillata', and recent coarse and glazed ware.
2. Pockets of whitish sandstone and fine gravel.
3. Topsoil like 1, but lighter, because it is mixed with sandstone gravel. It lies between the boulders and has a vertical demarcation against layer 1.
4. Like 1, but less compact, containing boulders, pieces of green andesite and sandstone.
5. Loose greenish sandy layer with more than 50% of green andesite chips and pieces and some marble chips. Also a few pieces of sandstone and lumps of claystone. The lowest course of sandstone ashlars is imbedded in this layer, which is seen in between the stones and above one of them.
6. Loose reddish sandy layer with pieces of sandstone with greyish, greenish and reddish particles. Pieces and chips of green andesite, a few marble chips, bits of lead and charcoal. Of pottery small fragments of black-glazed ware, and a considerable amount of local, burnished ware. Also two fragments of stucco with white, reddish and bluish particles and with a fine, smooth yellowish to white surface.

Newton's reason for leaving undisturbed a substantial part of the 'rubble wall' and the Maussollan fill below is certainly due to his correct observation that no remains from the Maussolleion could be found in the fill. Its interest today is due to this fill and its firm *ante quem* dating of the transverse corridor across the staircase. The structure Cb1 was destroyed together with the aqueduct UG:B, but for some reason it was considered necessary to secure admission from the Main Corridor into a hastily built corridor that gave access only to the SW corner of the Maussolleion podium in green andesite (see below Ch. 6.2.2).

Description of the strata in elevation and section A-a of the rubble wall and soil profile in the southern staircase, Fig 2.6.3+4.

Description of the stones in the rubble wall (besides one piece of white marble and minor pieces of green andesite):
B. Greyish andesite
C. Like B but lighter in colour
D. Blue limestone
E. Boulder, bluish and reddish
S. Sandstone

The lower part, Layer 5 together with the lowest string of four sandstone ashlars plus one in greyish andesite embedded in it, dates to the time of the building of the Maussolleion. The south limit of this layer (Fig. 2.6.4) denotes the limit of Newton's excavation, clearly indicated also on Pullan's plan. The upper part of the wall is inseparable from Layer 3 and was also spared by Newton. It consists of various kinds of stones,

Fig. 2.6.3. View of transverse rough wall and fill in staircase in Cb1. 1:50.

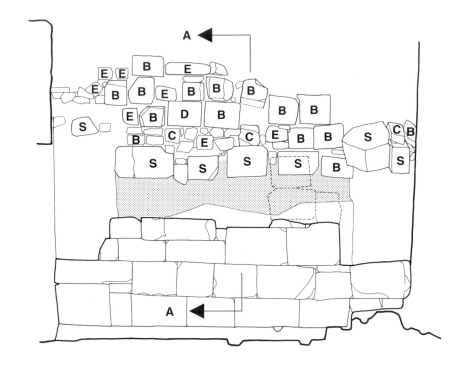

Fig. 2.6.4. North-south section A-A in staircase in Cb1. 1:50.

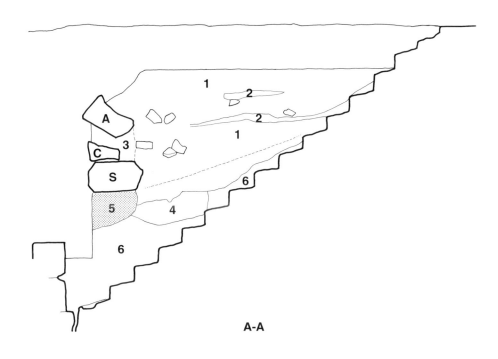

A-A

Fig. 2.6.5. The bottom part of the staircase of Cb1. The south wall of the transverse corridor rests on the fill in the bothros, and to the right on the fill above steps 15-16. 1973.

but not of sandstone as in the bottom 'course'. Most probably, the upper part of the rubble wall was piled up by the Hospitallers as a kind of protection against the soil balk to the south, when they pillaged the bottom of the foundations of the Maussolleion.

Newton spared pockets of the original fill in the staircase above the level of the greenish layer 5. One pocket on the steps 5, 6 and 7 along the west parapet was substantial. It consisted of typical Maussolleion fill, compact decomposed sandstone with brown veins.

During our excavation of the 15th and 16th steps in the western part of the staircase, a cutting 1 m wide × 0.73 m north-south and 1.02 m deep appeared (Figs. 5.1.2 and 4). It was partly buried below the ashlar-built wall of the corridor intersecting Cb1 (cf. below Ch. 6.2.2.). This remarkable cutting was immediately termed a

bothros. Its fill formed a continuation of Layer 6, described above, but along the short sides and below the wall, it became very compact and contained fairly big pieces of sandstone placed as a kind of support for the wall above. Most remarkable, however, is that the layer downwards gradually consisted almost only of pottery, mainly local burnished ware but also black-blazed ware, as well as a few terracottas and glass pendants. Many vessels have been reconstructed. The same fill was also preserved in the bottom of the new transverse corridor, see below, p. 130. The findings are published in their totality by Leif Erik Vaag 2002.[45] See below, p. 82 for a discussion of the bothros in its architectural context close to the door from Chamber 1 into the Upper Gallery B, through which water was conveyed to the place.

51

3. The drain around the Quadrangle of the Maussolleion: the Lower Gallery

The Lower Gallery consists of two parts, one that surrounds the foundation cutting of the Maussolleion, and another, separately cut course, into which both the former and a built channel from within the Maussolleion come together, and which formed the outlet of the otherwise closed system. It is cut in the bedrock, is man-high (with an average height of about 1.6 m) and flat-bottomed. The highest point is in the NW (c. 4.6 m a.s.l.), from where it slopes towards the east and south towards the outlet in the SE (3.88 m a.s.l.). Ten shafts provided access to the gallery at varying intervals. The burial chamber of Maussollos was connected to the gallery both towards the east and the west by means of narrow channels, built in andesite.

The British team encountered the gallery already in the first weeks of the excavation.[46] It was completely emptied and was measured September 24-25, 1857 by Murdoch Smith,[47] immediately after which Newton sent a sketch plan to the Earl of Clarendon.[18] Newton describes the gallery in *P*15: 47-48, in *FP*16: 89, as well as in *HD*: 142-145 with the plan and sections (our Fig. 1.2.1 and Pl. 1) and two sections by Pullan.[49] A brief account is also given in *TD*: 207-208.

Murdoch Smith's plan is fairly reliable, but for two strange errors. The gallery traverses the Western Staircase at right-angles, whereas he shows its course obliquely. The confluence shaft, L10, is cut in the top of the 1.8 m wide bedrock ridge or 'bench' east of the Maussolleion. In Murdoch Smith's plan, however, it overlaps both the terrace wall TW1 and the vertical east side of the 'bench'.

3.1. General description

We investigated the gallery during the campaigns of 1973, 1974 and 1976. It was everywhere filled almost to the ceiling with stratified soil of varying density, cf. Figs. 3.1.8: section S2 and Fig. 3.2.6: section W1. The position of all the shafts was duly recorded, of Shafts L1 and L3, however, only *in* the gallery and of Shafts L4 and L5 only their openings. Shaft L3 is situated below a house terrace, and having excavated the main part of the circuit, we considered the effort of emptying the northern part a waste of time. It is regrettable, however, that the 'blind alley', in the north re-entrant of the Western Staircase, had to be left unexcavated. The lower part of the re-entrant is cut in the very friable claystone. We feared that the free-standing re-entrant might break down if we emptied the gallery, the west side of which was already ruined. In order to study the relation between gallery and staircase, a hole was cut down through the claystone to the gallery south of Shaft L1.

Parts are cut completely in the solid sandstone, others in claystone, e.g. from south of MauTb to Shaft L3 and around L9. In the area around Shaft L6, see Figs. 3.1.3 and 5, both stones are seen divided by a horizontal fault, claystone below and sandstone above.

The state of preservation varies according to the stone. The original surface of the claystone is everywhere gone and the present one is very friable. The original outlines of Shafts L2 and L9 are almost completely ruined.

The procedure and techniques of cutting the Lower Gallery – and the Upper Gallery and the

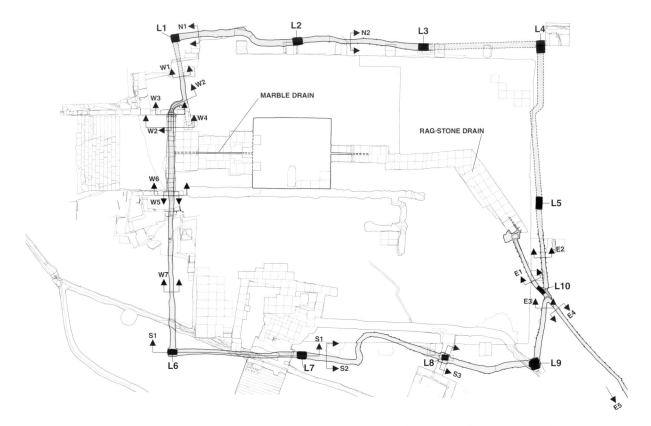

Fig. 3.1.1. Plan of the Lower Gallery with signatures and the position of sections. The unexcavated parts are reconstructed from *HD* pl. III-IV = Fig. 1.2.1 (broken line).

corridors as well (below, p. 115) – conform to general practice in Antiquity, most recently described by Klaus Grewe.[50]

Access to the gallery was provided by vertical shafts at varying intervals, one at each corner, and two more along the north, south, and east sides (Shafts L1-L10). They are situated 1 to 3 m outside the Quadrangle at level 9.6-9.7 m a.s.l. (L1, L4-L8) and c. 9.0 m a.s.l. (L9-L10). Only Shaft L2 is situated markedly lower down than the rest due to its position in the depression along the NW edge of the Quadrangle (top level c. 7.04 m a.s.l.). The bottom level in the gallery varies from c. 4.6 m a.s.l. to 3.65 m a.s.l. Altogether, the height of the shafts varies considerably, from only c. 2.6 m (L2) to 6.2 m (L7).

The distance between the corner shafts L1-L4, L6-L9 (the width of the shafts included) is very regular, 43 m E-W and 36.5 m (L1-L6) and 37.5 m (L4-L9 outline effaced) N-S. Most probably, therefore, the marking of their position was the first step in the construction. A regular system also appears from the location of Shafts

L2 and L3 that divide the north course into three parts of almost equal size. On the south side Shaft L7 corresponds to L2, but L8 is displaced towards the east. At this point it cuts through a pre-Maussollan corridor (see below, p. 133), the position of which must have been known (the peculiar character of this shaft will be discussed below, p. 59). On the west side there are no shafts. On the east side there are two, but they are different in character. Like the shafts on the north and south sides, L5 is positioned in line with the course of the gallery below. Shaft L10, however, has another orientation and follows the line of the outlet from the tomb chamber of Maussollos towards the SE, the direction of which is continued in the outlet of the whole system.

The size of the shafts varies considerably (L4: 1.35 m × 1.00 m; L7: 1.25 m × 0.92 m; L8: 1.45 m (reduced to 0.90 m) × 0.65 m; L10: 1.10 m × 0.50 m; L9 forms an exception N 1.15 m, E 1.05 m, S 1.0 m, W 0.97 m, see below, p. 60). Their tops are prepared with a ledge (best preserved at L6, see Figs. 3.1.3. and 5) for cover slabs, a few of which in green andesite are preserved. However, the top of L4 is plain. The cover slabs have been roughly treated with the pointed chisel, and there is neither anathyrosis nor clamp-holes. The two preserved slabs still partly *in situ* at Shaft L4 measure 1.42 m × 0.78 m × 0.30 m and 1.48 m × 0.97 m × 0.31 m. A slab measuring 1.0 m × 0.95 m × 0.3 m was found *ex situ* close to L10. In Murdoch Smith's section E-F in Pl. 1 a slab is shown *in situ* on top of Shaft L3.

The SW corner of the opening of Shaft L2 is hidden by Pillar P3, cf. Jeppesen 2000: 44, 45, Fig. 1.14 (the opening of the shaft visible below and to the right of the pillar). The shaft is cut in claystone and is badly damaged, so its exact original size is unknown. Most likely, however, the shaft predates the pillar. If the pillar were already there, the shaft could easily have been moved slightly to the east. This was not the case with the pillars that on both the north and the south side are placed at approximately equal intervals and opposite each other.[51] Anyhow, this shaft was certainly used only for the cutting of the gallery. Soon after, the whole area was filled with some 3.5 m fill up to the level of the euthynteria of the peribolos wall.

In all shafts there are cuttings for steps opposite each other on the long sides, cf. L6, Fig. 3.1.3 and 6, and L8, Fig. 3.1.9, to facilitate access during construction and, probably, maintenance later on.

Throughout the gallery there are chisel- or pickaxe-marks on the sides from the flat bottom to the top of the rounded ceiling. By this means, the direction of the working teams can easily be ascertained. This way of construction, which hardly surprises one, also appears from other observations. Conspicuous are the deviations from the line of several of the shafts (L1 and L2, L4 and L5, L7 and L8, L8 and L9), that can result only from sloppy planning of the direction of work, because there are no geological obstacles that might necessitate this. Only after they were quite close to each other did the teams realize that corrections had to be made. South of L1 the work in a wrong direction resulted in a 'blind alley' and the work was resumed from a point nearly 2.5 m before the ultimate point reached. The relation between the Lower Gallery and the Western Staircase is discussed in detail below. The meeting-points between two groups are further characterized by a narrowing of the sides, lowering of the ceiling and also a settling of the floor level. Between Shafts L6 and L7 the groups succeeded without a swerve, but the chisel-marks and the narrowing mark the place very clearly, Fig. 3.1.3.

The study of the chisel-marks also furnishes important evidence for the relation between the 'circuit gallery'- and the 'outlet gallery' where they joined close to Shaft L10, Fig. 3.1.12-13 and 14. The workmen proceeded from both the north and the south side towards the shaft and the 'outlet gallery' that, accordingly, had been executed – at least partly – in advance. The branch from the north met the 'outlet gallery' at level 4.54 m a.s.l., the one from the south at level 3.79 m a.s.l. The chisel-marks show moreover that Shaft L10 was the starting-point for the cutting of the 'outlet gallery' in both directions, towards the NW into the Quadrangle and towards the SE.

Throughout the gallery there are lamp-holes at irregular intervals, normally only on one side – and then on the left side of the cutting direction – but sometimes on both sides.

In two places the course of the gallery penetrates within the line of the Quadrangle. In both cases, however, only for a short stretch and not beyond the line of the crepis of the Maussolleion. Time has shown that the thickness of the bedrock, c. 2.5 m, was strong enough to carry the weight of the euthynteria course and crepidoma of the Maussolleion. The first penetration, see the plan Fig. 3.1.1 – between Shafts L7 and L8 – is certainly the result of a serious miscalculation, which may have been brought about by the situation and the floor level of Chamber 2, cf. the section Fig. 5.3.3. The other in the 'outlet branch', NW of Shaft L10 was beyond doubt intentional and will be discussed below.

The builders also had problems with establishing the correct level of the bottom in relation to the level in the outlet channel of c. 3.90 m a.s.l. The level on the north and the NE sides is very stable, with a decline of only c. 0.06 m (despite a possible slight depression around L2). The level on the whole south side, however, turned out very badly: the whole stretch from a few metres north of L6 to L10 lies 4 cm to 25 cm (3.65 m a.s.l.) lower down than the outlet channel. Of

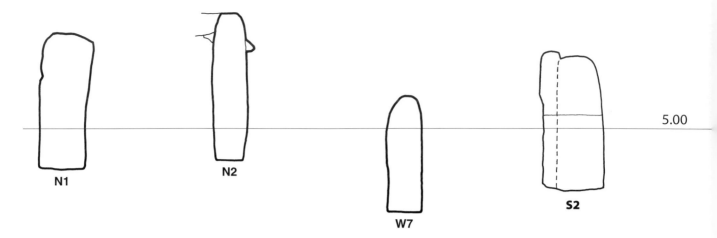

5.00

N1   N2   W7   S2

Fig. 3.1.2. Sections in the north, east and southwest course of the Lower Gallery. 1:50. See Fig. 3.1.4 for the east side and Fig. 3.2.4 and 3.2.6 for the area of the Western Staircase, MauTb. 1:50.

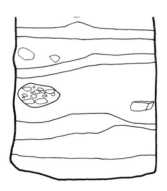

Fig. 3.1.2a.
Section S2 in LG. 1:20

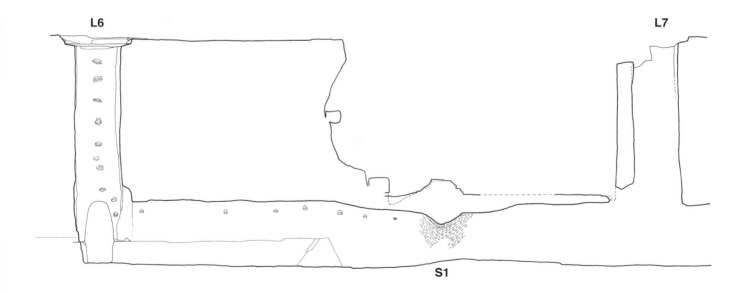

L6   L7   S1

Fig. 3.1.3. Section S1 through Shaft L6, Chamber 1 and Shaft L7. The ashlar-built transverse corridor in Cb1 is not shown. The meeting-point of the two crews is ascertained from the chisel-marks and the narrowing of the passage, cf. Fig. 3.1.7. 1:100.

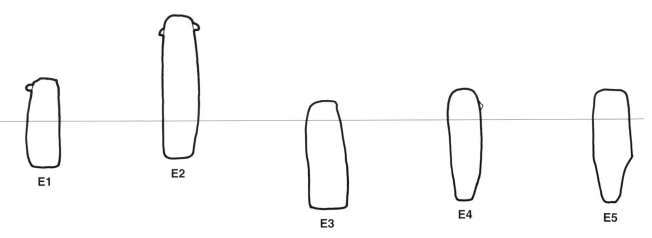

E1   E2   E3   E4   E5

Fig. 3.1.4. Sections in the southeast course of the lower Gallery. 1:50.

course, the mistake had no great consequences for the outlet of the water. If the level of the water rose above 3.90 m a.s.l., it would run away as intended.

The explanation of this odd situation is linked up with the pre-Maussollan structures. A detail in Shaft L6 and also in L7 seems to indicate that the problems raised by Cb1 were realized very late in the working process, Fig. 3.1.3 and 7. Above the opening of the gallery from Shaft L6

towards the east, there is a cutting, 0.45 m high and 0.3 m deep. It repeats the top of the gallery below and cannot but indicate that the level of the gallery was planned to be higher up than actually happened. Without the lowering of the gallery, its top would have cut through the floor of Cb1. There is again an oblique cutting in the west side of Shaft L7 at exactly the same level, and this indicates a similar procedure, when the workmen started to work towards the west. This

Fig. 3.1.5. The top opening of Shaft L6 with ledge for top block(s). 1973.

Fig. 3.1.6. Shaft L6 with four steps seen from the north in LG:w. Note the fault line between sandstone, above, and claystone, below. 1976.

Below, left. Fig. 3.1.7. Detail in Shaft L6 with the cutting of the ceiling of the gallery towards the east. The cutting, 0.45 m high and 0.3 m deep, denotes the planned top level of the gallery before it was lowered. 1976.

Below, right. Fig. 3.1.8. LG:s between Shafts L6 and L7. View east. The meeting-point of the two crews working towards each other is clearly seen. 1976.

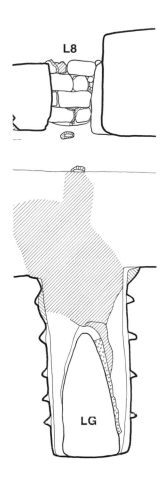

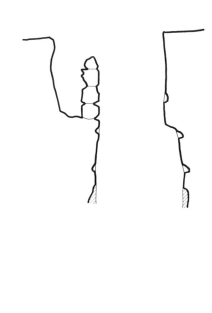

Fig. 3.1.9. Section S3 in Shaft L8 with east-west section of the built upper part in the east side of the shaft. 1:50

cutting, however, made a hole in the floor into the east side of Chamber 1, where the thickness of the floor was only 8 cm because of the presence of a 12 cm deep channel, Figs. 5.1.3 and 5.1.14. The workmen were apparently not aware of the pre-Maussollan chamber, but they solved the problem by lowering the ceiling by 0.50 m. The concurrent lowering of the floor in the gallery inevitably resulted in the unhappy base level of this part of the Lower Gallery in relation to the outlet branch. In Shaft L6 towards the north, there is no correction in the top of the gallery, so it was cut after the work towards the east had begun.[52]

The peculiar features of the top of Shaft L8 reflect an encounter with another pre-Maussollan structure, the corridor connecting Upper Gallery B2 with the subterranean Chamber 2. The evidence, however, appears ambiguous with regard to whether it was known of beforehand or discovered only during the work.

The position of the shaft is not centred between Shaft L7 and the corner Shaft L9, like

Shaft L3 on the north side of the Quadrangle (between L2 and L4). Above, it was suggested that the position of the shaft was moved towards the east because of the very corridor. Fig. 3.1.9 and 10. The top opening of the shaft, 1.45 m × 0.65 m, however, only partly overlaps the corridor and was 1.1 m down shortened to only 0.90 m by a course ashlar wall, with the consequence that its east side came in line with the side of the corridor below. Apparently, the *exact* position of the corridor was not known, when the position of the shaft was decided upon. From this observation it can be concluded that the present opening of the corridor towards the Quadrangle was not visible, either because the area had not yet been prepared for the foundation blocks of the Maussolleion, or, alternatively, because they were already in position when the gallery was cut. The fill behind the coarse wall included many fragments and chippings of green andesite, a feature that confirms the dating of the construction to the time of the construction of the podium of the Maussolleion.

Fig. 3.1.10. The top opening of Shaft L8. The original size of the shaft was diminished when the pre-Maussollan corridor was encountered c. 1 m below the surface.1974.

Fig. 3.1.11. View down in Shaft L9 with, to the left, the floor of UG:B2 and, below, the openings of LG towards west and north. 1973.

A look at the orientation of Shaft L8 bears out the idea that the character of the pre-Maussollan structures was only vaguely known to the workmen of the gallery. As a rule, the shafts follow the line of the gallery below. The top of Shaft L8 closely follows the line of L6, L7 and L9, but its lower part conforms to both the orientation and dimensions of the corridor. So does the gallery below, the line of which almost conforms to the line of the north side in Cb2. In conclusion, first the workmen adjusted the position and the size of the shaft to the corridor and afterwards, also the line of the gallery, for fear of cutting into floor and benches in Chamber 2. This change to another direction, moreover, resulted in the above-mentioned interference of the gallery with the Quadrangle.

Also the Shaft L9 cut through the ceiling and bottom of a pre-Maussollan gallery, UG:B2. The whole upper part of the shaft is badly damaged, Fig. 3.1.11. The east side is missing due to the proximity to the vertical side of the rock to the east and because a shallow sandstone stratum, only c. 0.95 m thick, formed the very top. Climbing-holes are preserved in the lower part of the south and north sides. Peculiar is a kind of ledge with holes around the shaft, in line with the bottom of the Upper Gallery, Fig. 6.2.3.3. The evidence points to a kind of ceiling – probably to hold boards to carry a British windlass, see p. 115 and 133. A ceiling with the purpose of securing a flow of water in UG:B2 can be excluded, because the gallery is effectively blocked up by the andesite ashlars of the foundation a few metres to the NW.

The confluence of the outlet axis and the branches of the circuit is very revealing of the working process, Fig. 3.1.12-14.

The orientation of Shaft L10 follows the line of the 'outlet gallery' below, and the chisel-marks show that the shaft was the starting-point for the cutting in both directions. The bottom level of the shaft and the narrow, only 1.18 m high course towards the Rag Stone Drain (4.32 m a.s.l., ceiling 5.5 m a.s.l.) are precisely cut with regard to the position and level of the built drain coming from the tomb chamber. Also the almost straight outlet towards the SE is precisely cut. It is, however, 1.46 m high, and the almost horizontal floor

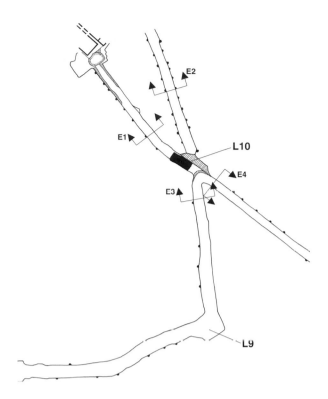

Fig. 3.1.12. Plan, west of Shaft L9 to the north of Shaft L10, including the SE end of the Rag-Stone Drain.

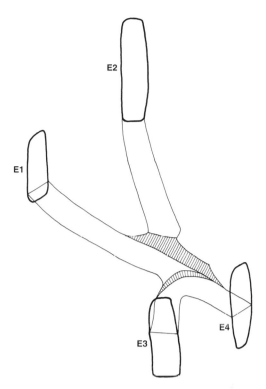

Fig. 3.1.13. The confluence of the 'circuit gallery' with the 'outlet gallery' showing the relative levels and sizes of the parts.

lies at a level (W 3.90 m – E 3.88 m a.s.l.) about 42 cm lower down. A roughly cut step forms the transition between the two levels.

The level of the branch coming from the north towards Shaft L10 is 4.49 m a.s.l., and with a height of 1.86 m it is much higher than the outlet branch. Just before reaching Shaft L10, the ceiling was lowered, and the difference of floor level of about 17 cm caused no problem. The edge between the two floors was cut obliquely, and the water could easily find its way.

The level of the branch from the south, however, is at 3.74 m a.s.l., 57 cm lower down. It joins the outlet below the 42 cm high step, and its channel turns sharply round the corner towards the SE. The roughly cut step was certainly made to adjust the 'outlet gallery' to the south circuit, but not quite down to the level in its course from Shaft L9.

Fig. 3.1.14. View of the north end of the south circuit towards Shaft L10. In front, above, the opening into the north circuit. 1976.

61

The 'outlet channel' runs c. 24 m towards the SE from Shaft L10 and the chisel-marks show that it was also the cutting direction the whole way.

In Trench Q_6 it appears at a level (3.88 m a.s.l.), about 1.1 m below the east termination of the East Corridor (level 4.98 m a.s.l.), Fig. 2.4.1 (plan) and 2.4.8 (photo). At this point it takes a more easterly direction, and first its south side fades away, then its bottom and probably also its north side. The continuation of both galleries is not known (see above, p. 42).

3.2. The relationship between the Lower Gallery and the tomb of Maussollos

The relationship between the Lower Gallery and the tomb of Maussollos is of special interest for their relative dating within the period of construction of the huge building. There are three points of close connection.

1-2) The tomb chamber proper was connected to the gallery through built outlets from the chamber both to the west and the east. Newton termed the western one "The Marble Drain" and the eastern one "The Rag Stone Drain".

3) The gallery crosses the landing of the Western Staircase, its ceiling being constructed of andesite slabs at a lower level than in the subterranean sections to the north and south.

Newton discovered the staircase within the first weeks of the excavation.[53] Even if he did not discover the tomb chamber proper, he was convinced that the staircase formed the entrance of the tomb of Maussollos.

Jeppesen presents a concise description and analysis of the tomb of Maussollos.[54] The sacrificial bones and the heavy sealing above that Newton left undisturbed in the landing were excavated by F. Højlund and have been published by him and K. Aaris-Sørensen.[55]

For a proper understanding of the Lower Gallery's crossing of the landing of the Western Staircase, a short description of this part of the tomb structure appears useful. At the same time, also the results of an investigation of the fill to the north of the staircase will be presented, Fig. 3.2.1-2 and 9.

The dromos of the tomb measures c. 8.6 m in width and includes a staircase of 12 steps and a landing traversed by the gallery. The steps are partly cut in the natural rock, partly built of ashlars in the same material. This is also the case with the parapets that frame the staircase and the landing on both sides. The margin of the landing towards the Maussolleion is irregular, because the bedrock to the north of the entrance to the tomb-chamber is situated 1 m farther to the east than on the south side.

The uneven floor of the landing is cut in the bedrock (sandstone and claystone) and slopes towards the east from c. 5.8 m to c. 5.35 m a.s.l. at the level of the top surface of the andesite slabs that cover the gallery, Fig. 3.2.1-7. These slabs are placed on a ledge, 0.30 m high and 0.15 m wide on the west side and also on the east side except in its central part. Here the ceiling slabs were placed and fitted in to form the continuation of the single layer of slabs of the rectangular platform in front of the entrance to the tomb.[56] The difference in character between the slabs in the platform and those of the gallery is remarkable. The former are clamped together and precisely cut, the latter are roughly cut, of varying size and thickness and are placed side by side without bonding. The three northernmost are thinner than the rest.

The overall character of the dromos is of irregularity and thrift. Most remarkable is the asymmetric layout, the economical exploitation of the native rock in the construction, and also the irregular sizes of the wall ashlars, with the result that the north and south parapet walls are very dissimilar.

The gallery traversing the landing is cut as an open, shallow 'ditch', 0.68 m wide and 0.68-72 m high up to the ledge on which the ceiling slabs are placed. The bottom level of the gallery is at 4.36 m a.s.l., the ceiling accordingly at 5.02-06 m.

Fig. 3.2.1. Plan of the landing of MauTb with the line of ceiling blocks of LG. The area Z is shown in Fig. 7.1.3. 1:100

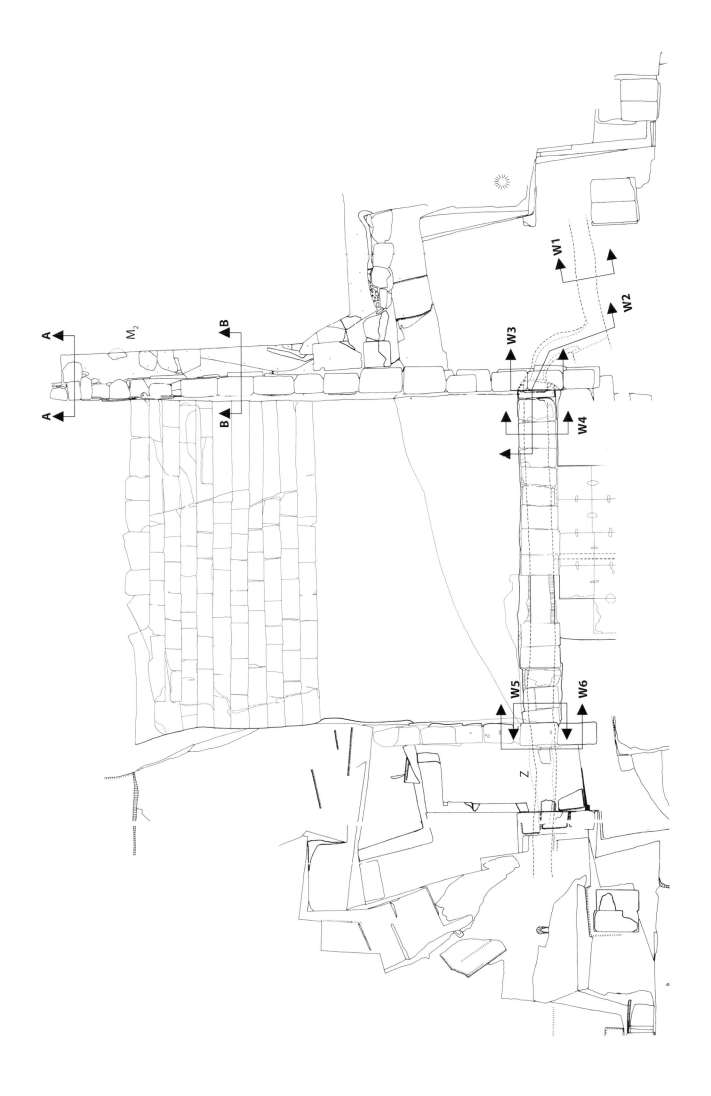

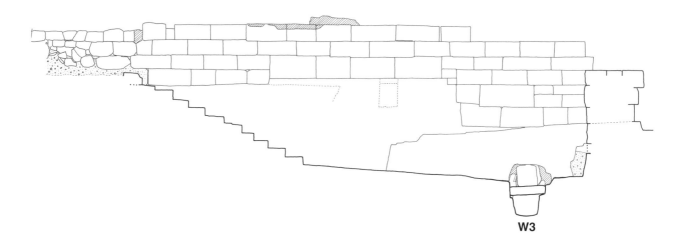

W3

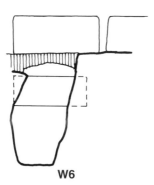

W5

Fig. 3.2.2. Elevation of the façade of the north parapet in the landing of MauTb with section in the LG below. 1:100.

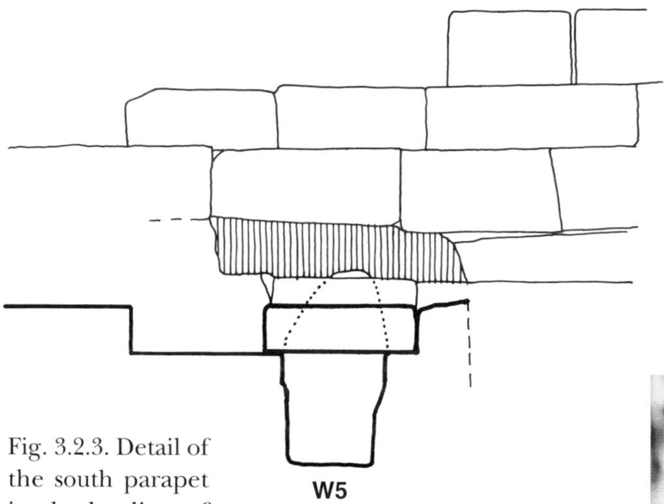

Fig. 3.2.3. Detail of the south parapet in the landing of MauTb with section W5. 1:50.

Fig. 3.2.4. Section W6, just south of the south parapet wall of MauTb. 1:50.

W6

Fig. 3.2.5. The fragile claystone ceiling in the LG below the south parapet of MauTb. The difference in height between the part cut in the bedrock and the andesite ceiling where the LG crosses the landing is 0.4 m. 1973.

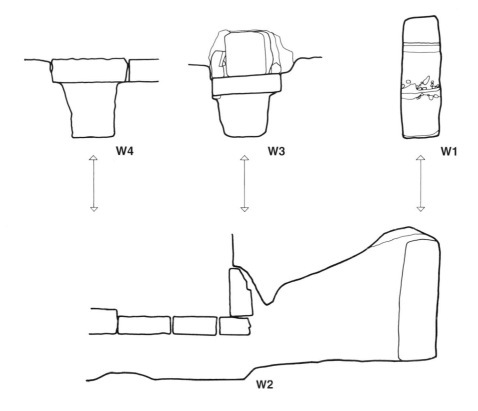

Fig. 3.2.6. Sections W1-W4 north of MauTb and in part of its landing. Three cross-sections and one longitudinal. 1:50.

With regard to technique, size and levels, this short stretch differs markedly from the rock-cut gallery immediately to the south and north of the landing. Very similar, however, is the way the encounter between rock-cut and built gallery was worked out. It is of great interest, moreover, that the cutting-direction of the chisel-marks shows conclusively that the Lower Gallery was cut from both Shafts L6 and L1 towards the staircase.

To the south the ceiling height in the gallery drops twice close to the staircase: first by 0.2 m about 2 m before the parapet at the encounter with the quarry area: secondly, exactly below the parapet, Fig. 3.2.3-5, the ceiling in claystone drops about 0.30 m to adjust to the top level of the southernmost andesite slab. The bottom level of this slab is again situated 0.32 m lower. The very top of the gallery in claystone, however, is ruined, for which reason it shows up in the view of the parapet, Fig. 3.2.3, and light enters the gallery from above in Fig. 3.2.5.

To the north, the ceiling height in the subterranean gallery is 1.15 m higher up than in the built channel, and also the floor level is higher up, albeit only 0.30 m, Figs. 3.2.6 and 8. In order to create a smooth transition, the ceiling slopes down towards the parapet and finally drops markedly close to a point where also the floor slides down. However, a part of the claystone parapet fell down and was replaced by an andesite block, placed on top of the northernmost ceiling slab in the landing, Fig. 3.2.6-7.[57] A similar drop in the ceiling height at the point of transition between cut and built parts of a subterranean gallery is seen in UG:C, Fig. 6.3.8 and 10.

The evidence demonstrates conclusively that the builders of the gallery adjusted themselves to the landing of the staircase – whether this was already in existence or was under construction. Beyond doubt, both the width and the floor level of the landing as well as the bottom level in the gallery were accomplished facts.

▲ Fig. 3.2.7. The northernmost ceiling blocks of LG in the landing of MauTb and the 'plug-block' hiding a breach in the fragile claystone of the parapet. To the right the breach into the blind alley of the LG. 1974.

◄ Fig. 3.2.8. The sloping ceiling of LG below the north parapet of MauTb. View SW. 1976.

Jeppesen has recently conjectured the existence of a shaft that was obliterated when the staircase was executed.[58] This implies 1) that the area was covered by the bedrock when the gallery was cut, which is unlikely and at least not documented (see above, p. 22), and – not least – 2) that the gallery was older than the staircase and landing, which was certainly not the case. Finally, there is no trace of a shaft either in the sides or bottom of the gallery where it traverses the landing or in the quarry just to the south (cf. Fig. 7.1.3).

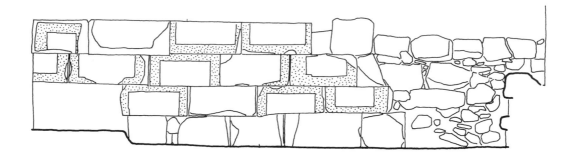

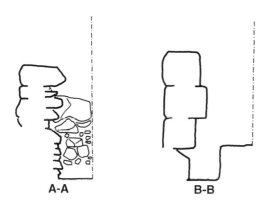

▲ Fig. 3.2.9. Elevation of the western end of the back wall of the north parapet of the staircase of MauTb. Several of the ashlars display an anathyrosis. 1:50.

A-A   B-B

◄ Fig. 3.2.10. Sections A-A and B-B in the north parapet of the staircase of MauTb. The wall is placed in a 0.15 m deep ledge. 1:50.

Digression: Stratigraphical evidence for the dating of the staircase and landing

The area behind the south parapet is very irregular with plenty of traces of quarrying, including rows of wedge-holes (see below, Ch. 7.1 with Fig. 7.1.3). It was completely covered by recent soil.

We concentrated upon a study of the area immediately behind the north parapet in the hope of finding stratigraphical evidence for the date of the construction of the staircase. Although Newton had cleared the eastern part, a close study of the soil between the ashlars of the wall was revealing. Fortunately, to the west, on a higher level, we could excavate undisturbed fill. A short description of the area appears necessary Fig. 3.2.1.9-10.

The ashlars of the eastern part of the north parapet wall and of the re-entrant rest on top of the claystone stratum at level c. 7.0 m a.s.l. This stratum also forms the ground in the open space north of the wall. Towards the west, the rock rises stepwise to about 8.20 m and 9.20 m a.s.l. and forms an irregular crag crowned by a crude wall at right-angles to the staircase.[59] This

crude wall, only one course high, and its back were investigated along with the excavation of a 0.80 m wide, nearly 7 m long and c. 1.6 deep Trench M₂ behind the staircase wall, Figs. 3.2.1 + 3.2.10.

The fill was made up by a uniform, undisturbed layer of whitish or light brown soil with several stones of various kinds, fragments of the local sandstone, of limestone, of green andesite (one piece measuring 27 cm × 23 cm × 32 cm), and of marble. The largest of these measured 26 cm × 20 cm × 6 cm and had marks from a pickaxe or the pointed chisel on two sides. Chippings of both green andesite and marble occurred regularly and also in lumps. In short, the fill conforms to the Maussollan fill, so often described by Newton, Biliotti and also ascertained by us, e.g. in Trenches Q₆ and Q₇ and in the staircase of Cb1 (above, Ch. 2). Also in the chinks between the ashlars in the east end of the back-wall of the parapet there was an abundance of andesite and marble chippings. In two places each a marble piece was firmly fixed *in situ* between the ashlars.

The dating of two red-figure crater rim fragments, of two black-glaze fragments (kylikes) and also a fragmentary terracotta figure (and other finds as well) is moreover in complete accordance with the stratigraphical and architectural evidence.[60] The Western Staircase is beyond doubt contemporaneous with the building of the Maussolleion.

The Marble Drain and the Lower Gallery in the landing

The features of the Marble Drain are carefully documented by Jeppesen.[61]

Below the platform in front of the entrance the drain is cut as a channel, 0.27 m high and 0.25 m wide, covered by andesite slabs. In the entrance, corridor and anteroom, andesite slabs also constitute its sides, about 0.30 m high. At the point where this channel opens into the Lower Gallery, its level is 4.83 m a.s.l., whereas the bottom level in the chamber is 4.78 m a.s.l. The change in level occurs below the entrance from corridor to anteroom. This odd feature caused Jeppesen to conclude that the Marble Drain did not drain the chamber, "but quite the opposite" drain the anteroom through the chamber to the Rag-Stone Drain. Consequently, the western part below corridor and platform served only this narrow area. This conclusion appears too categorical. Whatever the reason for the change of level (concurrently with a change of thickness of the andesite slabs), the consequence was hardly of any consequence. If the water level rose more than 4.5 cm, the water would escape also through the Marble Drain.[62]

The Rag-Stone Drain and the Lower Gallery close to Shaft L10

The Rag-Stone Drain opens towards the east on line with the Marble Drain. Its main part is now hidden by up to nine courses of andesite slabs laid in an open trench, which runs from the tomb chamber to a point a few metres from the east side of the Quadrangle. The north and east sides were cut vertically right down to the bottom, whereas the other side narrows stepwise.

The top levels and the western part are documented by Jeppesen.[63] The channel is two courses high, 0.63 m, and 0.25 m wide. The bottom level

Fig. 3.2.11. View through opening of LG:e towards the lowermost three courses of the west side of the end of the Rag-stone Drain. 1976.

again is flush with the floor of the chamber, 4.74 m a.s.l.

The bottom east end, where the built drain empties itself into the 'outlet gallery' of the Lower Gallery, can now be reached only from Shaft L10 through the gallery. The direction of cutting is from the shaft, and it opens after c. 6.2 m into a kind of shallow cave at level 4.38 m, Fig. 3.2.11-12. All around, the edge of the opening is set off from the side of the cave, the bottom of which is irregular and lies 0.39 m lower down. In front is the bottom end of the built Rag-Stone Drain, six courses high = 2.02 m, and about 2.0 m wide. The floor of the drain proper, two courses high, is at

Fig. 3.2.12. The opening, two courses high, of the built channel from the tomb chamber of Maussollos into LG: e (Rag Stone Drain). Course 1 and 2. 1976.

4.34 m a.s.l., its top at 5.03 m a.s.l. Whereas the opening and sides of the channel are carefully dressed, the 'façade' of the slabs is only roughly dressed and somewhat irregular. The bottom slab adds to the layers enumerated by Jeppesen 2000: 11, and the level 4.34 m should be termed 'Layer -1'.

During the course of the building of the east end of the Rag-Stone Drain, it was gradually closed. No efforts were taken to establish the outlet further SE. As mentioned, this was accomplished only from the east through the gallery and by another team of workmen.

One feature is of the highest interest and has important implications. The level of the opening of the Rag-Stone Drain channel, 4.34 m a.s.l., matches exactly the level in the Lower Gallery in the landing of the Western Staircase where

the Marble Drain empties itself (4.32 m a.s.l.). This complete accordance cannot be fortuitous and points to the conclusion that the extreme levels in the building's east-west axis were decided upon together with the level in the tomb chamber. This work was probably the very first to be accomplished when the final plan of the building was decided upon, and Maussollos had given his ultimate approval of the plans.

3.3. The chronology and function(s) of the Lower Gallery

Already Newton explained the Lower Gallery as a drain of the Maussolleion.[64] In addition he argued that it received the external drainage of the building, even if he (like us) found no evidence for it. Parts of the gallery could possibly have been cut before the Maussolleion, because of the bends and swerves in the course of the Gallery *where parallelism might have been expected* if it were contemporaneous. Also the evidence of the Pillar P3 on top of Shaft L2 and the execution of the gallery in the Western Staircase could point in the same direction.

Jeppesen briefly discussed the gallery.[65] Evidently it is a drain to prevent flooding of the tomb chamber of the Maussolleion, and there is no evidence whatsoever for an earlier dating. Moreover, the gallery may have served to drain away the groundwater to permit building on the site. Therefore the circuit and outlet were executed as the very first, and the position of the tomb chamber may have been decided later.

The geologist John A. Gifford brings forth an additional reason for the construction of the Lower Gallery.[66] The hydraulic pressure would force the ground water into the galleries, whereby the claystone and sandstone bedrock around the Maussolleion would be stabilized. "Over the months [of construction] the Mausoleum builders must have closely watched the water level in the Lower Gallery and the alignment of the foundation itself for indications of differential settling."

The present investigation has proved beyond doubt that the Lower Gallery was constructed in its entirety to serve the Maussolleion as a drain.

Its parts are closely linked to the layout of the tomb building and no part can derive from an older construction. The possible functions of the gallery are well explained by Jeppesen and Gifford. Perhaps, however, they overrate the risk for a high level of groundwater. The floor level of the pre-Maussollan subterranean chamber Cb2 is 9 cm below the floor in the Maussollan tomb chamber and, apparently, it needed no outlet. Also the ravines to the east and south of the Maussolleion site will have minimized the risk.

In modern terms, the drain is a 'perimeter drain', which is currently quite commonly used. The Maussollan structure, however, is unique in the Ancient World.[67]

The detailed analysis of all parts of the gallery has provided firm ground for a thorough understanding of the complicated history of its construction within the first year(s) of the building of the Maussolleion.

1. The gallery was cut in three parts.
2. The central axis (the Western Staircase, the Marble Drain, the tomb chamber, the Rag-Stone Drain and the outlet with Shaft L10) was planned and at least partly executed before the circuit.
3. The circuit consists of two parts, a northern and a southern. Both in the area of the Western Staircase and of the confluence close to Shaft L10, the workmen of the circuit adjusted to the features of the central axis.
4. All the same, the circuit was part of the initial plan and was executed very early in the process, before the pillars and before the cutting of the Quadrangle were accomplished.
5. The existence of previous structures along the south fringe of the Quadrangle caused problems and resulted in several odd solutions.
6. There is a marked contrast between the exact work in the axis (level of LG west 4.32 m and east 4.34 m a.s.l.) and the deficiencies in planning and execution along the south side. Maybe different teams of workmen were in charge.
7. The features of the Western Staircase determined the execution of the W gallery both to the south and the north. At the same time, the andesite slabs of the platform in front of the entrance determined the outline of the ceiling slabs of the Lower Gallery.
8. The fill behind the north parapet of the staircase dates its construction to the period of the building of the Maussolleion.
9. The workmanship and the use of local stone in the staircase and landing of the Western Staircase are careless, especially when compared with the Maussolleion proper. This is the more surprising, because the stairwell must have been open to the sky for a certain period until the burial of Maussollos or Artemisia in 353 BC and 351 BC respectively.

4. The terrace walls along the east and south sides of the Quadrangle of the Maussolleion

The British excavations uncovered long stretches of two different terrace walls to the east and south of the Maussolleion. They run parallel to the Quadrangle – and to the Hecatomnid street plan of Halikarnassos – and it is of obvious interest to clarify their dating and function in relation to the Maussolleion – and to the pre-Maussollan structures.

The first terrace wall, TW1, runs along the east and south sides of the Quadrangle, the façades at a distance of 2.75 m and 13.6 m respectively. Only three short stretches were investigated during the Danish excavations: in Trench P$_9$,[68] in Trench P$_{11}$ (see above, p. 31), and in Trench P$_{10}$ (see above, p. 33). Important evidence resulted from this, which enables us with fair confidence to comprehend the reports of Newton and Biliotti.

The second terrace wall, TW2, runs only on the east side of the Quadrangle, about 10.50 m from its side and on a much lower level. It was not investigated during the recent excavations.

4.1. Terrace Wall 1

Newton discusses the ashlar wall in several places.[69] It figures on Murdoch Smith's plan Fig. 1.2.1, in his sections C-D and E-F on Pl. 1, and a view of the southern course is shown in the watercolour by Pullan, Pl. 2. The wall was also photographed, and prints of one part of the east wall are preserved in the British Museum and in the British Library, Fig. 4.1.1. Biliotti investigated the southern course of the wall between March 31 and April 29, 1865.[70]

The stone is volcanic, grey-brownish and contains black, white and micaceous particles. The wall is built with only stretchers of irregular length, 0.30 m and 0.38 m high, thickness c. 0.30 m. They are jointed by means of a 5-10 cm

broad *anathyrosis*. The front face of the stone is roughly prepared into a kind of rusticate. The back is very irregular, and the stability of the wall depends on the filling around the blocks during the course of construction. The east wall consists of one line of blocks, whereas on the south side it was partially built as a double wall.

On the east side, it rests directly on the levelled bedrock in a bedding on a slightly lower level than the ground to the east. On the south side, it rests in addition partly on a built foundation and partly on the ceiling slabs of the East Corridor.

The façade of *the east wall* runs north-south c. 2.75 m east of the Quadrangle. To the north (in Trench P$_9$) it abuts on the inner face of the peribolos wall, unfortunately at a point which, perhaps in Roman times, was completely remodelled. Although the single block *in situ* (ground level 8.6 m a.s.l.) is furnished with *anathyrosis* also in its north end, it was not possible to ascertain whether the wall originally continued further north or was planned to abut on the peribolos wall. Its top level is 8.9 m a.s.l. In Trench P$_{11}$ the three courses *in situ* rest on level 7.73 m a.s.l. The top level of the wall is 8.84 m a.s.l. and is prepared for another course. With the addition of this, the wall would be flush with the top of the bedrock 'bench' behind. Undoubtedly, the function of the wall was to conceal the irregularly cut east face of this 1.8 m wide 'bench' along the east side of the Quadrangle. Newton notes that the height of the bench varied from 5′ to 10′ (3.05 m).[71] The latter height was not verified and is surprising, to judge from the bottom levels in Trench P$_9$, P$_{11}$ and Q$_7$.

The façade of *the south wall* runs E-W at a distance of 13.60 m to the south of the Quadrangle. Newton traced it for about 80′ [24.38 m], Fig. 1.2.1,

Fig. 4.1.1. View of the Terrace wall, TW1e, towards the north. Unpublished photograph from 1857. By courtesy of the Trustees of the British Museum.

but Biliotti followed it about 25 m further to the west,[72] to a few feet west of Nalban's SW-oriented house. Their information is crucial for an understanding and is quoted below.

Newton:

At a distance of 40′ [12.2 m] from the south side of the Quadrangle, the rocky platform suddenly terminates in a vertical cutting, running east and west. This cutting was faced by a wall of isodomous masonry running parallel to it. The southern face of this wall was composed of square blocks beautifully jointed, but roughly dressed. The space between this face and the cutting was filled with rubble. The thickness of the wall was 1′ 10″ [0.56 m]; its height 7′ [2.13 m], distributed over eight courses of masonry. It rose within 2′ [0.61 m] of the rocky platform behind it, and from its construction and position seems to have been built

as a terrace-wall, to conceal the irregular and unsightly face of the vertical cutting.

As the southern or exterior side of the wall was evidently built so as to be seen, it may be presumed that its line marked a change of level in the platform of the peribolus. This wall was traced for about 80′.(HD: 130-131)

Biliotti confirms Newton's information on the relation of bedrock and wall:

Discovered in the rock forming the platform a vertical cutting running E. & W., and about 2 feet S. from it a wall, which is the continuation towards the W. of that discovered by Mr. Newton at about 40 feet S. of the Quadrangle. The description and details he gives of it in Vol. II part 1st page 130, and following, corresponds exactly to what we find. (Diary 1865.03.31)[73]

Cut a trench about 6 feet wide on the S. side of the wall

discovered yesterday and cleared six courses of square stones. The soil along this wall is whittish intermixed with splinters of rock, and as we proceed deeper with fragments of pottery. A few pieces of stucco have also been found. (Diary 1865.04.01) [74]

We continue the work in the trench and clear the two other courses of stones; then we meet the rock on which they rest, but which seems to be cut again vertically. The total height of the wall is about 8 feet in the places where the eight courses occur. (Diary 1865.04.03) [75]

The upper part of the gallery [UG:C] *which passes under the E. angle of Hagi Nalban's* [SW] *house is built, and on it rests the Ashlar wall. The rock does not appear on the west side of the gallery, and there, there is an additional lower course of stones in the Ashlar wall which rests on rubble. There are six complete courses besides the additional one just mentioned and now and then occurs a stone of another course raising the Ashlar wall to the level of the platform. At 16′* [4.88 m] *from the surface we are prevented from continuing the excavation any deeper on account of water springing up. We are 3′* [0.92 m] *lower than the foundation of the Ashlar wall,* ⋯ (*Diary* 1865.04.17) [76]

Concerning the position and character of the very west end of the wall, Biliotti states:
The Ashlar wall was traced under, and only a few feet W. of Nalban's house. ⋯ *The foundations of the Ashlar wall gradually rise, and there are only four courses at this point. No return of the Ashlar wall has been discovered towards the West. (Diary 1865.04.28-29)* [77]

In Trench P$_{10}$ the wall intersects Chamber 3, and it is carried on a 1.6 m high, free-standing foundation, so a double-wall appeared necessary, the back-wall consisting of limestone ashlars. The total width is 0.60 m or a little less, a number that matches well with Newton's: 1′ 10″ / 0.56 m. The top level of the foundation is at 6.96 m a.s.l. Two courses are documented as well as the bedding for a third one in the top surface of the ceiling slabs of the East Corridor. Five limestone slabs were purposely selected to carry the wall over the corridor (see below, p. 107), which therefore functioned at the same time as the terrace wall. At this point the level is 7.54 m a.s.l.

Pullan's watercolour, Pl. 2, shows the wall, eight courses high on a foundation, towards the west. Murdoch Smith's plan and section show that it rests on a kind of shelf in the bedrock, the level of which is at c. 5.25 m a.s.l. in continuation of the level in Chamber 3. In his section of the wall, Murdoch Smith does not distinguish between the wall proper and its foundation, and very little is shown of the bedrock shelf. However, in his original plan and section published in *FP*16, Pl. 1, the shelf appears to be at least 3 m wide.

Biliotti also ascertained up to eight courses further to the west. At a certain point, though, the level of the bedrock may have now risen because 'the stones rest on the rock' *which seems to be cut again vertically.* Beyond, i.e. west of the passing over the aqueduct UG:C (at 7.40 m a.s.l., see below), however (1865.04.17), the rock did not appear again and there was an *additional lower course* (compared to east of the aqueduct) resting on a "rubble" foundation, that reaches more than 1.2 m down, that is below 6.20 m a.s.l. Further west *the foundations gradually rise and there are only four courses.* We understand this slightly ambiguous statement to mean that the level of the bedrock rises, so the lower courses of the wall gradually disappear.

The relation between the wall and the aqueduct UG:C appears well documented, but is unfortunately ambiguous. Biliotti states (*Diary* 1865.04.17, quoted above), that the wall rests on the aqueduct, and it appears from his careful explanations (1865.04.20), see p. 136, below, and Fig. 6.3.6, that the top level of the ceiling block of the aqueduct is at 7.45 m a.s.l. while the level of the surface above is at 11.40 m a.s.l. Moreover it is clear (1865.04.17) that also the level of "the foundation" of the wall to the west of the aqueduct is at about 7.45 m a.s.l. (13′ / 3.95 m below ground level).

During our excavation we established three fix-points that allow certain conclusions.
1+2. The distance of 13.60 m from the Quadrangle to the façade of the wall (in Trench P$_{10}$), the distance of 13.0 m from the Quadrangle to the point where UG:C abandons the bedrock, which is cut vertically, and is built for the next 11 m. By this means, Biliotti's statement that the wall rests on the aqueduct seems to be confirmed. Although we could not establish the exact course of the wall from its sparse appearance in Trench P$_{10}$ alone, a line drawn through the remains and

at right-angles to the East Terrace Wall 1 both crosses the aqueduct at the point stated by Biliotti and runs parallel to the south side of the Quadrangle.

3. The level is 5.25 m a.s.l. of the bedrock bottom in the aqueduct, the sides of which are ashlar-built. Accordingly we *know* that the level in the aqueduct corresponds exactly with the level in Chamber 3 and the bottom of the foundation of the terrace wall. This level *could* be the surface level of the ravine in the period before the building of the aqueduct and terrace wall, from where there was access into Cb3. Also the bottom level in the built section of UG:C to the SE of Cb3 at c. 4.80 m a.s.l. conforms to this idea.

For a proper understanding of the history of the area, the British observations of the soil along the south side of the terrace wall are also of great interest. Newton[78] and, in more detail, Biliotti agree that the area was filled with the characteristic whitish Maussollan fill with splinters of rock up to c. 9.60 m a.s.l. (6 feet / 1.83 m below the surface level at c. 11.40 m). Moreover, Biliotti describes the fill along the wall very precisely, and he does not distinguish between strata down to 20′ / 6.1 m down (level c. 5.3 m a.s.l.).[79] On the basis of this information, the ravine would have been filled up in one operation to the level of the bedrock to the south of the Maussolleion.

Ambiguous, though, are the notices of several slabs in green andesite that both Newton and Biliotti found on the surface of the whitish fill, and which Pedersen[80] considers to be remnants of an andesite pavement of the platform. Biliotti noted that our terrace wall at a certain point was higher than the slabs:

It must be observed that the slabs just discovered run over the Ashlar wall & meet the rocky platform, while on the W of this row of stone slabs the ashlar wall was higher than them.[81]

Pedersen explains this by suggesting a stairway or ramp through the terrace wall at this point. However, the evidence of the scattered andesite slabs is uncertain and can bear no conclusions on the relative dating of the wall and the Maussollan fill. Jeppesen, in my opinion correctly, rejects the idea that the andesite ashlars in question can have formed a pavement.[82]

The southeast corner of the terrace wall

Newton was not able to study the SE corner, because the owner would not give up the house on the very spot, but he excavated all around and left it on an elevation (Pl. 6). Biliotti, however, obtained the house and cleared the ground but found nothing. Their observations appear somewhat contradictory, but still allow for certain conclusions.

Newton states:

We were unable to explore its course further to the east [from its passing over the East Corridor], *not having possession of the ground; but, if the wall was continued beyond this point, its lowest course must have been about 6′* [1.83 m] *higher than the rest of the wall.* (*HD*: 131)

The top level of the foundation of the wall where it crosses Cb3 is at 6.92 m a.s.l. Adding 1.83 m we get 8.75 m a.s.l. This conforms to his statement:

There is, however, this difficulty – that at the two points to which the southern wall has been traced, and at the southern extremity of the eastern wall, the vertical cutting ceases, and the rock reappears at the same level, or nearly so, as the margin of the Quadrangle. (*HD*: 132)

The level 8.75 m matches well the level of the bedrock near the SE corner of the Quadrangle.

In 1865 Biliotti excavated the very spot where the east and south walls would meet, and he confirms the observations of Newton:

At a depth of about 5 feet [1.52 m] *from the surface we find the rocky platform which in one place, towards the S.E. angle of the house is irregularly cut deeper, about 10 feet* [3.05 m]. *We meet here one of the galleries which passed under the house. No traces have been discovered of the ashlar walls described by Mr. Newton as running parallel to the E. and S. sides of the Quadrangle. ⋯. It must be observed, however, that the surface of the rock here, is nearly at the same level as the margin of the Quadrangle.* (*Diary* 1865.03.22[83])

The gallery under the house can only be the East Corridor. Biliotti did not state which part of the corridor he encountered, but it could very well be in the east end of the subterranean part of the East Corridor, where it is filled with soil from above (see below, p. 109). The floor level at this point is at 5.17 m a.s.l., so the rock above was at least at 8.21 m a.s.l. (5.17 m + 10′). The measure could have been taken higher up, but it

Fig. 4.1.2. Top of Shaft L9 and the north-south edge east of the Quadrangle. View south. 1973. Cf. Jeppesen 2000, end plate.

is hardly important for the argument. Undoubtedly the level of the bedrock was fairly high, certainly higher than in both Trenches P_{10} and P_{11} and probably as high as 8.75 m a.s.l.

How do their observations fit in with our results? In the NE corner of Trench P_{10} the level of the bedrock is 8.50 m a.s.l., and the bottom level of the terrace wall, where it crosses the East Corridor, is at c. 7.56 m a.s.l. However, in the west end of Trench Q_7 we ascertained the edge of Biliotti's trench along the wall, cf. Fig. 2.5.2. At this point, just about 0.6 m from the wall and 2.5 m away from the presumed corner, the level is only at 7.08 m a.s.l.

As we have seen above, there is in both Trenches P_9 and P_{11} a vertical cutting behind the terrace wall, cf. Fig. 4.1.2. and according to Newton this cutting ceases further south. This statement, however, appears contradicted in the East Corridor, where the ceiling, almost on line with the cutting, is lowered from 7.2 m a.s.l. to

6.82 m a.s.l. There are therefore reasons to conjecture that the vertical cutting continues south and beyond the line of the southern terrace wall, TW1s. However, the difference in level is hardly 0.40 m.

On balance, the congruent statements of Newton and Biliotti concerning the level of the bedrock in the area of the corner should be accepted. Biliotti found *no traces* of the wall in the place of the corner. Was it never built here, were the ashlars removed when the Maussolleion was built (like the ceiling blocks in the east end of the East Corridor and UG:B), or have they been robbed by the Hospitallers? Unfortunately, Biliotti's remark on the stratigraphy close to the house is ambiguous with regard to dating: *At six feet deep we met the primitive soil, namely that formed with fragments of stone &, in which we found, however, human bones, some rusty pieces, and fragments of pottery.*[84] The soil he describes *might* be Maussollan fill, but on the day before, he terms black earth

75

primitive. Be that as it may, considering the fact that the wall on the east side is preserved up to c. 8.9 m a.s.l. and according to Newton and Biliotti (see below) reached c. 9.30 m a.s.l. on the south side, we can take for granted that a corner was at least intended as part of the terrace project.

Evidence for a north and a west course of the terrace wall?

Neither Newton nor Biliotti managed to establish the exact termination of the western and northern ends of the preserved walls. Nor did they find any clues to the course of any west or north walls – if these ever existed. Newton shows a c. 110′ / 33.5 m long stretch of a "rough rubble wall", situated c. 18.5′ / 5.65 m to the north of the Quadrangle, Fig. 1.2.1 and Pl. 1. The continuation of this wall towards the west was apparently discovered in Trenches M_1 and K_1 and has neither in technique nor material anything to do with our terrace wall.[85]

As for a west wall, there are two possibilities to consider, neither of which is convincing, because their sparse remains are unlike the well-documented terrace wall. Biliotti encountered the foundations of a north-south running wall about 41′ / 12.5 m west of but *not quite parallel to the W. side of Quadrangle*.[86] It is connected with another wall at right-angles and is built with rough stones.

The other wall has been opted for by P. Pedersen, who discusses the terrace wall, TW1, to some extent.[87] He argues that our "frail rustica wall" was contemporaneous with the Maussolleion and should "be regarded as a revetment wall for a filled-up plateau around the Maussolleion building".[88] Tentatively, he reconstructs a terrace, c. 107 m E-W, and 50 m N-S, limited on the east and south sides by our wall and on the north side by the peribolos wall. As for the west side, he proposes a wall of which only the careless foundation – and a robber's trench – is preserved.[89] Its possible relation to the peribolos wall is not known.

Neither of these walls can with any conviction be related to TW1, and the ground to the west and north hardly calls for terrace walls. Towards the west, where the level seems fairly even, the south wall may have died out, and the same may have been the case towards the north, where the peribolos may have interrupted its course. Towards the ravines to the east and south, however, the wall makes good sense, demarcating the elevated plateau of the site of the Maussolleion.

Function and chronology

The terrace wall was preserved up to eight courses high, as is documented by Newton, Pullan and Biliotti, and according to the latter it reached along the south side up to the level of the bedrock behind. We ascertained the level of the bedrock at 9.25 m a.s.l. to the south of Chamber 2[90] and at c. 9.85 m a.s.l. just south of Shaft U7. On the east side the wall is preserved up to c. 0.3 m below the bedrock. Undoubtedly its function was to conceal both the irregularly cut faces of the bedrock and the cutting of the courtyard, Cb3. Its original – or planned – height can only be guessed. In order to create an even surface behind the wall, parts of the bedrock would have been hidden below a fill.

The level of the bottom course of the wall differs markedly. Towards the west, it gradually rises, and further to the east and north several levels are documented, as shown above. A terrace wall with such an uneven bottom line appears relative crude and is hardly reconcilable with the through-going euthynteria and the masterly treatment of the ashlars of the Maussolleion and of the peribolos. Pedersen argues, as mentioned, that the wall formed a low terrace with a bottom at 9.40 m a.s.l. and a top at 10.00 m a.s.l. that formed the transition from the level of the huge platform to a narrow terrace on a level with the Maussolleion euthynteria. The juxtaposition of refined marble ashlars and grey, rusticated andesite (in the area of Trench P_9) has nothing to recommend it. This applies also for the consequence that a great part of the wall, c. 2.5 m (from level 6.92 m up to 9.4 m a.s.l.) from the beginning was never meant to be seen and was to be buried below the ground.

The orientation of the walls conforms to that of the Maussolleion, which again conforms perfectly to the Maussollan city plan (to the ascertainment of which it played a certain part). P. Pedersen has established its 'grid units' to measure 36.4 ×

54.6 m or 120 by 180 modules of 30.2 cm.[91] The huge Maussollan terrace conforms well to the grid on the north, the east and the south sides (but not on the west side). The position of the terrace walls stands in no clear relation to the peribolos. TW1 south runs 50 m to the south of this – corresponding to 165.56 modules (11:12 grid). TW1 east runs 29 m inside the east peribolos wall – corresponding to 96 modules (4:5 grid). However, the Maussolleion itself, being situated respectively 3.6 m, c. 12 modules (1:15 grid) and 32 m, c. 106 modules (1:8.6 grid) inside the peribolos, also seems fairly independent, so no conclusions with regard to any contemporaneity can be drawn. The planners of the area were presumably more concerned with the earlier remains when they laid out the walls than with subtleties within the system of grid units and their division.

A certain overlap or relationship seems to exist between the wall and the three pre-Maussollan chambers on the south side of the Quadrangle. Its orientation differs markedly, and the south wall blocked the (presumably) original entrance to Chamber 3 from the south. However, the wall is situated so that the three chambers are included within the wall. If the only concern was a low terrace along the sides of the Maussolleion, the wall could easily have been erected at the same distance from the Maussolleion as along the east side. Moreover, the East Corridor certainly opened into Cb3, because five ceiling slabs in the East Corridor were specially selected and prepared to carry the wall. Because the corridor was abolished when the Maussolleion was built, a 'co-existence' certainly was obtained before then. This conclusion is confirmed by the construction of the back of the wall where it crosses Cb3. Now Cb3 was a courtyard closed on all four sides (see below, p. 104) and with access both to the East Corridor and the Main Corridor. The three pre-Maussollan structures apparently were still in use – or could have functioned – after the terrace wall was built.

Finally it should be noted that Newton's and Biliotti's findings with regard to Maussollan fill right up to the top of the preserved wall along the south side were confirmed by us. Along the east side, in Trench Q$_7$, we ascertained the Maussolleion fill at level 8.82 m a.s.l. very close to the wall. This fact does not make for clarity. See below, Ch. 8, for an essay to understand what took place in the area within a presumably very short span of time.

4.2. Terrace Wall 2

This wall is known only from the investigations of Newton in 1857, his reports in *Pl* 3: 30, *FP* 16: 93 and *HD*: 119-121 with Pullan's views Pls. 3-6. It is moreover shown on the plan Fig. 1.2.1 and in the section C-D in Pl. 1.

Newton's description in *HD* deserves to be quoted in full:

After having laid down and measured this wall, we continued to advance eastward, finding at an average depth of 10′ [3.05 m] the rocky platform ⋯.

At a distance of about 29′ [8.85 m] from the eastern side of the Quadrangle, the rocky platform terminated abruptly in a vertical cutting running parallel to the wall just described [TW1].

On digging down here I found a trench 4′ wide [1.22 m] with an average depth of 25′ [7.62 m], which had been cut into beds of different levels, as if for the reception of a wall. This trench extended from the north wall of the peribolus, which it met at a right angle, nearly to a house marked in Plate II. The east side of this trench was formed by a wall of isodomous masonry, consisting of a single course of squared blocks, averaging in size 2′ by 18″ by 15″ [0.61 m × 0.46 m × 0.38 m[92]]. These blocks were dressed only on their eastern or outer face, and were nearly all of the native rock of the platform; but among the lowest courses were two limestone blocks, which had been evidently taken from some earlier building, and one of which had a fine joint all round. The masonry of this wall was very coarse and careless, and presented no characteristic of good Hellenic work. The space between the wall and the cutting I found filled with earth. To the south, within a few feet of the point where the wall ceased, this trench rose by steps to a much higher level. ⋯.

The wall ran 157′ [47.85 m] due south, beyond which we could not trace it, as the house marked in Plate II. stood in our way. No trace of a return, however, appeared on the south side. (*HD*: 119-121).

From this description (as well as from Murdoch Smith's plan) we know that the wall runs north-south for altogether 47.85 m. It is situated at a distance of c. 10.50 m (*34½ feet*[93]) from the Quadrangle and 7.75 m from Terrace Wall 1. Newton writes that it runs 15′ / 4.57 m below the level of TW1, but he also states that the bedrock was cut into beds of different levels. In Murdoch Smith's section the difference in height is indicated as 12 feet / 3.66 m. Both may be right, because also the area or plateau of TW1 was irregular and sloped about 1.5 m from the north towards the south (8.6 m a.s.l. in Trench P_9, 7.73 m a.s.l. in Trench P_{11}, and 7.08 m a.s.l. in Trench Q_7). We are accordingly left with several variables for the level of the wall, but where Murdoch Smith measured the level of the bottom of the wall it may well have been c. 4.50 m a.s.l.

Newton and Murdoch Smith agree that the wall extended from the north peribolos wall. We know, however, that the level of the bedrock in both sides of TW2 (in Trench P_9 and Trench Q_5) was on a much higher level, 8.6 m and 8.0 m a.s.l., respectively.[94] Be that as it may, the bottom of the wall was at least at a certain point c. 5.00 m below the euthynteria of the north peribolos wall of 9.40 m a.s.l. Still, it is situated about 1.9 m above the bottom level of the East Terrace Wall, at 2.64 m a.s.l., located 21.50 m to the east.

According to Murdoch Smith's plan, he also seems to agree with Newton that the gap or "trench" between the wall and the bedrock towards the south *rises by steps to the level of the native rock, and appears to die away into it*.[95] Also Pullan confirms this.

Pullan illustrated the wall in four closely connected watercolours made in January 1858. He shows four ashlar courses to the north – extending apparently from a soil profile and not from the peribolos (Pl. 3). Soon it steps two courses down, but a fifth, bottom course appears (Pl. 4), an indication of a change in level. At this point, however, another wall just in front of the first one, so to speak takes over and rises from one course up to eight (or more?) courses – apparently up to the level of the bedrock to the west. Further to the south, this second wall (Pls. 5-6), now only three courses high, terminates on the higher ground just to the north of the outlet of Upper Gallery B2. The top course here is clearly shown to be the continuation of the top course shown in Pl. 4: the stepwise rising of the bedrock explains why the wall to the south is much lower.

This interpretation is confirmed by the statement of Newton that the sarcophagus shown in Pls. 5-6, lying well below the bottom of the wall at 23′ / 7.01 m below the surface none the less is situated 2 feet higher up than the bottom of the wall in the north end (at 25′ / 7.62 m below the surface).[96]

The parallel course of two lines of ashlars, shown by Pullan, explains the surprising thickness of the wall in Murdoch Smith's plan and section (Fig. 1.2.1 and Pl. 1), and it contrasts with the description given by Newton, quoted above. According to him the ashlars were fairly short and rather alike in thickness and height, being 0.61 m × 0.46 m in plan and 0.38 m in height. In Pullan's watercolours one notices a difference between the first and the second wall. The former appears to be thicker and have a rusticated façade towards the east (Pl. 4) compared with the clear-cut ashlars of the second wall. Finally it should be noted that the two walls, where they run parallel to each other, are not bonded.

Chronology and function

It is clear from Newton's remarks on levels and his careful description of the stratigraphy in the area of the wall that the wall was buried deep below the waste and fill from the building of the Maussolleion and therefore, beyond doubt, was constructed before the Maussolleion:

It is specially to be observed that these zigzag strata [with *veins of chippings of green stone*] *rose fully to the level of the rocky margin west of the trench, and such an artificial stratification proves that the wall was intentionally concealed at the time of the making of the platform, in the level of which it consequently does not mark a change.*

I am therefore inclined to think that this wall has no connection with the plan of the Mausoleum, and that it is anterior to it. What its purpose may have been, it is difficult to conjecture. (*HD*: 120-121).

Unfortunately, we have only little other evidence for a relative dating of the wall. Newton's statement that it "extended from the north wall of the peribolos" may be true but does not seem confirmed by Pullan, and might not help us any further. Anyhow, although the local stone is the same, our wall is completely different from the foundation of the peribolos, whose courses, 1.7 m-2.0 m wide, consist of a row of bonders and a row of stretchers.[97] It is remarkable, however, that our wall runs at right-angles to the peribolos and parallel to both TW1 and the Quadrangle. Its stepwise termination towards the south mirrors what we have seen in TW1. Neither the distance between the two terrace walls, 7.75 m = 25.6 modules, nor the distance from the wall to the peribolos, 21.5 m = 71 modules, has a clear relation to the grid width of 120 modules of the city plan.

We have no means to decide if the wall was ever finished, or if some of its ashlars were taken away before it was covered by the thick Maussollan fill layers. Nor can we decide whether the wall was planned as a foundation for a wall or was planned to be a wall in its own right. Could the easternmost course of ashlars be the remains of the façade, whereas the other was (planned as)

a backing in order to withstand the pressure of the fill behind the wall?

Just as TW1, the wall is placed in front of a vertical cutting in the native rock and most probably was built as a terrace wall and to conceal the features of the former quarry (see Ch. 7.1). The irregular cuttings both behind and in front (on a lower level) of the wall were probably also meant to be hidden below a fill. The wall, therefore, should be dated to *after* the quarrying.

E. Krüger[98] interpreted the wall as the continuation of Terrace Wall 1 (see below, p. 170 and Fig. 8.1). Its distance of 10.5 m from the Quadrangle does seem more appropriate when seen together with TW1's distance of 13.75 m. However, whether our wall is considered to be a foundation or a wall in its own right, the differences in technique and building material(s) exclude this possibility.

5. The pre-Maussollan structures along the south side of the Quadrangle

Newton excavated three rock-cut structures situated along the south side of the Quadrangle and oblique to its line, having a NNE orientation. He ascertained a stair of fifteen steps that through a gallery gave access to two chambers, "the subterranean chamber" and "the broken tomb", a structure with dromos and a chamber, the ceiling of which was broken. Newton correctly interpreted the structures as pre-Maussollan, and Pullan recorded them in several measured drawings and watercolours.

The three structures, two subterranean chambers and (it will be argued) a courtyard, were

connected by the subterranean Main Corridor and formed a remarkable whole, albeit with certain irregularities. The line of the corridor bends slightly by the shaft, and is not quite parallel to the chambers. Chambers, courtyard and corridor were undoubtedly created together with the aqueduct, the Upper Gallery, which is described below in Ch. 6. For the sake of convenience, all three structures are in the following termed chambers (abbreviated Cb1-Cb3).

Cb1 and Cb2 were re-excavated in 1972 and 1973, and the chamber in Cb1, overlooked by Newton, to which the southern staircase led, was

Fig. 5.1.1. View south in Cb1 with the opening into the Main Corridor and (to right) into UG:B1. In the centre, the transverse corridor from the time of the Maussolleion. 1973.

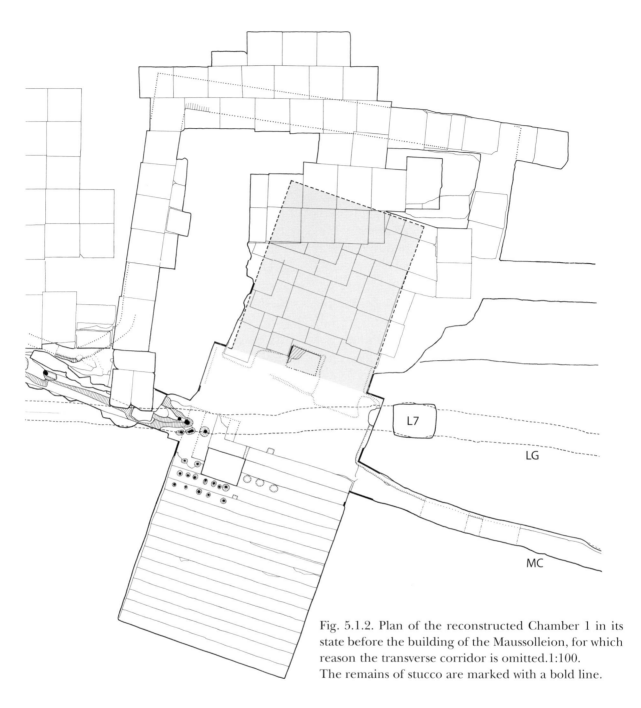

Fig. 5.1.2. Plan of the reconstructed Chamber 1 in its state before the building of the Maussolleion, for which reason the transverse corridor is omitted.1:100. The remains of stucco are marked with a bold line.

ascertained. The subterranean chamber, Cb2, was partly emptied, but of Cb3 only a small corner was re-excavated in connection with the investigation of the East Corridor (cf. above, p. 35, Trench P₁₀).

5.1. Chamber 1

Newton only briefly mentioned the southern staircase, *FP*16: 86; and *HD*: 127, 146, 152 with Murdoch Smith's plan, Fig. 1.2.1, and the fine measured drawings by Pullan, Pl. 7. He was unable to explain the structure adequately, because none of them ascertained the presence of the chamber.

The structure was cut in the bedrock and consisted of three parts: a staircase of 18 steps with a wing of the bottom three steps on the west side, a landing and a chamber. The length was altogether c. 12.45 m. Both staircase and landing were open to the sky, whereas the chamber was doubtless subterranean. The floor of both landing and chamber is at 5.55 / 5.50 m a.s.l.,

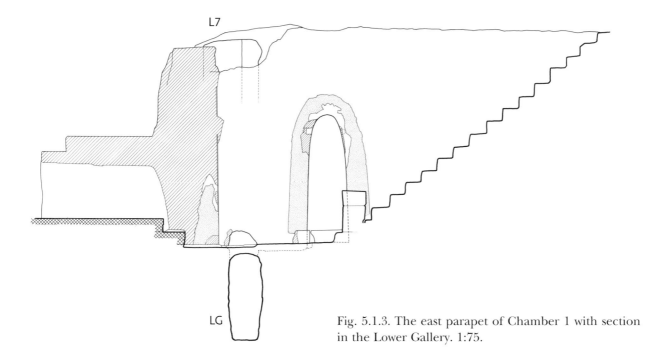

L7

LG

Fig. 5.1.3. The east parapet of Chamber 1 with section in the Lower Gallery. 1:75.

c. 4.30 m below the ancient level of the bedrock preserved around the staircase and along the east side of the landing (c. 9.85 m a.s.l.). There was access to the subterranean galleries on both sides. To the west though a door into the aqueduct UG:B1 (below p. 121). To the east, one could enter the Main Corridor, through which the Chambers 2 and 3 could be reached.

The lower two steps and a part of the landing are partially hidden below a built corridor (contemporaneous with the building of the Maussolleion, see below, p. 125). The builders of the Maussolleion also partly cut away, partly filled up, the landing and the chamber. Two crucial features for the reconstruction of the inner parts, however, are sufficiently preserved. A central pil-

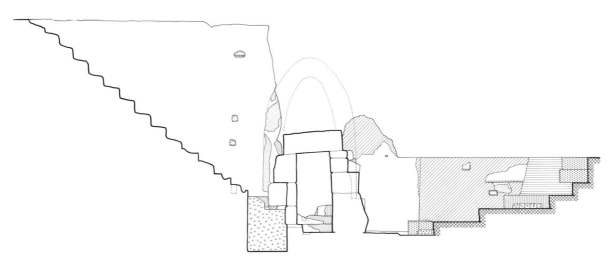

Fig. 5.1.4. The west parapet of Chamber 1 with section in the bothros and the Maussollan transverse corridor. Behind, the estimated outline of the opening into the Upper Gallery:B. 1:75.

83

lar in the opening of the chamber helps us to ascertain its façade; and the oblique orientation of four courses (3-6) of foundation blocks indicates the size of the chamber, of the back-wall of which only a small part is preserved in the bedrock.

The staircase

The staircase is 4.7 m wide, 5.45 m long and comprises 18 steps, each c. 0.32 m broad. Along the east parapet the steps are well preserved, but they are otherwise rather worn, as already noticed by Newton. The original height and width of the steps were respectively c. 0.25 m and 0.30-0.34 m.

Several cuttings in both the west parapet and in the west part of the steps 13-16 testify to activities connected to the wing of the staircase and the access into the aqueduct UG:B1.

Prominent is a square, flat-bottomed cutting in the steps 15 and 16, Fig. 5.1.4. It measures 0.75 m by 1.0 m. Its bottom is at 5.20 m a.s.l., 1.10 m below step 15, and to the N, two steps lower down, its side is only 0.56 m high. A shallow channel, 8 cm high and 10 cm wide, cuts through step 17 and would lead overflow to the floor of the landing. The cutting has from its discovery in 1972 been termed a bothros. Its content of pottery was sealed by the above-mentioned built corridor, see below, p. 51.

The west side of the bothros is almost on line with the transition from step 16 to step 17 in the wing of the steps 15-17, that protrudes in the west side and is closely connected with an opening into the aqueduct UG:B1. These steps are much worn, and the top one, step 15, is completely destroyed, presumably deliberately in connection with the building of the transverse corridor contemporaneous with the Maussolleion (see below, p. 125). Its original level was at c. 6.25 m a.s.l. The ends of the three steps of the wing are hidden below the north wall of the built corridor, and the shape of their termination is unknown.

Already Newton observed the evidence for a doorway that gave access from the staircase into the aqueduct, and details were measured by Pullan, Pl. 7. Only the lower south side of the cutting for a doorway, 0.80 m high, is preserved, Fig 5.1.5 and 9. A ledge, 0.40 m wide and 0.10 m deep, for the insertion of a separate door-frame, and in its bottom, a cutting, 0.14 m by 0.14 m and 0.1 m deep, for the insertion of a threshold with top level at 6.47 m a.s.l., are preserved. The whole upper and northern part of the door is destroyed, so the shape of the top of the door is open to conjecture. However, stucco is partly preserved in a c. 0.40 m broad band on both sides of the opening into the UG:B from the staircase. On the south side it starts at level 6.4 m a.s.l. and is preserved up to 8.55 m a.s.l., at which point it curves. On analogy with the better-preserved stucco band around the opening into the Main Corridor, this evidence suggests a curved and presumably also rock-cut opening into the aqueduct. Unfortunately, we have no means to determine the relation between this opening and the inserted, presumably rectangular door-frame.

The part of the gallery just inside the doorway is completely destroyed except, on the north side, for a patch of stucco 0.70 m from the line of the staircase Fig. 6.2.2.7.

On three sides of the bothros in the steps 13, 14, and 15 there are altogether 17 flat or conical cuttings. In the steps of the wing there are more depressions, one in step 16 is certain, while in step 17 there are possibly three more. Because of the wear of the surface of the steps, their depth has to be reconstructed. The three flat ones in step 15 have a diameter of c. 0.15 m and may have been c. 0.1 m deep. The conical ones are deeper, 0.14 m-0.18 m, and have a rounded bottom, c. 6/7 cm in diameter. Their surface is fairly smooth. They may have served the placing of flat-bottomed and rounded vessels. The rounded holes may, perhaps, also have served as containers for liquids. This explanation may at least apply to the elongated holes in the top step (15) of the wing and situated just inside the threshold of the door into the aqueduct.

In step 14, 1.80 m from the west parapet, is a 0.20 m deep square cutting, 0.125 m by 0.10 m, with stucco preserved on the east side. On line with this are three holes in the vertical west parapet. They are situated almost, but not quite, above one another. The lowest two are almost square and regular, 0.12 m by 0.12 m, and respectively 0.12 m (below) and 0.16 m (above) deep. The third hole is different, elongated and pointed, 0.12 m deep. Its purpose is uncertain,

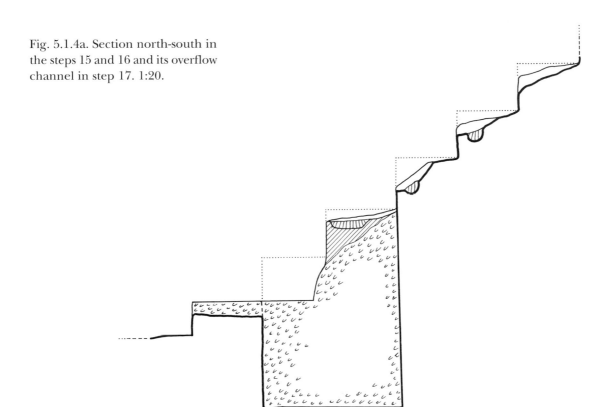

Fig. 5.1.4a. Section north-south in the steps 15 and 16 and its overflow channel in step 17. 1:20.

Fig. 5.1.5. Section east-west in Chamber 1 with the opening of the Main Corridor and of the ruined opening into UG:B1. The staircase behind the south wall of the transverse corridor is not shown. 1:50. A shows the position of the cutting for door post and sill, and B a section of the cuttings. 1:20.

Fig. 5.1.6. Detail of staircase, bothros, and UG in Cb1 seen from above. a-b-c mark the 1st, 2nd and 3rd steps of the staircase wing, that gave access into UG:B. On the steps, depressions for offerings. A part of the bothros is visible in the lower right corner. 1973.

Fig. 5.1.7. Part of the staircase and landing in Cb1, east side. View from above the opening into the Main Corridor. Between the walls of the transverse gallery, the bottom step of the staircase is visible. 1973.

whereas both the hole in step 14 and the two lowest ones in the parapet in all likelihood served the protection of the bothros – for the position of a kind of rail. A cutting in the floor of the landing contiguous with step 17 may have served a similar purpose. It is situated almost in the centre of the structure and measures 0.18 m by 0.14 m and is 0.09 m deep.

The bothros, the wing, the doorway, and the cuttings all combine to form a most interesting ensemble in their setting with the aqueduct and the chamber in Cb1 and the quite subterranean chamber Cb2. Important for the understanding of the rituals(?) performed are most probably also the contents of the bothros, which have been treated by L.E. Vaag[99], see also below, p. 168.

The landing

The landing is short, only 2.3 m deep, and 4.7 m wide in extension of the staircase. It is defined by the lowest step, by the sides cut in the bedrock, and to the north by re-entrants in both sides and a central pillar. The east side is preserved up to the ancient and present surface level. The west side, situated within the foundation cutting, was cut down to level 7.05 m a.s.l., and only the bottom part of c. 1.5 m was spared.

The floor is uneven and shows only a few features. The square cutting in the centre of the landing contiguous to step 17 has been mentioned above. Another shallow and irregular cutting is situated in the floor in the corner of the wing.

Fig. 5.1.8. View west in the transverse corridor in Cb1. The lowest step protrudes below the south wall; in front, the wing of 3 steps that gave access to UG:B1. 1973.

Finally, in the NE part of the landing there is an irregular depression, c. 1.3 m by 1.3 m and only c. 3 cm deep. Fig. 5.1.7. K. Jeppesen has convincingly interpreted the feature as the bedding for Pillar P14, one of the altogether 18 Maussollan pillars situated around the Maussolleion.[100]

Two areas are of special interest: the limit towards the chamber and the connection between the landing and the Main Corridor.
1. Below a slab in course 4 of the Maussolleion ashlars a rock-cut part of an architectural feature is preserved, 0.28 m high (Fig. 5.1.12). It faces west and is stuccoed. Beyond the protecting andesite ashlar, only the outline of the other sides survived destruction. The west side measured 0.55 m and the north side c. 0.82 m. The distance from this point to the east re-entrant mirrors the distance to the west, so a central pillar can be reconstructed with certainty.

Fig. 5.1.9. Cutting for door post and sill in opening between Cb1 and UG:B1. 1973.

The south side of the pillar is flush with the finely cut re-entrants in both side walls, by which means the width is reduced by 2 × 48 cm = 0.96 m. This line therefore marks the beginning of the inner part or chamber of the structure.

Substantial remains of wall stucco are preserved on the south and west faces of the east re-entrant. Stucco also remains on the south face of the west re-entrant, of which only the bottom is preserved, Fig. 5.1.2.
2. The opening of the Main Corridor is 2.56 m high. Around the opening there is – as in the opposite opening into UG:B1 – a c. 0.30 m wide stucco band. Moreover, all the way along the inside of the opening a similar band is preserved, but c. 0.60 m wide, which terminates 0.25 m above the floor. The stucco is coarse with red and black 'grains'. Both on the N and S sides are patches of the same stucco preserved immediately inside the band in the opening. There is hardly reason, though, to consider the walls of the corridor to have been completely stuccoed.

In the opening 2.2 m above the floor two holes are situated opposite each other, 0.1 m by 0.12 m and 0.1 m deep. They may have been instrumental for a kind of closing of the entrance into the corridor. This, though, can only have been provisional, because there is no other evidence for any closing.

Landing and corridor are closely connected. The floor slopes gently from c. 5.55 m a.s.l. in the landing down to the average level in the first part of the corridor of 5.49 m. Also a shallow, well-defined channel, c. 13 cm wide and 10 cm deep,

Fig. 5.1.10. The west side of the landing in Cb1 with ashlars of the Maussolleion foundation. View towards NW. Note above the 3rd course of the andesite the remains of the stucco of the wall of the chamber. 1972.

connects the two. The channel runs along the north side of the corridor, turns at right-angles into the landing and along its east side where it disappears in the area of the break into the ceiling of the Lower Gallery. On the other side of the break there is only a shallow depression, a couple of centimetres deep.

The channel was filled with a hard packing of whitish soil and was covered by the eastern-most ashlar in the built north wall of the corridor across the landing. Therefore, the channel must belong to the original, pre-Maussollan phase of the structure. How it ended – or rather begin – in the landing we shall never know, because this point was destroyed (see above p. 59). One could surmise that it emptied itself into the Lower Gallery – which would imply the co-existence of gallery, landing and corridor. This is, however, impossible, because both the Lower Gallery and the built corridor are Maussollan, and also for

technical reasons with regard to the cutting of the Lower Gallery. In the angle between Cb3 and the East Corridor, a pre-Maussollan wall (see below, p. 106), moreover, destroyed the continuation of the channel.

Both floor level and channel demonstrate a close connection between the landing and the Main Corridor. Therefore the awkward protrusion of 0.28 m by step 17 of the staircase into the opening is very surprising. UG:B1 and the Main Corridor are situated in line with each other, and on the west side the wing of three steps and the doorway into the aqueduct fit perfectly together. On the east side, however, the builders obviously forgot to allow for the length of the stair. Instead they secured an easy passage by widening the opening of the corridor to 0.75 m from the average 0.60 m. 1.8 m from the opening the corridor is only 0.5 m wide.

Fig. 5.1.11. The central part of the landing in Cb1 with ashlars of the Maussolleion foundation. View north. The lower 3 andesite courses follow the line of the earlier structure, while the courses above are adjusted to the E-W / N-S line of the Maussolleion. The claystone in the background, below the 4th course, indicates the approximate position of the rear wall of the chamber. To the right the east parapet with remains of stucco. 1972.

The chamber

The pillar divided the façade of the innermost part of Cb1 into two openings, each about 1.48 m wide. Hardly more than the outline of both west re-entrant and central pillar is preserved. The east re-entrant, however, is preserved 1.2 m up, and there are no traces of cuttings or holes for a locking device. The same applies to the floor, so the inner part appears to have been quite open towards the landing.

Fig. 5.1.12. Rest of stuccoed central pillar in the landing of Cb1. View north. 1974.

Fig. 5.1.13. The opening of the Main Corridor from Cb1. To the right, south ashlar wall of the transverse corridor on the lowest step of the staircase. In the lower left corner the breach into LG:s. View towards SE. 1974.

As in the landing, the Maussolleion builders cut the west side of the chamber down to level 7.06 m a.s.l. The remaining side was moreover dressed to fit in 4 courses of ashlars for the foundation, Fig. 5.1.10-11. Well-preserved is a shallow cutting on a level with its course 8. Fortunately a small stuccoed piece of the original west wall about 1.60 m inside the re-entrant and 0.90 m above the floor level establishes the line of the wall, Fig. 5.1.4 and 10. It is exactly in line with the reconstructed inner side of the re-entrant, by which means it is proved that the re-entrants were not just pillars but for certain establish the width of the chamber to be 3.75 m.

Only one other feature of the inside of the chamber is preserved in the west wall beside the just mentioned stuccoed area at a slightly lower level, 0.78 m above the floor: an 8 cm deep square depression, 10 cm × 16 cm, also partly stuccoed.

The greater part of the north side in the chamber is hidden below and behind the andesite ashlars, but a short stretch of the bedrock (claystone) is preserved close to the NE corner of the chamber and establishes the end wall, approximately 4.70 m inside the re-entrants. Up to this point the green andesite foundation blocks (courses 3-6) stick to the NNE orientation of the chamber, whereas the line of the ashlar courses 7-8 (above level 6.46 m a.s.l.) conforms with the regular E-W orientation of the Maussolleion. This feature delineates the cavity that the Maussolleion builders had to fill up, and this can be nothing but a chamber.

The east side of the chamber – in claystone – is completely destroyed except for the width of 0.6 m of the re-entrant. Andesite ashlars extend over the (supposed) line of the east side of the chamber. Therefore we have no means of deciding whether there was an opening also at this point into the gallery UG:B2, the floor level of which originally lay c. 0.75 m higher up, at c. 6.20 m a.s.l. (see below, p. 132). The possibility, however, cannot be excluded, because in Chamber 2 a plain opening and a short corridor secured a direct communication between chamber and aqueduct (see p. 132).

No traces of a ceiling are preserved, but one feature strongly indicates that the chamber was subterranean: the central, square pillar can hardly have had any other purpose than to support a ceiling. Also the fact that UG:B2 was subterranean strengthens this conclusion.

The surface level of the bedrock S, east and west of Chamber 1, is about 9.85 m a.s.l., and the floor level of the chamber is c. 5.50 m. The difference of 4.35 m leaves plenty of room for an interior height of more than 3.0 m, compared with the thickness of 1 m of the ceiling in Chamber 2.

Finally, it should be admitted that we have no means to decide whether the inner part was cut as one chamber, c. 4.5 m long (measured from the façade) and 3.8 m wide, or as two narrow chambers, c. 4.5 m long and only 1.48 m wide (like the openings). The latter solution, however, is quite unparalleled and is unnecessary for structural reasons.

Fig. 5.1.14. The shallow channel running from the Main Corridor into the landing of Cb1. Above, the breach into LG:s. 1974.

Fig. 5.2.1. View west in the Main Corridor. To the right, the door into Cb2 and further on, the light from above in the shaft. 1974.

5.2. The Main Corridor

The corridor is briefly mentioned by Newton, *HD*: 146-147, and illustrated in a sketch by Pullan, Pl. 8.

The course is about 19.4 m long and runs from Cb1 to Cb3 and also provides access through a doorway into Cb2. Only the last c. 0.5 m was not investigated by us. A rough wall that can only have been built by the British blocked the opening into Cb3. It is cut completely in sandstone, the surface of which is only partially preserved. In the E end, especially on the south side, large flakes have fallen down due to cracks and breaks in the bedrock, Fig. 5.2.1.

Cutting-marks in its upper part show the corridor to be cut in both directions from a shaft that is situated eccentrically, about 13 m from Cb1 and 5 m from Cb3, pl. 5.2. The lower c.

1.3 m is slightly set off from the upper part and shows irregular cutting-marks from both sides.

There are five lamp-holes in the west end of the corridor, three in the north side and two in the south side. They are situated high up in the wall, as shown in the section A, Fig. 5.2.2, as in the Upper Gallery. The third one, 3.7 m from the opening into Cb1, though, is situated 0.7 m below the ceiling. Also their almost alternating position and the absence of holes in the rest of the course sets this corridor apart from both the Lower and the Upper Gallery.

The shaft measures 1.25 m by 0.70 m and is 4.15 m high from the floor level to the top around which is cut a ledge 0.20-0.40 m wide and 0.15 m high. In the long sides of the shaft there are cuttings for steps, c. 0.40-0.50 m apart. Quite extraordinary is a 0.80 m deep cutting in its bottom with sloping sides in the short ends

91

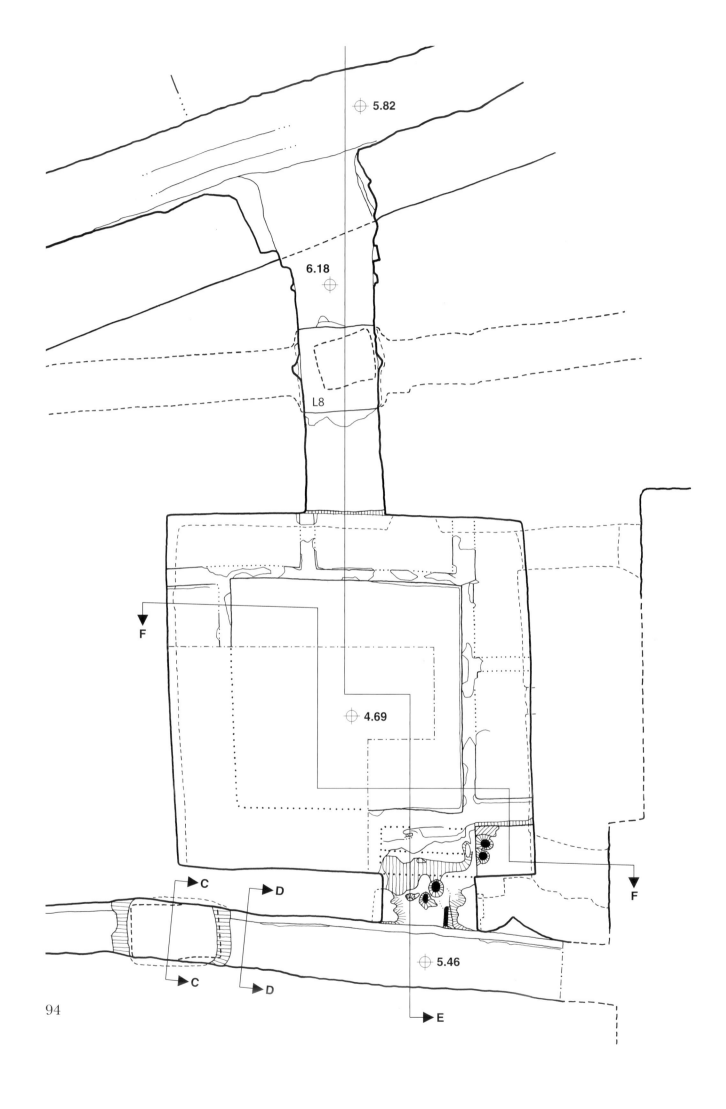

5.82

6.18

L8

F

4.69

C

C

D

D

F

5.46

E

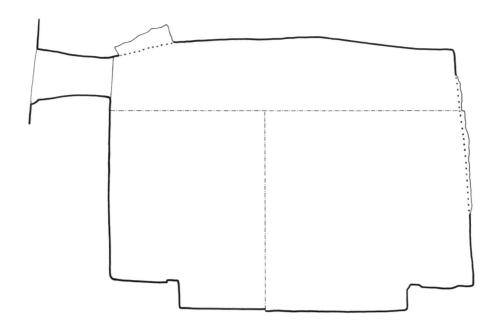

Fig. 5.3.2. Composite section F in the chamber Cb2, east-west. 1:50.

When we encountered the chamber in 1973, it was again almost full of white friable soil mixed with brownish veins, and their position showed that it had been filled up from the hole in the ceiling. According to Murdoch Smith, it was completely emptied through the same hole in February and March 1857.[101] We repeated the procedure, but, for security's sake, the chamber was only partly emptied.

The chamber is square but in plan slightly distorted, none of the corners being at right-angles. The sides slant inwards, as it appears from the measure c. 5.2 m by 5.2 m below and only 4.8 m by 4.8 m just below the ceiling. The floor level is 4.70 m a.s.l.; the height of the chamber in the centre reaches 3.6 m.

The state of preservation is not good. As already mentioned, there is a hole in the sandstone ceiling, but a large part of the remainder has flaked off. The original sides are flawed by

◄ Fig. 5.3.1. Plan of the subterranean chamber Cb2 with the openings into Cb3. Also shown is the corridor to the north and, to the south, part of the Main Corridor with shaft. 1:50.

faults and cracks, and across the chamber runs an E-W fault in the bedrock with the vulnerable claystone in the lower part of the northern half, clearly visible in the view Fig. 5.3.7-8 of the east side. This peculiar formation is mirrored in the west side of the adjacent Cb3, the wall being only c. 1.6 m thick, see below, p. 102. This situation explains why hardly any features are preserved in the surface of the walls. Only in the east wall below the square opening in the upper left corner (see below) are three cuttings preserved one above the other at a distance of about 0.55 m. The cuttings resemble the cuttings in the shafts of the galleries, but without corresponding ones within reach, as in the shafts, they can have been of no use. One could well conjecture that they are of the 19th Century, but it does not help to explain their function.

All around the chamber there is a 0.90 m wide and 0.45 m high bench cut in the solid rock, Fig. 5.3.4, reducing the floor to c. 3 m × 3 m. The outer border of the bench has a 0.16 m wide raised ledge, and likewise the bench is divided into compartments of slightly irregular length, 1.60 m-1.80 m. Four are visible and three more can be calculated to lie hidden below the unexcavated earth in the SW part of the chamber.

95

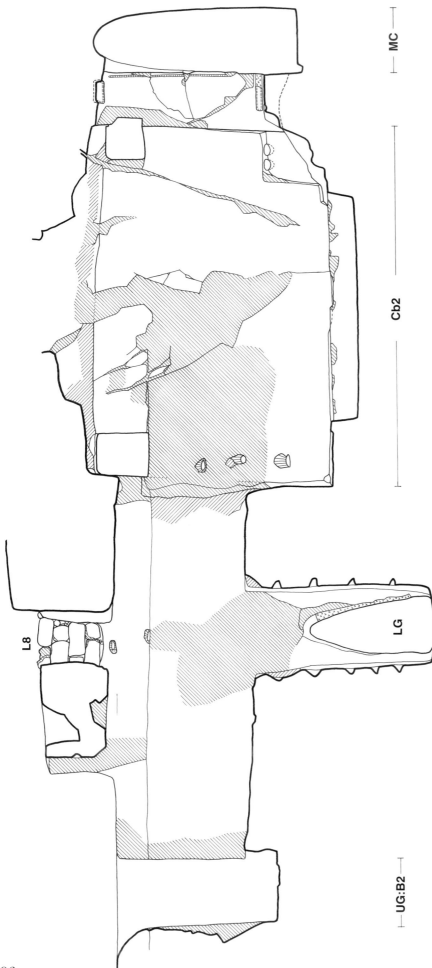

MC

Cb2

LG

L8

UG:B2

Fig. 5.3.3. North-south section through Upper Gallery B2, Shaft L8, the chamber Cb2 and the Main Corridor. 1:50.

Fig. 5.3.4. The bench along the east side of Cb2 with the podium and a part of the opening into the Main Corridor. View south. 1974.

Fig. 5.3.5. The SE corner of Chamber 2 with the podium and the opening into the Main Corridor. View south. 1974.

The bench is interrupted in the SE corner by a 0.80 m high podium and the staircase leading down from the door between the Main Corridor and the chamber. The podium measures c. 0.70 m by 0.70 m, and close to its west edge are two conical cuttings similar to those in the southern staircase.

The doorway between the Main Corridor and the chamber measures 2.2 m × 1.25 m and is 0.50 m deep. Its irregular bottom is 0.45 m above the floor in the corridor, and in the chamber, a staircase, 1.25 m high, of probably three steps, led down to the floor level. In the top and bottom of the sides of the doorway there are well-preserved cuttings for a separate threshold and a lintel – probably in wood because marble or limestone is too heavy for the friable sandstone. With the lintel and threshold in place,

the height would have been 2.06 m. In contrast to the opening between Cb1 and the aqueduct UG:B1, where a ledge testifies to the existence of posts, the sides are smooth. The E side of the doorway, though, is furnished with a vertical line that could mark the existence of posts that could have been fitted into lintel and threshold. Both the steps and the bedrock threshold were much worn already when excavated by Newton, as it appears from Pullan's watercolour Pl. 9. The wear of the latter is intriguing because it would have been protected by the inserted threshold,

In each upper corner of the east wall of Chamber 2, just below the ceiling, there is a square opening cut horizontally in the bedrock. Both openings reach into the west side of Chamber 3, the northernmost at a level with what Newton pre-

97

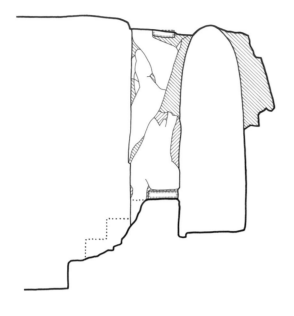

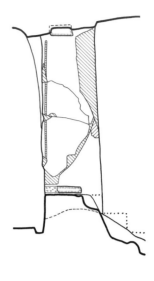

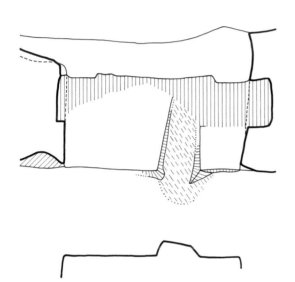

Fig. 5.3.6. Views and sections of the door between the Main Corridor and the subterranean chamber Cb2. 1:50. Detail of lap, 1:25.

sumed to be its ceiling, which therefore would already have been destroyed when the opening was cut (see below, p. 104, however).[102]

The northernmost opening, Fig. 5.3.7, is cut at right-angles to the E wall in continuation of the N wall of the chamber. The length is 1.4 m. Cutting-marks show that it was cut from west towards east, except in the eastern end where it widens slightly. It measures 0.70 m in height, and the width narrows upwards from 0.58 m to 0.52 m. In the wall below are the three stepping-holes (?), mentioned above.

The other square opening is situated on a slightly lower level. It measures 1 m in length,

c. 0.5 m in height and 0.48 m in width. Compared to the former opening, the execution is very sloppy. Its direction runs slightly oblique to the line of the wall, and the south side is both cut into the south wall of the chamber and widens stepwise towards the east from 0.48 m to 0.75 m. The sides are badly preserved, so the cutting direction cannot be established. The 'stepwise' cuttings, however, strongly indicate that the cutting (re-cutting?) was done from the east towards the west.

With regard to both openings, we were able to ascertain their eastern returns in Chamber 3, but they could not be studied in any detail,

Fig. 5.3.7. The NE corner of Cb2 with, left, the Short Corridor running north from Cb2 towards Shaft L8, and the northernmost 'window' connecting Cb2 and Cb3. 1974.

because the chamber was not re-excavated. Fortunately, the square cuttings in Chamber 3 figure on several of Pullan's drawings, Pl. 10-12, and their differences with regard to size and level are confirmed.

Newton discusses the openings only in connection with Cb3 and first understood them as windows: *Adjacent to this chamber on the south-east, and communicating with it by two small windows.*[103] However, he came to believe that they were secondary and in vague terms suggested that they could be *loculi*, made in a later period for burials. *Loculi* are characteristic of Hellenistic burials also in Halikarnassos, and there are several chamber tombs with *loculi* on the Göktepe. But the size of our openings excludes this possibility, the south one being only 1 m long, and their position in the tomb shows them to belong to the chamber. Below, it will be argued that Newton's claim of their secondary nature was founded on a wrong

understanding of the geological features. There is no evidence for their use later than in the period of the two structures they connect.

In the centre of the north wall in Cb2, 1.1 m above the bench and at right-angles, is the plain opening of a Short Corridor, 1.70 m high and 1.00 m wide. It runs 5 m to the Upper Gallery B2, which it reaches 0.38 m above its bottom. This conforms to the level of the footpath in the aqueduct, before the Maussolleion builders (see p. 132) cut it down.

Chamber and the Main Corridor on one side, and chamber, the Short Corridor and aqueduct on the other, are closely connected to each other and certainly functioned at the same time. By means of the Short Corridor there was direct access from the aqueduct to the chamber, but the lack of any architectural features in the corridor itself, the bottom, sides and ceiling of which are

99

Fig. 5.3.8. The NE corner of Cb2. View east. 1974.

Fig. 5.3.9. The corridor between Cb2 and UG:B2 with column drum and Shaft L8. View north. 1973.

plain, leaves us with no means to explain the character of the communication.

The Short Corridor was partly destroyed when Shaft L8 was cut down through its ceiling and floor. The shaft is clearly secondary to the corridor, because both its size and position were modified during construction (see above, p. 59). When the Quadrangle was cut for the foundation of the Maussolleion, also the ceiling in the northern 1.6 m of the corridor was cut away.

5.4. The Courtyard, Chamber 3

Newton mentions the structure three times: briefly in *Pl*6: 51 and in a short, precise account in *FP*16: 90, which is repeated almost literally in *HD*: 148-149. It moreover figures in several plans and drawings by Murdoch Smith and Pullan, to which he refers.

We excavated only a small area in its east side (Trench P$_{10}$, above p. 35) that among other things served to fix the east side and the opening into the East Corridor. Moreover, both the position of the north side and certain features of the W and N part of the structure were studied through the openings in the party wall between Cb2 and Cb3. On this basis we believed to have enough evidence to interpret and complete Newton's and especially Pullan's fairly detailed documentation. However, to understand what Newton and Pullan saw has long appeared as difficult as the evidence is crucial for an understanding of the history of the site before the building of the Maussolleion.

Newton's accounts are quoted in full.

Adjacent to this chamber [Cb2] on the south-east, and communicating with it by two small windows, was another larger chamber, about 22 feet by 14 feet broad. [6.71 m by 4.27 m]

This, like the smaller adjacent chamber, had been excavated out of the solid rock, but the roof had fallen in, and the interior was filled with large blocks of native rock, built up in irregular courses.

The southern end of this chamber is traversed by a wall of rustic work, described in my last General Report [Pl5: 47] as a terrace wall [TW1], running east and west, parallel with the south side of the Mausoleum.

It is evident that this wall was built subsequently to the chamber, as it destroys the regularity of its plan, running at an oblique angle to its southern side.

On the other hand, from the character of the masonry of this wall, I should consider that it is of the same period as the Mausoleum.

If such be the case, this chamber, and the smaller one adjacent to it, must belong to some cemetery earlier than the building erected by Artemisia. (P16: 51, 1857.12.10.)

The large oblong cavity, lying to the east of this chamber [Cb2], has been divided into two compartments at the point where nearly opposite returns are cut in its eastern and western sides. (See the Plan of this part, Plate XIII. and Plate III.)[Pl. 10 and Fig. 1.2.1]

The smaller of these two compartments is evidently a monolithic chamber, like the one contiguous to it on the west, as, on three sides, a return in the rock may be traced all round at the same height from the ground, showing where the line of the roof has been broken away. (See the Views, Plate XIV., and the Section, Plate XIII., of this chamber.) [Pl. 10-12]

On the west side of this second chamber are two square apertures cut through the rock into the contiguous monolithic chamber on the west. They are large enough to admit a man's body.

These apertures range immediately below the roof of the western chamber, but above the broken line of roof in the second chamber. It would seem, therefore, that they had been cut after this latter roof had been broken away.

On clearing out the second chamber, it was found to be partially filled with a rough wall of squared blocks of native rock similar in appearance to the walls at the foot of the two stairs already described. [Cb1 and MauTb]

The larger compartment, adjacent on the south to the second chamber, exhibited no trace of a roof, and may have been hypæthral.

The branch of the upper gallery, C, leading into this larger compartment from the west, is continued across it in an oblique direction by rubble walls carelessly built, and re-enters the rock on the opposite side.

It may be presumed that the rubble walls crossing this chamber are more recent than the chamber itself; they may be additions made at the same period as the rubble walls by which the gallery is prolonged across the foot of the south stair, which are similar in masonry. (FP16: 90, 1859.04.12, and HD: 148-149.)

Besides these two texts, the British documented the structure by means of the general plan by Murdoch Smith, and Pullan's two watercolours and his plan and view of the west side. The latter are dated October 10th and 12th, 1857 and reproduced as engravings in *HD*.

Murdoch Smith's plan, Fig. 1.2.1, is very schematic and shows a very regular layout. A narrow inner part is set apart from the rest by a pillar and a re-entrant opposite each other. Also the openings of the Main and East Corridors are shown on line. All four sides of the southern part are clearly indicated. The length, 11.28 m, can be calculated only from this plan.

Pullan's line drawing, Pl. 10, shows the measured plan and a view of the W side with a section of the terrace wall, TW1, in the S end and in the other a section of bedrock. The southern part, beyond TW1, is omitted. The overall impression is one of irregularity.

The line of the corridors crosses obliquely, and only a single stone(?) denotes the north side of Newton's rubble corridor connecting the Main and East Corridors. A dashed line indicates its line. The level of the floor south of the rubble wall is on a higher level than in the rest of the structure. The 'pillar' and re-entrant are not situated opposite each other and are not at right-angles to their respective sides. The sides in the inner part are shown to be eroded and the original line is indicated on the east side. The upper part of the west side appears fairly smooth whereas, to the north, it is clearly broken

Pullan's watercolour, Pl. 12, with a view towards the west, substantiates and adds to the above information but also differs in certain respects. Very clear is his distinction between sandstone and claystone. The geological features of the west side clearly mirror the other side of the party wall in Cb2, cf. above p. 95 and Pl. 9 and Fig. 5.3.3. The southern and upper part of the side (in sandstone) appears somewhat irregular and is smooth only beside and above the northern window into Cb2. The bottom of the window (correctly) goes with the top of the claystone, whereas it in the drawing is placed higher up. The claystone in the north side appears eroded, its bottom part still being *in situ*. The 'pillar' on the north side hardly figures. A new feature is the north edge of the crossing rubble-wall, still standing c. 0.5 m high.

Pullan's watercolour, Pl. 11, shows part of the west side, nearly the whole north side, and the east side with a part of the terrace wall, TW1. Beside the southern window appears the 'pillar' that hides the rest of the west side. The dividing line, the fault, between the broken sandstone, above, and the claystone, below, continues over the capstones of the East Corridor, as if they were covered by sandstone. The fault slants towards the west, in accordance with our observations along the south side of the Quadrangle from the SE angle and through the Short Corridor into Cb2, Fig. 5.3.3. The re-entrant on the east side is clearly shown. The state of the rubble wall is again new or rather blurred. The higher ground level to its south is indicated, but not the channel itself, so clearly shown on the other watercolour. And on what is the resting Turk seated? When compared with both the other watercolour and the plan, it cannot be the rubble wall.

Summing up, Newton and Pullan agree on important features such as the (correct) oblique course of the line of the Main and East Corridor, and also with Murdoch Smith on the inner part being narrower than the southern part. Many of Pullan's observations are verified, but several problems remain, of which the crucial ones are the plan arrangement and, closely related, Newton's reconstruction of an inner, roofed chamber. Also the evidence for the alleged corridor connecting the East and Main Corridors appears puzzling.

The plan arrangement and the dimensions

The length of the structure north of the rubble wall can be fairly precisely established, although we measured 0.2 m less than Newton and Pullan, and our measures of the width of both 'chamber' and dromos come 65 cm shorter than Pullan's. See the table, below, and the plan Fig. 5.4.2.

The different state of preservation of the sandstone and claystone explains the discrepancies. Just as in Cb2, cf. Fig. 5.3.7-8, the sandstone protrudes in front of the underlying claystone. For example in the northern window, Fig. 5.3.1, the sandstone protrudes 0.45 m (full line) in front of the claystone bottom (the dashed line). Also along the N side in Fig. 5.3.3 the different alignment of sand- and claystone, only 0.1 m, is clearly seen.

The geology and the state of preservation in Trench P_{10}, Fig. 2.3.1 and 4 (plan & photo) are also crucial for the understanding of the width and of the plan. The claystone side is much eroded and recedes about 0.60 m from the clear-cut transition from floor to side and up to the top, 2.28 m higher up. Pullan's larger width derives, we believe, from his taking his measurements not at the bottom but somewhere higher up the wall.

We were able to ascertain another error of Pullan. In the watercolour Pl. 11, the oblique fault between sandstone above and claystone below continues right to the opening into the East Corridor, across which the sandstone appears to cover the capstones. From Trench P_{10}, however, we know that soil covered the ceiling of the East Corridor and the c. 1.1 m broad ledge to its north, where the level of the sandstone rises from about 7.2 m to about 8.45 m a.s.l. On Pullan's watercolour this shift may correspond to the re-entrant in the bedrock shown to the left of the seated Turk. Only until this point did the sandstone protect the claystone below, and this explains the presumed re-entrant that in Pullan's plan, Pl. 10, appears irregular, a detail that renders a man-made and cut execution unlikely.

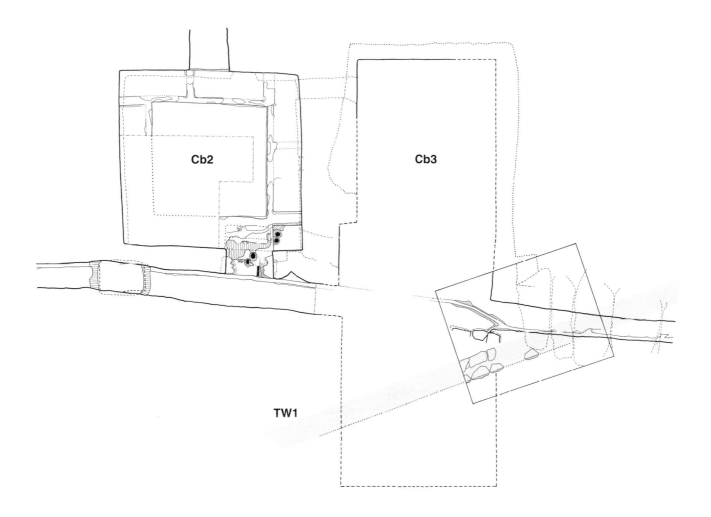

Fig. 5.4.1. The reconstructed outline of Cb3 in relation to Cb2 and the opening of the East Corridor as revealed in Trench P₁₀. The broken line indicates the bottom line, the dotted line is Pullan's outline that he measured higher up on the eroded sides of the chamber. His line matches neatly the upper part of the side, documented in P₁₀. 1:100.

The case for a re-entrant – but not for a pillar – on the west side of the chamber is compelling. We know the line in the sandstone around both windows. The southern window lies c. 0.45 m behind the other, and the recession north of the "pillar" is, as shown in the northern window (see above) due only to erosion. The north side of Pullan's "pillar" is nothing but the verti-cal line of the fault, which moreover does not continue upwards in the sandstone above the claystone.

On this basis, we reconstruct the plan of the structure as fairly regular with a re-entrant only in the W side. It rather sets off the opening into the Main Corridor than forms a feature of Chamber 3.

103

	Newton	Murdoch Smith	Pullan	Actual size
Length of Cb3		11.28 m		
Length of inner part, to line of the Main and the East Corridor	6.71 m	6.42 m	6.3 m 6.7 m	6.10 m to the Main Corridor 6.50 m to the East Corridor
Width of inner part	4.27 m	3.96 m	4.34 m	3.70 m
Width of S part		4.87 m	4.70 m	4.10 m

The ceiling and the openings between Cb2 and Cb3

Very intriguing is the case for a ceiling in the northern part of Cb3. Newton was not in doubt (full quotes, above):

1. *This, like the smaller adjacent chamber, had been excavated out of the solid rock, but the roof had fallen in, and the interior was filled with large blocks of native rock, built up in irregular courses.* (*Pl6*).

In *HD* the wording is changed (see above), and it becomes clear that the *large blocks* were found in the second, southern "chamber". They were not the remains of the broken ceiling and belonged to the rough wall running in the line of the Main and East Corridors:

2. *The smaller of these two compartments is evidently a monolithic chamber, like the one contiguous to it on the west, as, on three sides, a return in the rock may be traced all round at the same height from the ground, showing where the line of the roof has been broken away.*

3. *On the west side of this second chamber are two square apertures cut through the rock into the contiguous monolithic chamber on the west. They are large enough to admit a man's body.*

    These apertures range immediately below the roof of the western chamber, but above the broken line of roof in the second chamber. It would seem, therefore, that they had been cut after this latter roof had been broken away. (*HD*)

Newton's observation on the relative chronology of the ceiling and the openings appears correct, except that it can only pertain to the northern window. Although he is not saying anything on the possible south limit of the chamber, the southern window would evidently be outside the chamber, in the 'dromos'.

In the photo Fig. 5.4.2 a curved, c. 0.30 m wide and c. 0.12 m high cutting of this ceiling in sandstone is clearly seen. Marks of pointed chisels or the like are preserved – to the right is seen its broken edge. It was duly recorded by Pullan in his drawing Pl. 10. The distance down to the floor is 2.42 m, which would come close to the height of the chamber. Around the northern window there are no similar traces of a ceiling, only the marked different line of the claystone below and sandstone above. Pullan's watercolour, Pl. 12, confirms this observation. On the other hand, he is of no help with regard to the possible cutting on the east side of the chamber: the cutting for the ceiling does not figure on any of the watercolours, so it could just as well be on the east side.

Be that as it may, the evidence for a ceiling, whatever its extension and the shape of the chamber, is conclusive. We must imagine a phase with a chamber or a roofed area in this place. Newton considered the chamber to be contemporaneous with the subterranean chamber and the windows to be later. As he considers both subterranean chambers to be pre-Maussollan, the windows would be post-Maussollan. In our opinion, their position in the upper corners of the east side in Cb2 renders them inseparable from the period of use of chamber Cb2. Moreover, their differences in size and shape render any other common purpose impossible.

Two scenarios are feasible that both imply the decommissioning of the structures when the Maussolleion was built:

Fig. 5.4.2. View of the upper part of the north side in Cb3. 2003.

1. The chambers are contemporaneous. After the destruction of the ceiling, either both windows were cut or only the northern one.
2. The chamber Cb3 is older than Cb2, and the area was re-used as a courtyard in connection with the cutting of the chamber / corridor complex.

The irregular plan and the marked wear and decay of the bedrock may recommend the latter scenario.

Only an excavation may settle the matter.

Finally, two narrow cuttings in the back wall should be noted, one vertical, the other apparently square, that are indicated by Pullan in the section Pl. 10 and in the view Pl. 12. Their appearance in the eroded claystone is as enigmatic as is their purpose. In shape they are reminiscent of the cuttings in the eastern vertical side of the bedrock behind the terrace wall, TW2, Pl. 4.

The lower wall crossing Chamber 3

Two walls intersected the southern part of the rectangular cutting. The terrace wall, TW1, carried on a solid foundation, and facing south, has been treated above, p. 73. Now the focus is on Newton's contemporary rubble wall on a line with the south side in the East Corridor and the Main Corridor.

A short stretch of the construction was re-excavated in 1976 and is documented above, p. 35. The preserved lower two courses of the wall are built with various kinds of stones: sandstone and andesite of three slightly different colours. Also their sizes are remarkably varied, and they are irregularly placed when compared both with the back wall of TW1, just above (Fig. 2.3.3), and – not least – with the smooth inner faces of the built corridor in Chamber 1, Fig. 5.1.5 and 8.

The evidence adduced by Newton and Pullan and their interpretation of it must be scrutinized. The wall features in the two watercolours and in the measured drawing by Pullan, referred to above. In one watercolour, Pl. 12, two clearly distinguished sides of a corridor, perhaps about 0.5 m high, and divided by a 'channel' or void, span the courtyard from side to side, just as stated in Newton's text: *The branch of the upper gallery, C, leading into this larger compartment from the west, is continued across it in an oblique direction by rubble*

105

walls carelessly built, and re-enters the rock on the opposite side (*HD*: 149, full quote above).

On the other watercolour, Pl. 11, however, the line of the corridor does not attach to the north side of the opening into the Main Corridor, nor is the void between the walls indicated as in the other drawing. Instead, the area south of the line of the wall appears to form a 'platform' at the level of the low wall.

As noted above, the measured plan, Pl. 10, moreover clearly shows the whole north wall to be a conjecture, since it is indicated by a broken line and on the basis of what may be one block to the west. An unbroken line, however, indicates the line of the south wall of which we ascertained the east end. There is no corridor either in the plan or in the section. During our excavation in 1974 we ascertained no trace of the 'second' wall.

Newton in vague terms noted close similarities between the lower wall in Cb3 and both the corridor traversing Cb1 and the coarse wall crossing the Western Staircase.[104] However, the dressed inner face of the sandstone corridor in Cb1, Fig. 5.1.8, is very different from the roughly built wall in Cb3, Fig. 3.2.2, of various andesite stones. The lower wall is both in appearance and function quite different from the construction across Cb1. In Cb3 the wall probably served to limit the inner part of the structure, which due to the building of TW1 now had become a courtyard, closed on all four sides, except, of course, for the entrances into the Main Corridor and the East Corridor. Its height can only be conjectured. It may have completely hidden the back of TW1, or rather – considering the fairly diligent construction of the back of this wall in limestone – may have been only as high as up to the top level of the ceiling in the East Corridor, i.e. about 2 m high.

The place of connection between the wall and the c. 2.80 m high opening of the Main Corridor was not re-excavated (top level 8.17 m a.s.l.). From the drawings and from the silence in the written description, the opening appears to be plain, except perhaps for a notch in the right side, Pl. 10-11. Its level may correspond with the square cutting in both sides of the opening of the Main Corridor into Cb1.

Above, p. 35, with Fig. 2.3.1-2 is noted the shallow water channel that emerges from the East Corridor and divides into two branches. One of these turns south under both the above-mentioned wall and the foundation of TW1 that obstructs its course and is therefore later than the channel. The other branch turns slightly to the north, crosses the courtyard and connects to the channel in the Main Corridor. The channel definitely belongs to the period of use of the corridors and Cb3 before the reformulation of the area due to the building of the terrace wall, TW1.

The southern part of the courtyard Cb3

Terrace Wall 1 and the lower wall blocked the earlier passage or 'dromos' from the courtyard to its opening and the ravine to the south.

The original form of the southern part of the structure is open to conjecture, because the only evidence for its delimitation and shape comes from Murdoch Smith's plan. Newton does not mention the termination of the 'dromos' towards the south, nor does it figure on Pullan's plan.

In Murdoch Smith's published plan, Fig. 1.2.1, the 'dromos' stretches beyond the terrace wall, and the horizontal hatching indicates that the level of the courtyard continued also in this area. This level also conforms to the level west of the 'dromos' as it appears again from the section by Murdoch Smith, Pl. 1, E-F. Its east side is indicated by a full line, which most likely indicates that the dromos was cut down into the bedrock, which is higher to the east, cf. Fig. 2.3.3-5. The south side is also shown as a full line, but we have hardly any means of ascertaining the nature of the area to the south. The west side, however, is shown with a dashed line, whereby the demarcation of the dromos is blurred. This accords well with the evidence of the hatching and confirms that the level of the dromos continues to the west. On the original plan by Murdoch Smith, however, also a part of the south side is indicated with the dashed line. This conforms well to his original section, Pl.1 where the terrace on which the foundation for the terrace wall, TW1, rests is about 3 m wide. Therefore, also a part of the south limit of Cb3 (probably) had a smooth transition towards the terrace to the south.

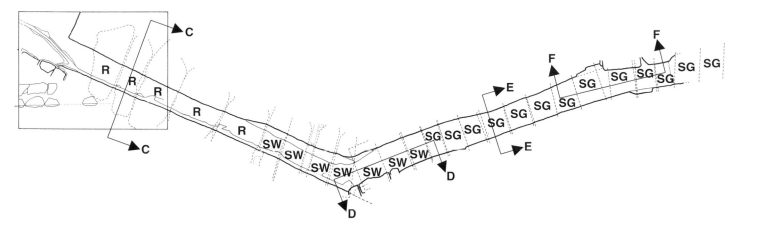

Fig. 5.5.1. Plan of Trench P$_{10}$ and the East Corridor with the ceiling slabs: R: limestone. SW: sandstone, whitish. SG: sandstone, greyish. The position of the sections and views C-F are indicated. 1:50.

5.5. The East Corridor

The line of the East Corridor continues the line of the Main Corridor. Whereas the fairly horizontal surface of the bedrock west of Cb3 is at c. 9.25 m a.s.l., the surface east of Cb3 is both lower down and slopes markedly towards the S, within Trench P$_{10}$ from c. 8.4 m a.s.l. to 7.8 m a.s.l. Presumably, the thickness of the bedrock was considered inadequate, and first a cutting, at present c. 2.5 m wide with a horizontal surface at 7.20 m a.s.l., was prepared, in which the East Corridor was cut like an open ditch, and on which the ceiling slabs of the corridor rested. Since the floor level of the corridor continues the gentle slope of the Main Corridor and Cb3, the corridor is only 1.84 m high, 1.07 m less than in the Main Corridor.

The course to the east is divided into two parts by a change in direction of c. 40° NE coinciding with the lowering of the ceiling from 1.84 m to only 1.55 m, due to a decrease in the level of the bedrock to 6.82 m a.s.l. The angle is situated 8.4 m from Cb3. At a point about 11 m further to the ENE, the corridor is blocked up by earth fallen from above, because the ceiling ashlars are missing.

The first part – 8.4 m long – was about 0.8 m wide (measured at the bottom, the claystone sides are badly damaged) and flat-bottomed. The channel along its south side continues the channel in the Main Corridor, now, however, running along the south side, see above. It is 14 cm wide and 10 cm deep. At the very point of the opening between the corridor and Cb3, a branch turns south around the corner underneath the built, transverse wall of the corridor and the foundation of TW1. Thereby its course is interrupted.

Terrace Wall 1 crosses the East Corridor on top of its ceiling, which was specially prepared to carry its weight. Five huge limestone slabs, more than 2 m long and c. 0.45 m thick, lie *in situ* where the wall crosses. A fifth, above the opening into Cb3, was found below in the corridor. Their tops are levelled (see above, p. 36) in a 0.40 m wide strip for the wall. East of the course of the wall, the ceiling consists of sandstone blocks that are far too weak to carry the wall. There is no doubt, therefore, that the East Corridor was in use contemporaneously with the terrace wall. At the same time, however, the terrace wall's foundation blocked the channel in its bottom. The wall, therefore, is later than the corridor, and as a consequence the limestone slabs must derive from a rebuilding. We have no means to decide if the beginning of the original corridor was subterranean or was covered with the same type of whitish sandstone that forms the ceiling

Fig. 5.5.2. View west in the East Corridor towards Chamber 3. 1976.

towards the east in continuation of the limestone slabs. In the former case the ditch would derive from the rebuilding phase, in the latter case it would have been widened to make room for the slabs.

In the angle of the corridor, there is on the east side a c. 1.50 m wide breach in the rock, Fig. 5.5.2. and 4, which has been blocked up with four courses of ashlars in sandstone and green andesite. On these rests the ceiling of the continuation of the corridor towards the ENE. The breach is situated exactly in line with the first part of the corridor, and its south side, though partly broken, continues beyond the new wall, and was ascertained for a further 1.30 m. Also the shallow channel disappears below the built wall. The combined evidence strongly indicates that the corridor originally continued in a straight line. Alternatively, the features testify to a radical change in the plans during construction.

From the angle, the corridor continues for 9.15 m (bottom) and 10.70 m (ceiling). It is quite flat-bottomed and also narrower, being reduced to only 0.5 m in width. The bottom level of the ceiling blocks is at 6.82 m a.s.l., so the height is reduced to 1.55 m. Only the three first are of the same white sandstone as just before the angle, while in the continuation they are of a

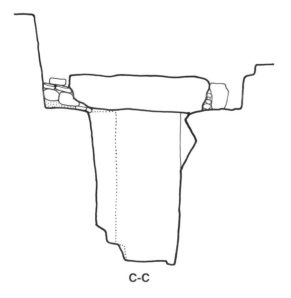

C-C

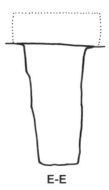

E-E

Fig. 5.5.3. Sections C and E in the East Corridor.

Fig. 5.5.4. View east in the East Corridor. Detail of built wall where the corridor turns towards NE. 1976.

Fig. 5.5.5. View NE in the East Corridor. Detail of built wall. 1976.

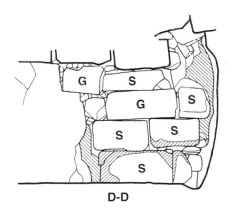

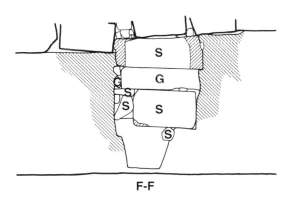

Fig. 5.5.4a. Section D in the East Corridor.

Fig. 5.5.5a. Section F in the East Corridor.

more greyish kind. In the north side, close to the interruption of its course, there is another built section, a repair of a break (?), 0.42 m wide below and about 1.10 m wide above, Fig. 5.5.5. On a 0.55 m high compact layer of decomposed bedrock rest three ashlars, two in sandstone and one in green andesite, closely packed with minor

pieces in the same materials, and a small piece in white marble. The face of the rock to both sides is fairly damaged, and the built section projects about 0.3 m into the line of the otherwise hewn side of the corridor.

The absence of ceiling blocks, whereby the corridor is blocked by earth from above, is very important for our understanding of the chronology of the corridor. In Trench Q_6 the continuation of the East Corridor appears as an open 'ditch' without ceiling-stones. The stratification shows that the ditch was covered by several thick layers of Maussolleion fill, a part of which (a layer of green andesite chippings) has fallen down on the sill accumulated since Newton's sappers passed through. The evidence points to the conclusion that this whole branch went out of use when the Maussolleion was built, and that some of its ceiling-blocks were allowed to be taken away, for which reason it must be earlier.

The evidence for a change of direction, for rebuilding of the corridor and for it being earlier than the Terrace Wall 1 confirms this conclusion and demonstrates that the East Corridor will have existed for a considerable period. How long, we have few means to determine. The use of green andesite in both repairs in the corridor and in the transverse wall in Cb3, though, may indicate a date close to the building of the Maussolleion. This is a fair conclusion, but we do not *know* if the Kuyunbaba green andesite quarry north of Myndos (Gümüslük) was exploited already in pre-Maussollan times.

The beginning of the East Corridor, or perhaps rather its first and second openings towards the east, is quite obscure. The first and southern one would be in the SE and could open into the south ravine with access from the east. However, the deep level, 3.35 m a.s.l., in the SW corner of Trench Q_6, does not make for clarity. The continuation of the second, and more NE course of the corridor was revealed in Trench Q_6, but was completely destroyed first by the outlet of the Lower Gallery and later by the Hospitallers' spoliation of Building C and its surroundings.

5.6. The chronology and function of the pre-Maussollan structures

The complex structure comprised a subterranean chamber flanked by a courtyard (Cb2 and 3) and a semi-subterranean structure (Cb1). They were connected by means of a corridor (Main Corridor), and two of them had access to a subterranean aqueduct (UG:B) through a doorway (Cb1) or a corridor (Cb2). Close to the doorway in Cb1, substantial evidence for rituals is preserved: a bothros and cuttings for placing of offerings. Evidence for the latter is also preserved in the SE corner of Cb2. A bench or *kline* along the four sides of this chamber is of major importance for the understanding of the use of the whole structure.

Despite being subterranean, the structure was easily accessible from the outside at different levels. Cb1 could be entered by means of the staircase from the top of the natural plateau. There are no cuttings for a closing, only evidence for protection of the offering's area. Cb3 could be entered both from the ravine to the south and through the East Corridor. The possible ways of access to these entrances, however, are unknown, but will be discussed below in Chapter 8.

Neither end of the Main Corridor was equipped for solid closing, in contrast to both the doorway into Cb2 and the one between Cb1 and the aqueduct, which were furnished with separate door frames. The substantial wear of the staircase, of the basin in the aqueduct (see below, p. 124), and of the steps inside the doorway in Cb2, all reveal a considerable use. In another sense, also the windows in Cb2 into Cb3 conform to the overall impression of accessibility.

The close connection of all the elements shows the structure to be the result of a single master plan, of which the aqueduct formed an integral part. Previously, though, we considered it possible that the line of the Main and East Corridors formed the original course of the aqueduct and that the chambers were cut later in order to use the water of the aqueduct, which was only then conducted around the Cb1 and further east along its present line. Along this line of thought, the course of the Main and East Corridors would have been re-cut, *i.e.* the floor would have been lowered and flattened. This might explain the awkward relation between the lower step in the staircase in Cb1 and the Main Corridor. The above-mentioned (p. 91) 'carination' in the sides of the Main Corridor would mark the transition from the earlier floor to the later one. Also the fact that Cb1, 2 and 3 are parallel to each other, whereas the openings of the Main Corridor and the East Corridor into Cb3 are not quite opposite each other, might point in the same direction. However, this idea of two phases can be conclusively refuted. In the UG, between shaft U6 and Cb1, the form of the gallery broadens, whereby place is created for the line of shallow basins that continues right up to the door into Cb1. The distance widens between the basins and the water channel that eventually turns north (around Cb1). The whole arrangement is undoubtedly made according to a single plan, with no traces of a re-cutting. The levels in the floor give no room for an original channel that continued straight on, see below, p. 125.

The date of the chamber and corridor structure is obviously pre-Maussollan, and its ENE orientation is paralleled in the foundations of the Sanctuary of Demeter and Persephone to the SE in Halikarnassos, where the majority of the finds are of the 5th Century BC.[105] We have no means of dating the construction to either the 6th Century or to sometime in the 5th Century BC. No finds of pottery, for example, contribute to dating, and both the horse-and-rider terracottas and the small lekanis from Cb2 were discovered in Maussollan fill. They can, however, together with other finds either *in* or *ex situ*, contribute to form a general idea of when the area experienced much activity. See for an appraisal, below, p. 168.

There can be no doubt that the chamber-corridor structure was destroyed when the Maussolleion was built. The aqueduct UG:B was cut off and partly filled in. Cb1 was filled with foundation slabs and waste from the stone-cutting.

Cb2 for certain and Cb3 most certainly were also filled in. Contemporaneous with this, though, a part of the Main Corridor on both sides of Cb1 was maintained in use by means of a built corridor across Cb1 (see below, p. 125).

However, there is substantial evidence for a pre-Maussolleion phase with a partial rebuilding of the east part of the chamber structure. This seems to be connected to its adjustment to or incorporation into the new orthogonal city plan by means of the Terrace Wall 1 and the almost certainly contemporaneous building of Branch C of the aqueduct, see below, p. 148. The relative chronology established between 1) the East Corridor and Cb3, 2) the subsequent erection of the Terrace Wall 1 with the necessary rebuilding in Cb3 and the East Corridor, and 3) finally the Maussollan fill to the east and SE of the Quadrangle, is crucial for the understanding of this phase, which is discussed further below, p. 175 and p. 177.

The purpose and use of the chamber-corridor structure is, of course, of paramount interest, but there are only few and inconclusive clues. We are not able to come up with an explanation, except a 'negative' one. The unique layout, its openness and the unparalleled importance of water in the activities excludes a sepulchral use. This notion seems corroborated but not proven by the finds in the bothros in the Cb1, for which see below, p. 168. The evidence has a general symposium character and nothing points to burials or sepulchral rites.

111

6. The aqueduct, 'Upper Gallery', and its branches

The subterranean network of both aqueducts and corridors giving passage to the rock-cut chambers comprised Newton's Upper Gallery and Short Gallery. The latter designation is, however, obsolete, because the corresponding stretch of gallery can now be explained as a part of the former. Moreover, Newton's lack of distinction between aqueducts and corridors or passages does not make for clarity. The designation 'Upper Gallery' (UG) is therefore in the present publication applied only to the aqueduct. The corridors have been treated above, together with the chambers to which they gave access.

The Upper Gallery served as an aqueduct conveying water both to the pre-Maussollan chambers and further to the east. It originates in an unknown place in the NW (branch A) and divides some 15 m west of the SW corner of the Quadrangle into the two branches, B and C. It slopes gently from NW towards SE. The level at the north end of A is 6.16 m a.s.l., at the east end of Branch B 5.78 m a.s.l., and at the east end of Branch C 4.74 m a.s.l. As a rule, the gallery is completely cut in the rock, but parts in UG:A and UG:B are cut as open trenches and were covered by ashlars or slabs. Moreover, parts of UG:C are built completely in ashlars, because it had to cross ravines or depressions in the bedrock. At its very end, in the SE, the aqueduct is carried on a several-metre high ashlar construction. The function appears from the channel in its bottom that would have been destined for the pipes in which the water was conveyed. However, neither Newton nor we discovered remains of terracotta pipes in the gallery (see below, p. 166, though). On the bottom and sides there are hardly traces of coating and, except in a few stretches, the surface is rough without lime deposition.

The British discovered the opening into Branch B in the SW corner of the Quadrangle during the second week of excavation.[106] It was only partly filled with earth and could easily be explored. Murdoch Smith gives a lively description of the excitement in *turning sometimes to the right and sometimes to the left, sometimes going straight onwards, and sometimes circling round about.* At the bottom of a shaft they pierced *upwards with boring irons*, and on the ground they could localize the sound near an old Turk's house. *At last the old Turk with a look of consternation which I shall never forget came and asked me into his house. On entering I at once saw the cause of his alarm, which was no other than Jenkins's boring iron jumping up and down right in the middle of the floor.*[107] However, in his plan, Fig. 1.2.1, no Turkish house is situated on top of a shaft on the plan of the area. Either the plan is inaccurate or the story surpasses reality. In the same letter Murdoch Smith gives some precise descriptions and also notes findings of fragments of sculptures from the Maussolleion and of the marble head of uncertain origin.[108] Newton records other finds as well, semi-precious stones,[109] and reports in fair detail in his preliminary papers[110] and in the final publication in 1862 with plans and sections.[111] Also Biliotti's investigations in 1865 south of the Maussolleion brought forth evidence about Branch C.[112]

The British investigated parts of the aqueduct, which we did not re-study. In the direction of Göktepe, in straight continuation of the part of Branch A seen by us, Newton traced the gallery for 58.5 m[113] beyond the modern road in the direction of the ancient theatre, and he suggested a connection *with a large and deep shaft in the upper part of the Theatre, towards which it points.* Also Murdoch Smith advocates the same idea.[114] Unfortunately, it was beyond the scope of the Danish project – as it was of the British – to study this important subject.

The above-mentioned distances conform well to the plan in *HD* pl. II, where the length of

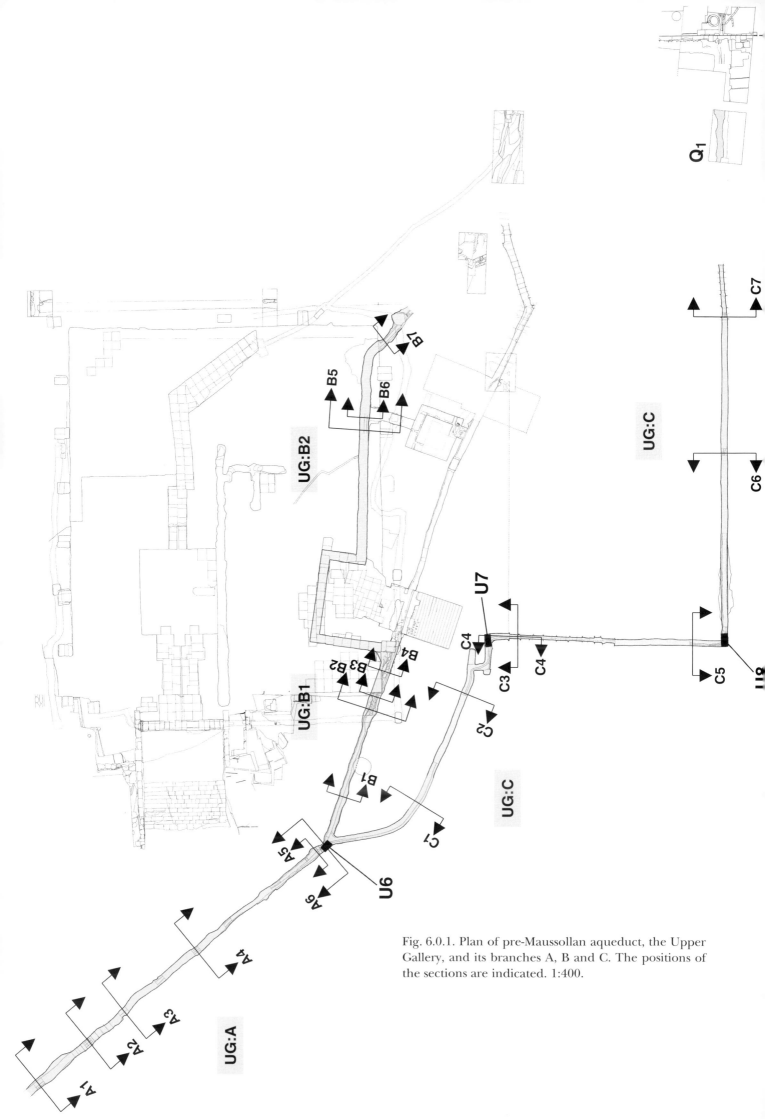

Fig. 6.0.1. Plan of pre-Maussollan aqueduct, the Upper Gallery, and its branches A, B and C. The positions of the sections are indicated. 1:400.

Branch A is shown as 320' = 97.50 m. Beyond the road, the gallery was larger than elsewhere and measured h: 8', w: 3' = c. 2.50 m × 0.95 m, and two pairs of shafts (U1-U4) at intervals of about 15.75 m (50')were noted (as was also the water channel in the floor) – but they are not shown on the plans. Newton ascertained a fifth shaft (U5), the position of which, on the line of the modern road, appears from Murdoch Smith's sketch plan of the site from September 1857, Fig. 1.2.3. Otherwise it is only briefly mentioned,[115] with reference to a section in the gallery, Fig. 6.1.1, with the caption: "Section 10 f. south of shaft 1".

We hoped to study the east course of Branch B in Trench Q_7, but in vain (see above p. 44), so the only documentation for this part of the course is the sparse evidence brought forth by the British (see below, p. 134).

Also a part of the SE course of Branch C was not investigated by us. Newton ascertained two enigmatic cross-walls (see below, p. 138) and Biliotti a shaft, U9, that was partly cut, partly built.[116] On the other hand, the Maussollan end of the branch was studied in 1967 in Trenches Q_1 and R_1. This evidence has been published by Pedersen in 1991 (see below p. 139 ff.).[117]

General description

When the Quadrangle was emptied in 1972, the openings into the branches of the gallery (and the corridors) were cleared for stone packings built by the British. Although some clearing was necessary in the shafts, there was free access. The state of preservation is generally fine in the parts cut in sandstone. Where it is cut in claystone it is bad, especially at the north end of Branch A, Fig. 6.1.3, which is completely ruined, and where there were apparently serious problems already in Antiquity. Also where Branch B is cut through by shaft L9, the upper parts are in a very poor condition. Even where the overlying sandstone stratum should have protected the claystone below, the sides are rather damaged, e.g. in Branch B, Fig. 6.2.3.4, which is very much like the situation in the first part of the East Corridor from Chamber 3, Fig. 5.5.3. Also both sides in Branch C, for a length of about 12 m east of shaft U8, are very fragmented.

The techniques of the execution of the shafts and the gallery come very close to those in the Lower Gallery, described above p. 53 ff., but there are some differences and peculiarities. However, the quality of the work is generally on a higher level and appears better planned.

Throughout, there are cuttings for lamps at more or less regular intervals; about 0.5 m appears to be the norm. As in the Lower Gallery, they are as a rule situated fairly high up in the left side of the cutting direction. Sometimes, however, two are very close or are situated almost one above the other. Murdoch Smith noted: *All along at various intervals on each side are small holes which seem to have been for the purpose of holding small lamps for the lighting of the passage as over each of them the rock naturally of a light brown colour is quite black as if it had been burned.*[118] We also ascertained dark colour in a few places.

The size and heights of the (only three) shafts we encountered conforms well to the Lower Gallery: U6 measures 1.13 m × 0.9 m (original height approx. 4.0 m), U7 measures 1.3 m × 0.62 m by 3.8 m, U8 1.38 m × 0.78 m by 4.0 m. They are furnished with cuttings for steps in both long sides, about 0.4 m above each other.

The top of U6 is ruined, but parts of fragmented sandstone ashlars were ascertained in the shaft and are most probably the capstones.[119] In fact, one in this material is preserved *in situ* in its ledge in the top of U7, Fig. 6.3.3. It measures 1.34 m × 0.70 m × 0.55 m. Part of a ledge is also preserved in the opening of U8. Peculiar are in U8 two pairs of cuttings opposite each other in the west and east sides of the shaft, Fig. 6.3.9. They testify to a kind of platform as in Shaft L9 (see p. 60 with Fig. 3.1.11): probably for the mounting of a windlass, mentioned by Newton (*Pl6*: 49). The use of sandstone for the capstones sets the Upper Gallery apart from the Lower Gallery, where green andesite was used.

The distance between the shafts is considerably greater than in the Lower Gallery, and the evidence of chisel-marks for the cutting-directions is somewhat obscure compared with the Lower Gallery. Whereas the latter gallery shows no evidence for repairs, there is ample evidence for this in the Upper Gallery, which functioned for several centuries. The ambiguous evidence of the cutting-directions may well derive from re-cutting.

115

Regular is the situation between U6 and the Chamber 1. The course is c. 22 m long and chisel-marks and a narrowing of the gallery show where two working-teams met about 14 m from shaft U6. The lamp-holes are, as they should be, situated in the left side of the cutting directions.

In Branch A the first 17.7 m from the shaft U6 was cut northwards, and the lamp-holes are mostly (16:3) on the west side. The next 12 m are cut southwards (lamp-holes mostly (8:3) on the east side). Between 29.6 m and 34.5 m from the shaft, the upper part is completely built, and this may explain the absence of a shaft in the whole course.

The distance between U6 and U7 is about 28 m in a straight line, but the course is – unique for all the galleries on the site – curved. In the east end there are two blind alleys, which should indicate that two teams have missed each other but by means of the short 'cross-gallery' established a connection. However, from the 'cross-gallery' the cutting direction is towards the NW, and most of the lamp-holes are in the SW side (29 compared with nine only in the NE side), which confirms the observation (as does, also, the lack of a meeting-point) that this whole section was cut from Shaft U7 towards Shaft U6. See below for a tentative interpretation of the blind alleys.

The distance between U7 and U8 is 24.3 m. Between 1.9 m and 12.9 m (from the north), the gallery is constructed in ashlars, cf. below and Fig. 6.3.3. The chisel-marks and the lamp-holes both show that the short stretch from U7 was cut from the shaft towards the south. Where the gallery re-enters the bedrock again to the south of the ravine, 13 lamp-holes are cut in the east side against only the first and the last and two in the middle in the west side. However, in two places, 2 m from the shaft and at the point where the gallery leaves the bedrock, the ceiling drops considerably. One would therefore expect the cutting-direction to be from Shaft U8 towards the north. But only the first 2 m were cut in this direction, as the lamp-hole shows. The last one shows only that a workman facing north did the final cutting of the ceiling and therefore needed a lamp-hole on his left side.

From U8 towards the east, we followed the gallery for 40 m until soil from a break in the ceiling and the side blocked the way. For 34.45 m the gallery is cut, but the last 5.55 m are constructed in ashlars. In this, the longest uninterrupted course in the galleries, the chisel-marks show surprisingly that the cutting-direction was from the east towards the shaft. And the lamp-holes are again, with a few exceptions, in the left (south) side. Only between 25.35 m and 27.50 m from U8 do the chisel-marks show the cutting-direction towards the east, but two lamp-holes are situated in the south side!

6.1. The main branch UG:A coming from the north-west

The NW tributary branch comes from the NW and ends in Shaft U6, where the aqueduct divides into the two courses, B and C. The Danish excavation traced its course for a distance of c. 41 m, slightly beyond the point where it intersects the line of the terrace wall. The gallery is man-high or a little higher and about 0.7 to 0.9 m wide.

The whole course is cut in the rock, except for a short stretch (c. 4.9 m, between 29.6 m and 34.5 m from Shaft U6), where the upper part of both sides (in claystone) is reinforced by slabs of green andesite. On top of these there are altogether eight re-used marble slabs with drafting and dowel-holes and one slab of grey andesite that form the ceiling, Fig. 6.1.4. They are partly fixed by means of a kind of mortar, partly encrusted with lime sediment. Their undersides are about 0.2 m higher up than the bedrock ceiling to the south, a difference that might indicate a repair. A repair is almost proven by the fact that most of the ceiling blocks are re-used.

The claystone continues towards the north from 34.5 m until 41 m, where both sides and the ceiling are ruined and form a kind of cave, Fig. 6.1.3, beyond which the gallery is completely blocked.

When our section A2 in the built part (Fig. 6.1.2) is compared with Newton's (Fig. 6.1.1), mentioned above, the construction appears similar, but he shows a second 'course' of marble, where we have sandstone, set off from the ruined claystone, below. But Newton locates his section some 3 m south of the main road,

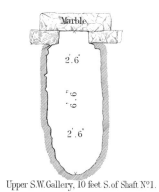

Upper S.W. Gallery, 10 feet S. of Shaft Nº 1.

Fig. 6.1.1. **Section** in UG:A. Measured drawing by R.D. Pullan, October 1857. Published in *HD* 1862, pl. XIII, bottom left.

which runs about 15 m to the north of our section. Most likely Newton is inaccurate. There is hardly reason to locate another built course in the gallery.

Newton's section shows a rounded bottom without channel and footpath, and we confirmed its correctness. In fact, the cutting of the bottom is irregular, which is probably due to a re-cutting that may have been executed in connection with the construction of a cross-wall where Branch A opens into Shaft U6 (see below).

At the edge of Shaft U6 the opening of Branch A is barred by a cross-wall, altogether 1.55 m high and c. 0.60 m wide, Fig. 6.1.5-9.[120] On its east side a vertical ledge has been cut in

the rock for the wall. This is completely covered by a thick layer of mortar and lime, and its construction is unknown, except for certain horizontal lines, suggesting courses, in the somewhat ruined uppermost part, about 12 cm high and only 22 cm thick. The wall is perforated by two holes furnished with terracotta pipes, diam. 10.5 cm, thickness 1.8 cm. The centre of the lowest hole, diam. 10.5 cm, is situated at 6.37 m a.s.l., while the centre of the second is at 7.07 m a.s.l. It could not be ascertained for certain whether a third pipe has been situated in the depression in the centre of the wall. The bottom of the shaft has a peculiar, oval shape, c. 0.25 m deep, and its sides are smooth and water-washed. This most probably derives from water pouring out through the pipes. However, a similar depression, about 0.40 m deep, was ascertained in Shaft U8.

The wall regulates the flow of the water into two levels, 6.37 m and 7.07 m a.s.l. How does this fit in with the water channel in Branch A? Its features are recorded in five sections, A1-A5, Fig. 6.1.2., besides where the wall is situated in the opening into Shaft U6, Fig. 6.1.6. The bottom level was recorded in three more places. It descends altogether 0.23 m, but only at both ends are there a path and regular channel, 0.45 m deep to the north (A3) and 0.74 m deep to the south. The level of the path at both ends is nearly identical, being, however, 7 cm higher at the south end. In between, the bottom is rounded, pointed or furnished with only a shallow channel. Presumably the original channel has been

Fig. 6.1.2. Sections A1-A5 in UG:A north of Shaft U6. 1:50.

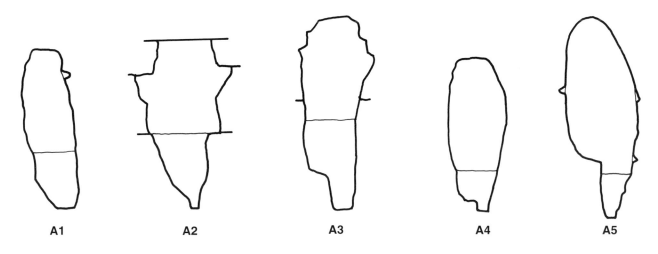

A1   A2   A3   A4   A5

117

Fig. 6.1.3. The ruined claystone 'cave' in UG:A and the present north end of the gallery strengthened with marble and andesite slabs. 1976.

Fig. 6.1.4. Marble ceiling blocks in the northern part of UG:A. 1976.

worn or cut away in connection with the destruction, which necessitated the repair of a section of the ceiling.

The bottom level in the channel close to the wall is at 5.94 m and thus lies 0.43 m below the lowest pipe in the wall. This is obviously later than the channel, because it blocked its course. A second, shallow wall, only c. 0.4 m high in the channel about 1.5 m north of the shaft, confirms the abolition of the channel.

Two branches continue the course of the aqueduct from the sides of Shaft U6; Branch B to the east, and Branch C to the south-east, Fig. 6.1.7. They bifurcate very regularly by 58° and 63°, respectively. The evidence from the levels in the three branches appears revealing and in fact is crucial for an understanding of the history of the aqueduct.

The level of the ceiling in Branch A just to the north of the cross-wall is 8.4 m a.s.l., of the channel 5.94 m a.s.l., and of the footpath 6.68 m a.s.l. The respective levels are in B 8.4 m / 6.33 m / 6.79 m, and in Branch C 7.8 m / 5.81 m / 6.14 m a.s.l. (sections B1, Fig. 6.2.1.2 and C1, Fig. 6.3.1). The bottom level in Branch C thus conforms to Branch A, but with regard to top level, Branch B comes much closer to A than C does. And the level of both footpath and channel in Branch B is higher than in A (and C). The flow in C is in a perfect continuation of A, but the water could not run from A to B.

The evidence for a relative chronology can be summed up:

1. There is a gentle flow right from the beginning of Branch A across Shaft U6 into C. Remarkable, however, is the marked difference in ceiling levels of A and C.

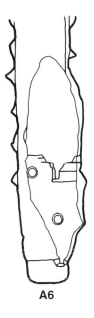

Fig. 6.1.5. View in UG:A towards Shaft U6 with the cross-wall with pipes. Bottom left the channel, to the right the ledge or footpath. In the background the opening into UG:C, the ceiling of which lies 0.60 m lower down than in UG:A. 1976.

Fig. 6.1.6. 1:50.

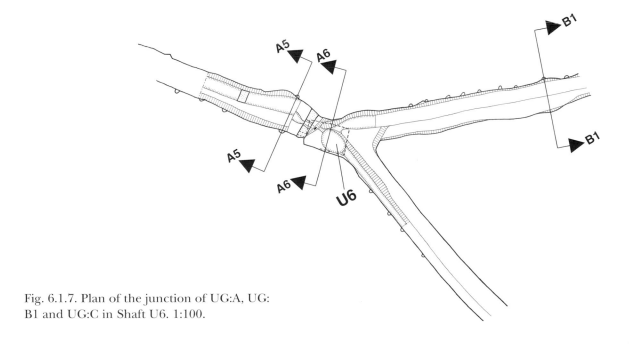

Fig. 6.1.7. Plan of the junction of UG:A, UG: B1 and UG:C in Shaft U6. 1:100.

119

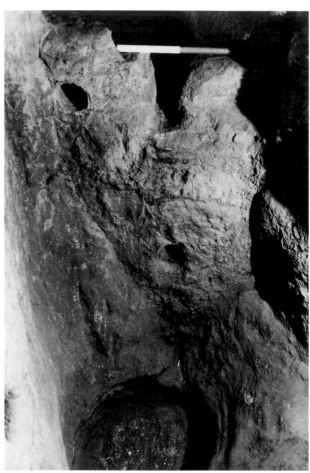

Fig. 6.1.8. Shaft U6 and cross-wall with pipes. View west from UG:B1. Several steps are recognizable, but the upper part of the shaft is blocked by one of the top-blocks that has fallen down. 1976.

Fig. 6.1.9. Detail of south side of cross-wall with pipes in Shaft U6. Below, the eroded or water-washed bottom of Shaft U6. 1976.

2. The level of the channel in Branch A close to Shaft U6 lies 0.39 m *below* the level in Branch B. Throughout A's course it runs at a lower level than in B. Also the level of the footpath in B is higher than in A (c. 10 cm). However, the complete accordance in ceiling heights between A and B is remarkable.

3. Because Branch B for obvious reasons must have been fed through Branch A, the latter's level must have been cut down. In fact, there is evidence for re-cutting throughout most of its course. The obvious connection from A to C explains the re-cutting, and at the same time indicates that C is later than B

4. The regular branching out ± 60° seems to point to a close relation, but a contemporaneity of B and C is hard to bear out.

How does the cross-wall with pipes relate to the above tentative conclusions?

1. The wall blocks the original free course of water from A into C. It is therefore a later addition.

2. The level of the lowest terracotta pipe is 6.37 m a.s.l., which matches perfectly with the level of the channel in B. By this means water could be led into Branch B. The idea presupposes that the wall raises the level of the water that flows freely in the channel without pipes. However, it would result in the flooding of a major part of Branch A, at least for a length of about 33 m.

3. Cross-walls with pipes are not known in pre-Roman aqueducts.[121] From evidence from Roman times one would expect such

a construction at the end of an aqueduct for the purpose of distributing the water to different consumers (*castellum divisorium*). Its position, therefore, should imply that water was to be led into B. This, however, appears most unlikely, because B was blocked by the building of the Maussolleion. However, between Shaft U6 and the Maussolleion (see below) there is a well (post-Antique) that could have been fed by this means.

4. The lowest pipe would be sufficient to lead water into B, and the other pipe (on a higher level) remains unexplained. The oval depression in the bottom of Shaft U6 might testify to water that has poured down from this or both pipes. Quite the same oval depression, however, is also found in Shaft U8 – without any wall and 'spouts'.

Newton discovered two more walls with pipes in Branch C. They were unfortunately not rediscovered by us, but for obvious reasons the evidence from all three walls has to be collated for their use to be understood. See below, p. 138.

6.2. The branch UG:B serving the pre-Maussollan chambers

The branch runs ESE from Shaft U6. The first part, termed B1 and c. 24 m long, reached Chamber 1, from where the gallery was accessible through a doorway. It continued north (B2) around the chamber and further on in Newton's *Short Gallery* to a point SE of the Maussolleion.

When the Maussolleion was built the gallery was interrupted by the SW corner of the foundation, and within the Quadrangle the ceiling and the upper part of the sides were cut off and its floor levelled, the resulting 'ditch' being filled with foundation slabs of green andesite. These are still preserved in three courses, where the gallery encircles the north end of Chamber 1, whereas in its continuation it was completely emptied by the Hospitallers.

The original character of the aqueduct with channel and footpath (as in Branch A) is well preserved respectively in B1 (bottom level 6.33-6.28 m) and in the east in B2 (5.82 m a.s.l.) outside the perimeter of the Maussolleion.

6.2.1 The branch B1 conducting water to Chamber 1

The shape of the first part of the gallery comes very close to that of Branch A, as appears from the plan, Fig. 6.1.6, and section B1, Fig. 6.2.1.2.

Between 8.5 m and 10.00 m from U6 there is a breach in the south side due to a presumably Turkish well, 'Ismael's well', already ascertained by Murdoch Smith and shown on the plan. *In the middle of the higher platform rock, there is a modern well, the sides of which contain pieces of marble and architectural fragments. In pursuing the passage it was found to run close past the side of the well into which we made an opening.*[122]

This clear statement, however, is hard to reconcile with the evidence: the circular well cuts away part of the footpath and into the chan-

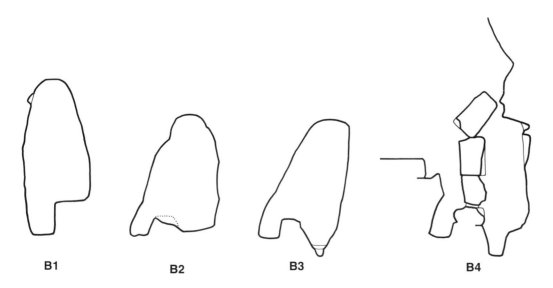

B1 B2 B3 B4

Fig. 6.2.1.2. Sections B1-B4. 1:50.

Fig. 6.2.1.1. UG:B1 between Shaft U6 and the Quadrangle. View west into U6, in which the cross-wall with circular holes is discernible, bottom right. 1976.

nel, so the opening between gallery and well must have existed before 1857. In fact, the well may have had a certain influx of water from the gallery. The British perhaps rediscovered the opening when they demolished the lining of the well in their search for marbles from the Maussolleion.

The gallery changes markedly at 14 m from U6 (Fig. 6.2.1.2, section B2): the ceiling height drops almost 0.40 m, the width of the gallery increases to 1.10 m, and the footpath widens and gives way to an irregular and interconnected series of water-washed depressions or pools parallel to the channel. The latter continues unchanged and well-defined along the north side of the gallery at a growing distance from the pool(s) and is soon separated from it by a ridge or a kind of (decayed) footpath. In the sides of the gallery this remarkable change coincides with

the meeting-point of two gangs coming from west and east, respectively: the chisel or pickaxe grooves meet each other in oblique lines from both sides.

In the bottom, close to this point, 14.5 m from the shaft, is the funnel-shaped opening of a vertical hole that connects to the Lower Gallery, where it appears in the ceiling, c. 2.8 m north of Shaft L6. Its length is c. 0.95 m, and the top and bottom diameter is 9.0 cm and 3.7 cm respectively. It was filled with dark soil and one chipping of green andesite. We believe the hole to have been made by one of Murdoch Smith's sappers. Had it been ancient, it would have been filled in for centuries and hardly discovered and re-opened by the British.

The understanding of the further course is complicated, because the gallery, 17 m from U6, was in the way of the SW corner of the Quadrangle. The north side and the top of the gallery were cut away, as were also a part of its bottom and a narrow strip of its south side. Five courses, nos. 5-9, of the Maussollan foundation slabs are still *in situ*, cf. Jeppesen 2000: 33, Fig. 1.59. The line of the ceiling and of the south side, however, can still be traced in the vertical cutting of the Quadrangle (Fig. 6.2.2.3), and the continuation of the bottom of the gallery with both channel and the irregular depression can also be studied. It does not make for clarity, though, that this c. 6.5 m long part of the gallery was partially restored immediately after its destruction, whereby a part of the original bottom was covered. The partly restored, partly brand-new corridor running between the SW corner of the Maussolleion and across the landing of Cb1 will be documented below in Ch. 6.2.2.

The evidence for the shape of the gallery close to Cb1 before the building of the Maussolleion is limited.

The above-mentioned series of water pools continue right to the doorway into Cb1. In the section B4, the width of the gallery has increased to 1.2 m. The upper north side and a part of

Fig. 6.2.1.3. The blocking of UG:B1 in the SW corner of the Quadrangle. View east. 1974.

Fig. 6.2.2.4. The junction between UG:B1 and Cb1 seen from above. To the left pillar P15, to the right the wall of the transverse corridor and the short stretch of wall between the two. a-b mark the 1st and the 2nd step in the wing of the staircase. 1973.

Fig. 6.2.2.5. Stretch of wall along the north side of UG:B1 that covers the lump of bedrock between Pillar 15 and the west side of Cb1 and abuts on the built channel. 1973.

128

Fig. 6.2.2.6. Bottom of UG:B1 just west of Cb1 partly unexcavated. Left, the cutting for the door between Cb1 and UG:B2 is discernible. 1973.

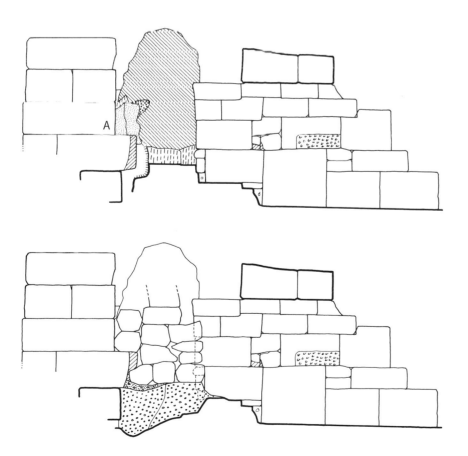

Fig. 6.2.2.7. Elevations of the south side of Pillar P15 and the north inner wall in transverse built corridor in Cb1. Below, with the rubble wall that connects the two and, above, with the wall removed and stucco, A, revealed. 1:50.

129

Fig. 6.3.4. View east into the northern 'blind alley' in UG:C. 1976.

Fig. 6.3.5. The ashlar-built section in UG:C between Shaft U7 and Shaft U8. View north. 1976.

We continue to clear the Ashlar wall [TW1, see below]. *Just in the N.E. Angle of Hagi Nalban's house the vertical cut in the rocky platform bends towards the N.W., while the ashlar wall continues in a due W. direction. The N. wall of Hagi Nalban's house followed the vertical cut in the rock.*[131]

This information also explains the blind alley and the cross-arm at right-angles. For fear of breaking yet another hole into the ravine, the course of the gallery was shifted 1.75 m to the north. Moreover, the extraordinary, curved course of the gallery towards the NW seems to run parallel to the line of Nalban's house and to the vertical face of the bedrock below.

Biliotti worked in the area from 28th March 1865, after having succeeded in purchasing Hagi Nalban's house, which was immediately demolished. He excavated along the south side of the terrace wall, TW1, and also further to the south

on a line with the Upper Gallery. At 6' [1.83 m] from the ashlar wall, he discovered a line of rough stones resting on a row of rectangular 1' thick green andesite slabs, and their exact position above the gallery appears from his fine section, Fig. 6.3.6. He does not give the number of slabs, but the length of the row may appear from his diary: *At 24 feet S.* [of the ashlar wall, TW1, 7.32 m] *and running parallel with it there is another rubble wall similar to that over the gallery but not resting on stone slabs. It joins this wall, altho' on a little higher level than it and extends for about 25 feet towards the West.*[132] The slabs, therefore, ran to a point at least 7.3 m south of the terrace wall. Their extension accordingly was 5.5 m, although it is not expressly stated that the row ended at this point.

The dimensions of the gallery in his measured drawing conform to our section C3, Fig. 6.3.1.

136

Fig. 6.3.6. Section in UG:C between Shaft U7 and Shaft U8 "together with the row of green stone slabs, & rubble wall above". From Biliotti, *Diary* 1865.04.20. a correction of *HD* pl. 13 below left.

The aqueduct, 1.93 m high internally, is covered by blocks 1.33 m × 0.66 m × 0.66 m. The top surface of the capstones can be established at 7.40 m a.s.l. and the level of the surface at 11.36 m a.s.l. ('7.4 m + 2' + 1' + 10').

Fig. 6.3.7. View north from Shaft U8 showing the lowering of ceiling height with a breach. 1976.

The gallery was full of water, so he did not realize that it is completely built. The construction of the ceiling, 2' high, is precisely shown. On top of it follows 2' of earth and splinters of rock, then the andesite slabs of 1' and a layer of rough stones forming a kind of wall, 2 or 3 feet high. The ground level, finally, is 10' above the slabs. Because we know the floor level in the gallery, the level of the features in his drawing can be determined as well as the surface at this time, ca. 11.40 m a.s.l.

The row of slabs follows the line of the gallery, but only for 5.5 m, half of the length of its built section. The top level of the slabs is at 8.40 m a.s.l. about 1 m above the bottom course of the terrace wall (where it crosses the gallery, see above, p. 73) and about 1 m below the surface of the white fill of the Maussolleion terrace. The slabs apparently relate to nothing, and their purpose is therefore enigmatic. The other wall at right-angles cannot be explained either. It may have a counterpart in the coarse wall in Trench Q7, see above, p. 46, Fig. 2.5.2.4-5.

The bedrock floor level in the gallery is 5.21 m a.s.l. This matches exactly the level in Chamber 3 and the bedrock on which the foundation of the terrace wall TW1 rests. The bottom level further to the SE, where the aqueduct again is built, is only slightly lower, at c. 4.75 m. The level may be the ground level of the ravine along the south side of the pre-Maussollan salient of the bedrock. This was most probably limited by a vertical and chisel-cut face of the bedrock, as along the east side of the Maussolleion. Where the built part in Branch C ends and the gallery re-enters the rock, the ceiling height drops c. 0.80 m. Although the level of the bedrock rose, it was not sufficient for

137

Fig. 6.3.8. View into Shaft U8 from the east. 1976. The cuttings testify to the mounting of a windlass used by Newton's sappers.

Fig. 6.3.9. Transition from cut to built course of UG:C east of Shaft U8. View east. The level of the ceiling is 0.38 m lower in the built part than in the cut part. The ceiling is formed by one block spanning from side to side and rounded below. 1976.

the full height of the gallery. Only 2 m before Shaft U8, the ceiling was again heightened by c. 0.7 m, Fig. 6.3.7. The hole shows how thin the bedrock is at this point.

The two walls with pipes east of Shaft U8

Difficult to explain is the following information given by Newton. He states in *Pl5: 48* that he traced the gallery 126′ [38.40 m] due east of Shaft U8. A few feet beyond *[the course] came to an abrupt termination ···, being closed up by a solid wall. This wall was pierced by four circular apertures, each containing an earthen pipe. These openings were made at intervals, in the manner represented in the photograph which I have the honour to inclose. (Pl6: 49)*

Fig. 6.3.10 shows a "tracing" of the wall, a section in the gallery, 1.4 m high, 0.46 m wide (below) and with four pipes, 8.9 cm in diameter. The pipes are placed at regular intervals, the uppermost just below the ceiling. The bottom is shown as flat, but we know for sure that the gallery had a water-channel. The dimensions of the gallery are shown in our sections, Fig. 6.3.1, and the section C7 in the built part comes fairly close, except for the channel, measuring 0.16 m. Most probably the spot was not carefully cleaned for a close study. Nor was it drawn or noted in the text that this part of the gallery is built.

The distance, 38.40 m, almost conforms to the place in the built part where we were stopped because it is blocked by soil from a breach in the

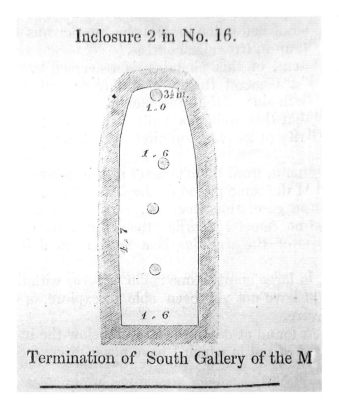

Inclosure 2 in No. 16.

Termination of South Gallery of the M

Fig. 6.3.10. Section in UG:C east of Shaft U8 with cross-wall with four pipes. *P*16, 1857.12.10: 49, Inclosure 2: "Tracing of Termination of South Gallery of the Mausoleum."

ceiling and in the side. However, we ascertained no traces of the wall, so it was probably situated further to the east.

Again in *P*16: 49 (dated 1857.12.10) Newton states:

The great distance of this wall from the shaft at which our windlass was at work, induced me to defer breaking through it till further operations had facilitated this labour. I ascertained, however, in the course of driving a mine with a different object, that the gallery, though partially closed up by this barrier, is continued for a few feet east of this point, where it is again interrupted by a solid wall, pierced with earthen pipes, in the same manner as the first wall.

Apparently, he did not break down the wall, but later, through another mine, 149 feet long in a SW direction from the east terrace wall, he encountered the gallery again, and now discovered a second similar wall situated a few feet east of the first.[133]

In a later report of 1858.04.12, however, he asserts *at a distance of 80 feet* [= 24.4 m east of Shaft U8] *it is closed by a double partition-wall, consisting of two party-walls pierced with pipes and separated from one another by an interval of 12 feet* [= 3.66 m].[134] In his major book of 1862, he repeats this information and also notes the similarities of the walls to the one in Shaft U6 noted above, p. 117.[135]

This information is seriously at variance with the first report. The distance is now stated to be 14 m closer to Shaft U8. Probably, the first report with the measured drawing comes close to the truth, because of its details and its size, which fit the gallery noticed by us. The wrong position stated in the second report also casts doubt about the distance between the two walls. In the first report the distance appears to be only a few feet. This may be more correct than the 12′ given in the second report. We have no means to determine the use and function of the walls, except for various options of stemming up the water. Some access would appear necessary to regulate the pipes, perhaps through the square Shaft U9 that was noticed by Biliotti. This shaft *appeared to be cut in the rock, but it proved that the upper part was built*.[136] However, Newton does not mention the shaft and Biliotti not the wall(s). Be that as it may, Biliotti's latter statement may imply that the gallery re-entered the rock again, before it was again carried forwards on a high substructure to the terrace wall. As for the second partition wall, it is tempting to guess that the sappers, when driving their long tunnel met only the east side of the first wall. The report is confused, and two partition walls close to each other hardly make sense.

6.4. The built part of UG:C towards the south-east and its termination

Important evidence on the end of the aqueduct appeared during the excavations 1966-1967 in Trench Q_1 and in Trench R_1, where the underside of the euthynteria of the Maussollan terrace wall is at 2.64 m a.s.l. (Figs. 6.4.1 and 4). In the northern part of Trench R_1 the euthynteria rests on the bedrock, but at a certain point it descends about 1.2 m, and the bottom of its sandstone foundation, two courses high, reaches

Fig. 6.4.3. The south side of the built aqueduct and part of the backing wall of the east terrace wall onto which it abuts. 1966.

sessment of the relative chronology of the two constructions.

An outlet channel is hewn in the top of a sandstone ashlar and a limestone bonder in the terrace wall. The latter, 0.5 m wide and 0.6 m high, is both fragmentary (its façade is completely missing) and eroded (Fig. 6.4.2.4-6).[140] The segment of the channel (with a rough surface with marks of the pointed chisel) in its top surface with a restored diameter of c. 15 cm is situated eccentrically in the southern half of the ashlar at level

4.50 m a.s.l., about 1.85 m above the bottom of the euthynteria. It appears odd that the water was not carried through the wall in a straight line, but a preserved sandstone bonder on this line shows that this was never the case. Instead, its course bends slightly to the north. According to Jeppesen (1968: 44), it may have ended in a gargoyle in the wall, perhaps in the form of a lion's head, as suggested by Pedersen. They both take it for granted that the outlet is contemporaneous with the construction of the terrace wall.

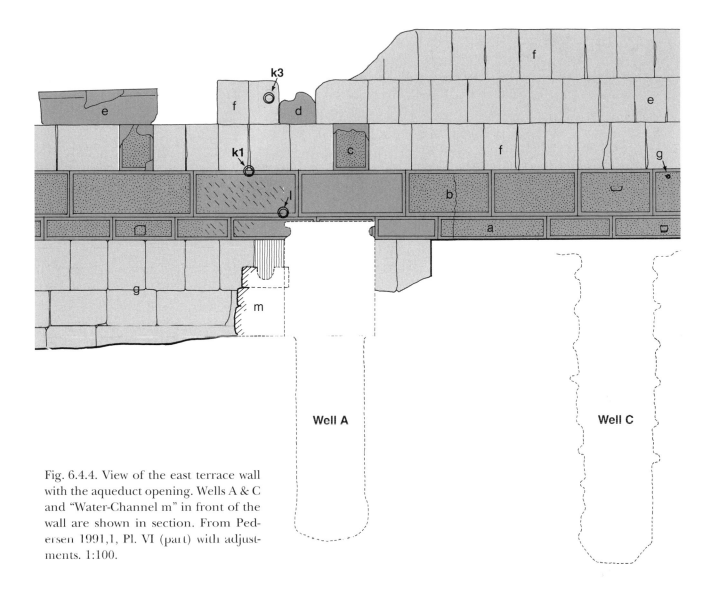

Fig. 6.4.4. View of the east terrace wall with the aqueduct opening. Wells A & C and "Water-Channel m" in front of the wall are shown in section. From Pedersen 1991,1, Pl. VI (part) with adjustments. 1:100.

The situation in front of the wall with regard to what has happened with the water is complicated, due to several phases and to destructions already in the middle of the 2nd Century BC, as well as by the Hospitallers around 1500 AD, and finally by Murdoch Smith's sappers.[141] The area in question, Trench R_1, is documented and discussed by Pedersen 1991.[142] In the trench are a well (Well A), the "Water-channel M", as well as several pipes that are all to be discussed and explained in relation to one another and not least to the terrace wall and the aqueduct. Vaag publishes a selection of finds from Trench R_1.[143]

No container or basin from the 4th BC was preserved below the outlet of the aqueduct. However, two sandstone blocks, 0.58 m wide, Fig. 6.4.5-6, were discovered walled up to the

terrace wall with strong lime mortar and hid a section of the euthynteria and the lowest ashlar course. The eroded surface of the said ashlars further south indicates that the sandstone blocks continued further on, forming an altogether 3.3 m long construction.[144] In Pedersen's opinion the blocks may have carried a basin, the shape of which would be very narrow and trough-like. However, because the sandstone foundation is almost centred in relation to the Well A and eccentric (towards the north) in relation to the outlet, there is no reason to relate it to the latter. Not least, the absence of an overflow conduit from the hypothetical basin renders the idea of a basin impossible. As for the dating of the construction, we know only that it predates "Pipe l" (see below), which runs close to the euthyn-

Fig. 6.4.5. The east terrace wall with the outlet of the aqueduct (arrow). Below are seen Well A and the sandstone ashlar that abuts on the second course of the blue limestone facing of the terrace wall. 1966.

teria and required the cutting away and partial destruction of the sandstones.

Preserved, though, were at least four terra-cotta pipelines at varying levels above each other, Figs. 6.4.1 and 4.

One ("Pipe l"), Fig. 6.4.6, level with the top of the euthynteria (2.92 m a.s.l.) and c. 1.6 m below the outlet, began only 0.2 m from the wall. According to the excavators, it was a pressure pipeline, with a lead pipe in terracotta casing that

again was firmly sealed with pink lime mortar.[145] Remains of this have not been identified among the findings.

Much better documented is the so-called "Pipe k", which is a collective name for several pipe-lines that all originated in the area of the outlet, but at different levels, and descended towards the east. More than 30 tubes were discovered *in situ*, positioned in the soil without bedding of any kind. They are wheel-made with notches in the

Fig. 6.4.6. The east terrace wall with the outlet of the aqueduct (arrow). Below, Well A and in the foreground the line of Pipe l, below which the stones of Water-channel m are discernible. 1966.

ends that were tightened with mortar or slaked lime. There are no hand-holes.

"Pipe k1" originated close to the terrace wall at level c. 3.4 m a.s.l. "k3" originated at level 4.6 m a.s.l. almost in prolongation of the outlet.[146] "k2" may also be *in situ* on a level between the two others, but only a small section was preserved 9 m from the wall. "Pipe k4" consisting of two straight tubes and one with an angle of 90° was not *in situ*. The latter is, however, the only pipe

among the preserved finds that can be exactly identified.

a. Fig. 6.4.7.[147] Its outer diam. is 14.5-14.8 cm, the inner c. 12 cm except in the partly preserved opening with a 3.3 cm wide adjoining ledge / socket where the inner diam. is only 9.5 cm. The distance from ledge to angle is 23.5 cm. The clay is reddish and slipped.

b. Fig. 6.4.8.[148] Slightly larger is another series with the length of the tubes of 37-37.5 cm.

Fig. 6.4.7. Water pipe.
Bodrum Museum. 2003.

Fig. 6.4.8. Water pipe.
Bodrum Museum. 2003.

Fig. 6.4.9. Water pipe.
Bodrum Museum. 2003.

The wider end has an outer diam. of 16 cm, an inner of 13.8 cm and a socket 3 cm deep. The other end measures 11.7 cm, 8.5 cm and 3 cm.

c. Fig. 6.4.9.[149] A third series of pipes is 39 cm long, but is narrower than the previous ones, with an outer diam. of 13.5 and 12.5 cm in the ends and with notches that fit into each other (inner diam. 8.2 cm, outer 7.5 cm).

Details of chronology are obscure, but the position of the pipes one above the other testifies to a remarkable filling-up of the area in front of the wall during a considerable period, which according to the stratigraphical finds ended early in the 1st Century BC.[150] This dating appears confirmed by their shape, which conforms to the Hellenistic one as it was already defined by E. Fabricius in 1884.[151] Due to the earlier spoliation, we have no certain means to reconstruct the kind(s) of connection between aqueduct and the lower-lying conduits, "Pipes k1 and k2" and "Pipe l" not to mention the "Water-channel m" (for which see below). The only way to feed the pipes with water will have been through a vertical conduit from the outlet down to first the pressure pipeline, "Pipe l", and later to "Pipe k1". The "Pipe k4" consisting of two straight sections and one with an angle of 90°, could very well be 'the missing link' but was *ex situ*.[152] Its diameter corresponds very well to the diameter, c. 15 cm, of the 'spout' in the limestone bonder.

Beyond doubt, the pipes testify to the use of Branch C of the aqueduct – and therefore, of course, of Branch A as well – several centuries after the Maussolleion was built.[153]

Certainly of the 4th Century BC are three wells that testify to the fetching of water in the area. Their settings have been presented by Pedersen,[154] and their rich contents have recently been published by J. Lund and V. Nørskov.[155]

Well A, Figs. 6.4.2 and 4-6, in Trench R_1 is situated 0.9 m from the terrace wall and its south edge is on line with the outlet of the aqueduct. It consists of two parts: below, a rock-cut part with a top level at 1.40 m a.s.l. and a terracotta wellhead, 1.53 m high, protruding 0.29 m above the bottom of the euthynteria. In order to place the well-head in position, the "Water-channel M" (for which see below) was destroyed and both

water-channel and most of the well-head were buried in the fill, when the surface level of c. 2.64 m a.s.l. was established.[156] By this means the builders obviously adjusted to the level of the terrace wall, so the well cannot be older.

Well C, Fig. 6.4.2 and 4, in Trench R_2 is situated c. 3 m north of Well A and 1.5 m from the terrace wall. Its opening in the bedrock is approximately level with the euthynteria.

Well B is located c. 25 m to the south, in Trench R_{11}. It is situated 1.85 m from the terrace wall and its opening in the bedrock lies c. 0.75 m below the euthynteria. There are no traces of a wellhead.

Because of their alignment along the wall, one would expect also the wells B and C to be contemporaneous with or later than the wall. This is also the opinion of Pedersen 1991 and Lund and Nørskov 2002.[157] The latter two have moreover established that the chronology of the contents of all three wells is compatible with this dating. They have furthermore concluded that the wells were in use only for a fairly short period. Well A was filled up already sometime in the 3rd quarter of the 4th Century (with an after-filling around 200 BC ± 25 years). Well C was filled in c. 300 BC at the latest (with a few sherds of the 3rd and early 2nd centuries BC in the uppermost layer). The evidence from Well B is less secure, but may well resemble the situation in Well C.

The date of the wells, coeval with the construction of the terrace wall, and only in use for few decennia, raises the question of their relationship to the aqueduct and the outlet situated just above Well A. This well and the outlet would seem to exclude each other, partly because they served the same purpose, whereby the well would be superfluous, partly because access to the outlet would have been hampered by the well. Lund and Nørskov argue that Well A (and the others as well) was constructed to serve a purpose during the building of the Maussolleion and that their filling in may have taken place along with the interments of Maussollos and Artemisia.[158] The choice of the earliest possible dating (from the evidence of the pottery), however, does not take account of the complicated archaeological evidence to be discussed in detail below. Moreover one would certainly expect a water basin into which the aqueduct would empty itself and from where the water could be fetched. As shown above, there is no evidence from the 4th Century BC for a basin, nor, of course, for a well-house (with a proper conduit for the waste water) that one would expect to be part of the original planning of the aqueduct.[159]

A key to an understanding of the situation in the 4th Century BC onwards comes from the above-mentioned gradual filling-in and degradation of the area in front of the wall, and from a close look at the outlet. As demonstrated above, the outlet is placed eccentrically with regard to both the line of the water channel in the aqueduct and in the limestone bonder in the top of which the water was carried forwards through the wall. The solution is certainly sloppy, considering the efforts invested in construction of the aqueduct, and can hardly have been intended from the outset. The lack of bond between aqueduct and wall corroborates the notion of incongruity between aqueduct and terrace wall. They may not be contemporaneous, in which case the wall would be the younger because it appears absurd to construct the long aqueduct, UG:C deep down in the Maussollan terrace fill with a planned termination in the sloppy outlet. Moreover, the aqueduct could easily have been directed right to the proper point, if the wall were already in existence or in course of construction.

If the outlet is hardly contemporaneous with the wall, the possibility for a secondary cutting of it should be considered. For technical reasons it is obvious that the establishment of the water channel would not be feasible if the altogether 1.6-1.8 m thick wall were intact. Very important, therefore, is the evidence from the area of 'Building C', only 10 m north of the outlet, for destructions already in the middle of the 2nd Century BC. Pedersen has ingeniously interpreted the complicated stratigraphy as evidence for a thorough removal of blocks from the building (explained by Jeppesen and Pedersen as the propylon to the terrace). Both west and east of the terrace wall, blocks were pillaged right down to the foundations, and the area was left to a gradual accumulation of soil strata rich in pottery, which effectively sealed the area and date the event to the middle of the 2nd Century BC.[160] Certainly the area was by this time utterly

devastated, and this may very well have affected also the area of the aqueduct, where, as mentioned, soil was allowed to accumulate in front of the wall.

The implementation of the sloppy outlet can be fully understood within this 'scenario', whereby it could have been done in the exposed top of the partly ruined wall. This reconstruction of the events has important consequences for our understanding of the history of the aqueduct. It implies that the built aqueduct is older than the terrace wall and, accordingly, that water was originally conveyed to the area before the building of the wall. This fits in with the ascertainment (above, Ch. 4 p. 73) that our branch of the aqueduct, UG:C, is contemporaneous with the terrace wall TW1, which can be dated to (shortly) before the Maussolleion.

The "Water-channel m" in front of the terrace wall also seems to favour a 'pre-terrace' dating of the built aqueduct, but the scant evidence unfortunately remains somewhat ambiguous.

Below the terrace wall, exactly in line with the aqueduct, and accordingly slightly to the south of the outlet, runs a wall of two courses at nearly right-angles to the wall, Fig. 6.4.4. On its top lies an ashlar, 0.6 m wide and 0.25 m high, with a hewn "Water-channel m", c. 20 cm wide and 15 cm deep (bottom level at 2.06 m a.s.l.). Whereas its foundation abuts on the protruding and roughly cut blocks of the foundation, the channel itself comes closer, and an ashlar in the wall was omitted, presumably to make room for it. The excavators stated that it did not continue under the euthynteria, but no details about the size of the void in the foundation or any suggestions about what purpose it may have served are given. No remains of a covering of the channel or of pipes were noted.

The shape of the channel fits well for an outlet of wastewater or overflow from a fountain. A similar one from the Tholos in Athens of the 5th Century BC was subterranean and covered with slabs and tiles.[161] Another of the 2nd Century BC, running from the South-East Fountain House, is an open stone gutter in the surface of the Agora.[162]

The excavators and also Pedersen were convinced that the "Water-channel m" is likely to be contemporaneous with the wall.[163] According to

Pedersen, it may have served as an outlet from the hypothetical, original basin below the spout, and because of its position c. 0.6 m below the euthynteria and the ground surface, it would have been furnished with terracotta pipes. Such an outlet from the presumed basin, however, is hardly likely, because its outlet would have been situated along its outer edges and not below and along its inner side towards the wall. Moreover, as mentioned above, the drain was both destroyed to give place for the terracotta wellhead of Well A and was buried in the fill around it, when the surface level of c. 2.64 m a.s.l. was established.[164]

For several reasons the 'scenario' of a Maussollan date of the channel is not feasible. The overflow channel would have functioned for only a very short period, and – not least – there is evidence for neither an appropriate outlet nor a basin. Finally, the setting up of the wells in the same period as the wall is incompatible with the notion of water pouring out from the façade of the terrace wall. Rather, the straightforward explanation of the wells as substitutes for the by now decommissioned aqueduct seems obvious. Moreover, both the relative dating of "Channel m" and the fact that it runs exactly on line with the aqueduct west of the terrace wall render a connection very likely.

This solution, however, does create problems. How did the water originally get down from level 4.50 m a.s.l. in the aqueduct to 2.06 m a.s.l. of "Water-channel m"? How can a transition from the aqueduct to the overflow or discharge gutter be imagined – in the shape of a fountain house or a basin exactly in the place of the later terrace wall? Be that as it may, the relative chronology as outlined here seems to be the only possible conclusion to be drawn from the complex evidence. The aqueduct was constructed as part of the grand design of the area along the lines of the new orthogonal city plan. This was, as shown above, soon given up in favour of a grand design of the Maussolleion and its terrace. The aqueduct was cut off and was re-established after the partial destruction of the terrace wall by means of the sloppy outlet.

The outlet served the pressure "Pipe 1" and "k1+3" that were fed by means of a kind of water tower or rather by a vertical tube. The evidence for pipelines, certainly, has important conse-

quences for the understanding of the function of the Upper Gallery in the late period. Certainly, by the 2nd Century BC, the aqueduct would have been furnished with pipes and such are, in fact, already documented in the two cross-walls, in Shaft U6 and in UG:C, not far from the outlet through the terrace wall. The diameter of their pipes is respectively 10.5 cm and 8.9 cm. Still, though, the purpose of the walls remains enigmatic.

Finally, it should be noted that one would expect the aqueduct to have had pipes from the beginning. This was the Greek practice from Eupalinos onwards, and there is hardly evidence (deposition, wear) for a free flow during centuries through the galleries. However, Newton did not mention and we did not find any fragments of pipes in the galleries, either from the old phase or from the Hellenistic. Only in Trench Q_7 were pipes found of a diameter of 18.7 cm. They would fit the channel in the floor of the galleries very well (see below, p. 166), but we have no evidence for their use. Only the smooth sides in the irregular, long basin in UG:B1 below the door into Chamber 1 testify to the wear of water.

6.5. The chronology of the aqueducts

The course of events in the area of the Quadrangle is considered well illuminated. The reconstruction of activities in the SE termination of Branch C is considered highly probable.

1. Construction of the Branches A and B in connection with the pre-Maussollan chamber and corridor complex. We know nothing of Branch B's outlet towards the east.
2. Construction of Branch C contemporaneous with terrace wall TW1 and continuing in "Water-channel m". The final aim / destination of the water-channel is unknown. The cancellation of the original outlet of Branch B2 probably took place in the same period.
3. Cutting-off of Branch B1 by the SW corner of the Maussolleion.
4. Cutting-off of Branch C by the east terrace wall. In compensation, construction of the Wells A, B and C, which were soon filled in.

Fig. 7.1.2. Detail of unfinished column drum in sandstone. 1976.

The situation east and south of the Maussolleion is known only from Newton's and Biliotti's reports.

Newton noticed extensive evidence for quarrying east of the Quadrangle and commented on the dual use of the site as cemetery and quarry.[170] In one place he could not make up his mind about the character of the cuttings. He tunnelled through the east course of UG:B2 that *leads into a large space, perhaps a sepulchral chamber on the eastern side. At the bottom* [25' = 7.6 m below the surface] *is an open trough, perhaps a sepulchral soros, about 7 feet long. It is cut out of stone; the ends are rounded. We are at present engaged in clearing out this supposed chamber.* (Pl5: 48, Sept. 1857).

In a later report, he states, though, that *the supposed chamber proved to be a rectangular cutting in the quarry.*[171] Finally in 1862, however, he in vague terms keeps open the possibility of also burials in this area to the east of the Maussolleion.[172] His

ambiguity is understandable, because of the discovery of the *soros* and close to it of a vase and a dagger (see below, p. 165, 167) and the fact that UG:B2 connected the area to the subterranean chamber, Cb2.

The sarcophagus or *soros*, which Newton discovered, is mentioned several times together with its stratigraphical context: *in a kind of soil in which I have never found any remains of the Mausoleum;*[173] *10' below the upper stratum of black earth*[174] and with *2 feet 6 inches soil below.*[175] It moreover figures in two watercolours by Pullan, Pl. 5-6. But very little information is given except its length of about 2.13 m. The material is stone and the corners are rounded.

In the east necropolis of Halikarnassos, along the road to Milas, Newton discovered two other stone *soroi*,[176] the circumstances of the find and the placement, however, are not stated. The larger *soros* measured 2 m by 0.74 m and 0.74 m. Neither stone nor shape is described, but the 1' high lid was gabled. The smaller is not described. Both contained one red-figure amphora each, the smaller also a kantharos.

In the same area, in 1989, was discovered the "Tomb of the Carian Princess". The rectangular sarcophagus in green andesite was encased in a roughly built, narrow chamber, and measures 2.2 m by 0.91 m and is 1.13 m high. The lid is gabled. Inside the sarcophagus plenty of jewellery was found, and outside the sarcophagus (at the foot end) was a single vase, a black-glazed oinochoe. The find is published by Özet 1994 and is dated to the latter part of the 4th Century BC.[177]

A reconstructed chamber tomb in the moat of the Bodrum castle contains a rectangular sarcophagus (in limestone) with a gabled lid.[178] It measures 2.3 m by 1.08 m and is 0.95 high. It was found in the same area.

Several more sarcophagi, most probably local but without known find spots, are exhibited in the castle and have been treated by Carstens 1999.[179] She has kindly informed me that none of them have rounded corners.

Beyond doubt, the type of plain sarcophagus is common in Halikarnassos, and ours may be the oldest datable, because it is from before the building of the Maussolleion. Unfortunately, it was out of context, since it stood in the quarry

Fig. 7.1.3. Part of the quarry to the south of MauTb with a breach in the fragile claystone ceiling of the Lower Gallery, cf. Fig. 3.2.1. 1973.

in Maussollan soil, was empty, and the lid was missing. If the censer and sword, which Newton found beside the *soros*, did belong to the original placement, the date of the sarcophagus will be the end of the 5th Century BC.

It is obvious also from Pullan's watercolours, Pl. 3-6, that a great part of the area between the Quadrangle and the Maussollan east terrace wall had been exploited extensively as a quarry. The vertical bedrock west of the terrace wall TW2 shows the characteristic horizontal lines from the cutting of courses of ashlars. The same lines are clearly seen in the vertical rock east of the same wall and close to the above-mentioned *soros*. Also the irregular zig-zag cuttings to the north of this place can derive only from quarry work.

The bottom level of the cuttings is documented in the recent excavations at c. 2.6 m and 1.5 m a.s.l.,[180] numbers that fit well with Newton's indications on the levels (see above Ch. 4). It is impossible to calculate the number of cubic me-

tres excavated, but given the rock level along the east side of the Quadrangle at 9.6 m descending to 8.9 m a.s.l. and in Trench Q_6 at 8.0 m a.s.l., it will be high.

We are hardly informed about quarry activities to the south of the Maussolleion. Biliotti, in his diary of 1865.04.21, states that *Irregular ledges are projecting from the vertical cut, but they cannot be ascribed to any purpose.*[181] As noted in Ch. 4, the ashlar wall, TW1 south, hides the vertical face of the rock, Pl. 2, and Biliotti reports on his work where wall and vertical bedrock divide west of Shaft U7, the bedrock turning towards the NW. His "irregular ledges" may well be the result of quarrying, as to the north and west of the Quadrangle, documented above. As for the vertical face of the bedrock between Shaft U7 and the courtyard Cb3, we have no means to ascertain if it derives from quarrying. Another possibility would be a dressing in connection with the pre-Maussollan chambers before or contemporaneous with the terrace wall TW1. The vertical

153

bedrock, 3 m high, in the SW corner of Trench Q_6 (above p. 42, Fig. 2.4.7) showed no trace of quarrying.

There is ample evidence for the use of sandstone in the Maussollan structures such as the Western Staircase (MauTb), the 18 pillars around the Quadrangle, the transverse corridor in Cb1, and not least in the foundation and terrace-wall backing of the peribolos wall. The sandstone, however, was also used for the pre-Maussollan structures: the unfinished(?) terrace wall TW2, a part of the ceiling in the East Corridor, as well as in the built parts of UG:C and in its built east termination up to the east terrace wall of the peribolos.

The employment of sandstone is thus very well documented both before and especially in connection with the erection of the Maussolleion structures. We have only a few possibilities, however, to date the quarrying by criteria independent of where the ashlars have been used. Moreover, the stones have not been subjected to analysis, and some may derive from another of several quarries in the vicinity, as noted by Pedersen 1991.[182]

1) The column drums can hardly have been intended for use in the area. They were left in a state apt for transport to another place.

2) North of the Maussolleion the peribolos euthynteria is carried on a foundation that bridges a gap towards the north. The level of this gap shows up both in the whole NW part of the Quadrangle and north of the Western Staircase, so this area most probably formed a part of the pre-Maussollan quarry.

3) East of the Maussolleion the extensive quarrying is definitely from before the Maussolleion proper, because it is deeply buried under Maussolleion chippings.

4) The aqueduct UG:B2 opens into the quarry east of TW2. This cannot be the original termination of the water conduit, so this part of the quarry will be contemporaneous with or later than the decommissioning of the aqueduct.

5) The terrace wall TW2 is aligned with the 4th Century city plan of Halikarnassos. It testifies to an intention to embellish the area and therefore to the termination of the quarry-

ing: both the narrow void behind the wall and the irregular area in front of it would have been meant to be filled in.

As a consequence of these observations, we can reconstruct the following sequence: the terrace wall is younger than the quarry, which again is younger than the aqueduct. This notion of destruction of the aqueduct earlier than the building of the Maussolleion conforms very well to the conclusions above, p. 149.

7.2. The 'Garbage' Chambers to the north of the Maussolleion

In August 1973 we were informed about a subterranean chamber situated close to the Maussolleion, above Turgut Reïs Caddesi 94/1 on a parcel at this time owned by Osman Sarselmaz. It was partly filled with soaked earth and garbage, filthy from a kitchen outlet, hence the name. The structure is briefly referred to by Jeppesen & Zahle 1975: 74. They were convinced that it formed part of the pre-Maussollan 'necropolis' of which Cb1-Cb3 are the best known.

The two chambers were only briefly described and photographed, Figs. 7.2.2-4, and regrettably (for lack of time and authorization) not recorded properly by means of a measured drawing. Fig. 7.2.1 only graphically sums up our observations. The orientation is oblique, 10° NNW, which varies from the pre-Maussollan structures Cb1-Cb3 at c. 14° NNE, and comes closer to the orthogonal town plan and the Maussolleion, 4° NNW.[183] The fairly hard bedrock is sedimentary, with strings or courses of gravel. The original

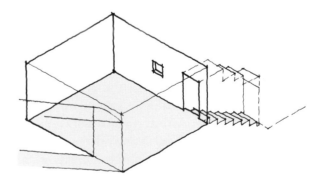

Fig. 7.2.1. Sketch plan of the 'Garbage tomb' with upper and lower chamber. Drawing Kjell Aage Nilson

Fig. 7.2.2. North wall of the 'Garbage Chambers' with niche and opening to staircase down to the second chamber. 1973.

Fig. 7.2.3. NE corner of the 'Garbage Champers' with opening to the staircase down to the second chamber. 1973.

Fig. 7.2.4. The staircase down to the second chamber partly uncovered. 1973.

155

ceiling splits and is well preserved only along the sides. The vertical sides are plain, with no traces of treatment.

The structure consists of a 'dromos', an upper chamber, and a stepped passage down to a lower chamber, which was quite filled with earth and was therefore inaccessible. The floor of the upper chamber could be studied only by means of a small trial excavation (1.35 m × 1.10 m) that was accomplished in its NE corner and in the upper part of the stepped passage.

The upper chamber is entered from above through an opening, 1.63 m wide, with its right side on line with the east side of the chamber. The upper or outer outline of the opening is completely worn. The chamber measures 4.85 m north-south by 5.30 m east-west, and in the NE corner the height was determined to be 2.85 m.

In the north wall is a niche, 1.6 m above the floor, 2.2 m and 2.7 m from respectively the west and east corners. It is 48 cm high, 45 cm wide, 23 cm deep below, and concave above.

The opening into the stepped passage is situated only 0.5 m from the NE corner of the chamber and measures at floor level 0.9 m in width but widens upwards. It is 1.85 m high. Five treads were cleared, each about 0.25 m high and about 0.45 m deep. Since the length of the passage is 3.3 m, there is room for altogether 8 treads down to the floor of the lower chamber. Also the ceiling is stepped, but only 3 times; the first step occurs at 1.4 m from the opening (above the 3rd tread).

Also the sides of the passage are plain, but for a hole, 9 cm × 9 cm, 1.76 m from the opening, above the 4th tread.

Nothing could be ascertained about the lower chamber.

In retrospect one can only regret that this structure was not properly studied. An excavation might not have produced any clue to the dating, but a precise knowledge of its plan and features would certainly have been very useful. Its plan and orientation, though, differ from those of the pre-Maussollan structures, Cb1-Cb3, and there appear to be no reasons to consider it together with these.

7.3. Finds of sculptures, terracottas, pottery, tiles, pipes, metal, etc.

For the present inquiry into the early history of the site, the pre-Maussollan finds are of great interest because they can provide an overall framework of activities in the area.

Throughout the British excavation reports references are given to finds. Unquestionably, the finds of sculptures from the Maussolleion had first priority,[184] but also other finds are mentioned and were even published by Newton. Several more entered the register of the Greek and Roman Department of the British Museum and have later been identified and published or are published below. Due to inconsistencies in Newton's recording, however, some identifications are tentative. Newton states, for example, the find-place of a terracotta figure to be the east of the Quadrangle, but in the museum register another find-place is recorded (see below). Some of the find-places should accordingly be understood as very likely rather than quite certain.

Below in the sections 1-6 follows a synopsis of certain groups of pre-Maussollan finds – according to categories – made both in 1857-1858 and 1865 and in 1966-1967 and 1970-1977.

7.3.1 Sculpture

a) Small archaic head of a sphinx? Fig. 7.3.1.1. BM G&R Reg. 1868.4-5.23.
Found by Biliotti 1865.07.24 close to the foundation of the Maussollan east terrace wall.[185]
Published by Ashmole 1950. Referred to by Bean & Cook 1955: 94-95 and Hornblower 1982: 245 n. 189 and p. 251.
H. 9.9 cm, w. 8.5 cm, diam. c. 6.0 cm, the ear 2.9 cm × 1.9 cm. White marble tinged with grey in parts, fine-grained, probably Asia Minor quarry (Ashmole).
The back of the head with left ear and chin is missing, the nose is mutilated. The details of the beardless head are soft and the eyes protrude. The mouth is straight. It is probably unfinished.
The hair above the forehead is shown like a cushion, set off from the face and the smooth

top of the head. It curves down on the temple, but leaves the (preserved right) ear free and continues down on the neck. On both sides the hair is divided by grooves parallel to the outline. Whether the 'cushion' indicates only hair or both hair and a ribbon is hard to tell. The ear is set off from the hair and cheek, but no details are shown.

The style of the head is local East Greek and is in no way 'Egyptianizing', as has been claimed. It is by Ashmole compared to sculptures found in Hieronda,[186] in Keramos,[187] and on Kalymnos.[188] A fairly close parallel is also the siren in the Ny Carlsberg Glyptotek in Copenhagen.[189] Their size is almost identical; the head of the siren being 11 cm. Ashmole suggested that the head could derive from a siren or a sphinx, a part of either

◀ Fig. 7.3.1.1. Archaic head of sphinx discovered by Biliotti east of the Maussolleion. In the British Museum. From a plaster cast.

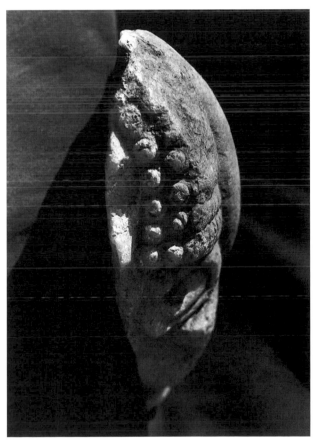

Fig. 7.3.1.2.a-b. Archaic female head in marble discovered in 1973 near the SE corner of the Quadrangle. Bodrum Museum inv. 6925. 1983.

than the sculptures from the tomb building. The head can hardly contribute to an understanding of the use of the site before the Maussolleion.

7.3.2 Terracottas

a) Remarkable among Newton's and Biliotti's small finds are 24 terracotta figures of the 'horse-and-rider' type, Fig. 7.3.2.1. They are published by Higgins 1954, Nos. 301-323. The 34 more specimens that turned up during the Danish excavations 1966-1967 and 1970-1976 are listed below.[201]

The statuettes are handmade and manufactured in the local, dark red, coarse and micaceous clay, the character of which is known also from the Red Burnished ware (Munsell 5YR 6/6, 7.5YR 6/2-4, 7.5YR 7/4).[202] They show a standing horse with mane and tail and with a separately made, bearded rider (without legs) on the back. He holds a small shield in his left arm, the right arm is raised, and he seems from the coarse shape of the head to be helmeted. The horse's mane, ears (no. 4) and tail may be separately made, occasionally also the neck of the horse (no. 6). Rarely the eyes are outlined and only once the horse's mouth is open and the nostrils are indicated.[203] Colour is sparsely used. On one specimen a white slip remains on one eye, on the top of the mane, and on the muzzle a chevron is painted.[204] On no. 20, below, there are reddish bands on the horse's chest and 2 horizontal and 3 vertical ones on the shield.

The average size is about 11 cm in both height and length, but several are larger. The horse no. 13 is 15.1 cm high and may originally have measured 20 cm in height. Also no. 21 is fairly large. Two pieces in the British Museum are quite extraordinary:

Head of horse, Fig. 7.3.2.1 bottom row, centre, h. 3.8 cm, l. 7.6 cm. Higgins 1954 No. 323, Fig. 7.3.2.1 bottom row, centre. It is fairly square in shape, the mouth is open, nostrils are indicated, and the eyes are outlined All other horses' heads are rounded and plain.

Body of man, head, arms and legs missing, the genitals separately made, h. 12.3, w. (shoulder) 6.7 cm, (legs) 7.5 cm. Higgins 1954, No. 321, Fig. 7.3.2.1 bottom row, right. The ubiquitous concave underside shows him to be a rider, but the legs and his nakedness are unique. The complete figure with horse would be c. 18 cm high.

None of the riders were found in a pre-Maussollan context and only a few in Maussollan fill: our no. 12 and the two *rude and grotesque terracotta figures* that Newton discovered in the subterranean chamber Cb2.[205] Nos. 20-25 derive from a late-Hellenistic context. Three times Biliotti notes the finding of *some* Terra Cotta *fragments*

Fig. 7.3.2.1. A selection of horse-and-rider figures discovered by Newton and Biliotti in the British Museum. Higgins 1954, Nos. 303, 304 308 (top row), 321, 323, 321 (bottom row). By courtesy of the Trustees of the British Museum. 2003.

Fig. 7.3.2.2a. Horse-and-rider terracotta statuettes, Nos. 21-27, below, discovered during the Danish excavations. Bodrum Museum.

Fig. 7.3.2.2b. Horse-and-rider terracotta statuettes, Nos. 3, 16, 12, 16, below, discovered during the Danish excavations. Bodrum Museum.

of human figures and animal (*Diary* 1865.04.18) that in two cases are labelled archaic (*Diary* 1865.05.17; 1865.07.17).[206] The contexts seem to be post-Antique (Hospitallers or Newton) and this may be the case for the rest of Newton's and Biliotti's finds, as it was for certain for all the rest of our finds.

The wide or 'un-focused' distribution of our finds is remarkable. The main bulk comes from the Quadrangle (1-16). Nos. 21-27, however, turned up about 90 m west of the Quadrangle and the rest were found close to the east terrace wall, Nos. 17-20, 32-33, and the south terrace wall Nos. 29-31 about 75 m to the SE.

Higgins dates the horse and rider statuettes to the 1st half of the 6th Century BC,[207] but specimens dated to the late Geometric period are very similar.[208]

161

f) Bearded head with pointed cap, hollow cast.
Fig. 7.3.2.3. H. 7.0 cm, w. 4.0 cm, l. 3.1 cm. Found in the Quadrangle Co8/12, in Newton fill.

g) Seven figurines were found in Maussolleion fill and are therefore from before c. 360 BC, but are of 4th Century types.[217]

The finds of the 2nd half of the 4th Century BC and later are substantial, and references are for the sake of convenience given to the ones in the British Museum.[218] They are mainly votive figures, standing and seated women, a male torso, many limbs, etc. They are all in the local, coarse and micaceous clay and derive from between c. 330/300 and the 1st Century BC.

The context of a few of them is known: the terracottas found by Newton on top of the marble- and green andesite chipping layers east of the Quadrangle (see above, p. 20) were published in *HD*: 125-126, pl. LX, figs. 1, 2, 3; 6, and are also mentioned *TD* II: 203. The specimens in question are Burn & Higgins 2001, nos. 2561, 2565, 2571 and 2573. With regard to no. 2571 they note, though, that it according to the Register was "found in mine under Hadji Nalban's house SW angle Mausoleum". One would expect the information published in *HD* to be correct, but we cannot know for sure.

One figure (head of woman) was excavated in the Western Staircase and published in *HD*: 93, pl. LX, Fig. 5. Burn & Higgins 2001 no. 2566.[219]

7.3.3 Pottery

Although both Newton, rarely,[220] and Biliotti (six times) refer to finds of pottery, only the find-spot of two vases is known.

a) Miniature lekanis, Fig. 7.3.3.1-2, G&R Reg. 1857.12-20.18 "Sepulcral chamber S.S. of Mausoleum."[221]

Low bowl with in-curved rim with a sharp edge to a broad flat upper surface. Two horizontal ribbon handles set just below the rim form a triangle seen from above. The ring base is hollowed out with little care. Diam. rim 6.3 cm, diam. with handles 9.5 cm, h. 2.9 cm. The surface is covered with a thin reddish-orange slip, at places turning light yellow.

Fig. 7.3.3.1. Lekanis and censer discovered 1857 by Newton in the subterranean chamber, Cb2, and east of the Quadrangle, respectively. By courtesy of the Trustees of the British Museum.

Fig. 7.3.3.2. Lekanis discovered 1857 by Newton in the subterranean chamber, Cb2. G&R 1857. 12-20.18. By courtesy of the Trustees of the British Museum.

The ware and the slip point towards a Hellenistic date, but no exact parallel could be found. The triangular handle is known on Crete in the 2nd Century BC, see Eiring, J. 2000, "Hellenistic Pottery from Pyrgos at Myrtos", Ε' Επιστημονική Συνάντηση για την Ελληνιστική Κεραμεική. *Αθήνα* 2000: 53-60. These bowls are dated as late as the first half of the second century BC.

East of the Quadrangle Newton discovered the above-mentioned *soros* and in the soil beside it a fine vase (and a sword or dagger, for which see below). The circumstances of the discovery together with the little information we have on the chest are discussed above, p. 152. The two small finds are mentioned in *FP*16: 91, and Newton published them with a fine drawing in both *HD*: 124 and *TD*: 204.

b) Censer in the shape of a female head, Fig. 7.3.3.1,3-4, G&R Reg. 1857.12-20.115. Higgins 1954, no. 444 pl. 62. His text "Excavated Halicarnassus (in a tomb) 1856" reflects Newton's first interpretation of the find-place. It is dated to the late 5th Century BC. The place of production is unknown. Because the clay contains mica, it might be East Greek.

Vaag, Nørskov & Lund estimate the total amount of sherds kept from the Danish excavation to be about 120.000.[222] In their publication they focus on finds from contexts closely related to the building of the Maussolleion, but in the beginning of their work they 'surveyed' all the finds, as we did ourselves in 1982 and 1986. Undoubtedly, therefore, their conclusion applies also to the site as a whole: "The pottery from our contexts comprises only a few fragments dating from the 6th century BC. There seems to be almost a complete lacuna during the first half of the 5th century BC, and the number of finds datable to the second half is relatively small."[223] In fact, of the Archaic period there are merely three Wild Goat fragments, one Attic Black-figure fragment, a possible Attic Red-figure fragment from before 450 BC and a fragment of a transport amphora of the early 5th Century.[224] Only from the late 5th Century and the 1st half of the 4th Century is there a steep increase in finds.

Vaag, Nørskov & Lund's analysis of the contents of seven contexts sealed by the building of the Maussolleion is very interesting. The percentage of coarse wares to fine wares is altogether remarkably low and the material "is largely made up of vessels that one would normally associate with banqueting".[225]

It is also worth noticing that all the pottery from before and contemporaneous with the Maussolleion is local or from the East Greek cities of the islands or in Asia Minor. Only one vase,

Fig. 7.3.3.3. Sword and censer in the form of a female head discovered in 1857 by Newton east of the Maussolleion. From *HD* 1862: 124 Fig. G&R 1857.12-20.204 and 12-20.115.

Fig. 7.3.3.4. Censer discovered by Newton east of the Maussolleion 1857. BM G&R, reg. no. 1857.12-20.115. Left profile. By courtesy of the Trustees of the British Museum.

165

the planned ground level, and the then c. 3 m high terrace wall would accentuate the natural platform with the chamber and corridor structure. The building of Branch C of the aqueduct moreover served to bring water to an unknown place further east. We have no means to reconstruct the master plan in detail, but it can hardly have been many years older than the grandiose and flamboyant Maussolleion project, which rendered the 'updating' of the old structure obsolete.

Phase 3

The building of the Tomb of Maussollos. The cutting of the Quadrangle for the foundation of the Maussolleion podium required the cutting away of the inner part of Cb1, of parts of both UG:B1 and B2, as well as of the natural rock further to the north. Also the area above and on both sides of the chamber-corridor structure will have been tidied up. Both the ruined bedrock and the surface layers were probably cleared into the ravine along TW1. The chambers Cb2 and Cb3 were filled in, presumably after having been emptied or plundered. The whole east end of UG:B2 as well as part of the East Corridor was pillaged of ceiling blocks. Coeval with the cutting of the stairwell and chamber of the Maussollan burial chamber proper a central drain or outlet was constructed towards the east.

Construction of a transverse corridor in Chamber 1. A part of the Main Corridor was re-used in connection with the building of a corridor across the landing of Cb1, and into which the original shaft of the Main Corridor formed the access. The purpose of the arrangement served to gain access to the SW side of the foundation – other explanations do not come to mind.

Construction of the Lower Gallery. Ten shafts formed the starting points for the cutting of the flat-bottomed subterranean drain, Lower Gallery, around the Quadrangle. The north and south branches joined the central outlet and emptied in the SE direction. The termination is unknown, due to various destruction where it converged with the abolished end of the East Corridor. There appears to be no parallel for this kind of 'perimeter drainage' in the ancient world.

Filling in of the Maussollan terrace. In connec-

tion with the building of the huge Maussolleion terrace and the raising of the surface to c. 9.4 m a.s.l., all the earlier structures were buried below several metres of fill. The area east of the Quadrangle was filled up with vast amounts of chippings from the building of the Maussolleion proper, whereas the whitish fill in the area to the south most probably derived from the cutting down of the earlier structures, of the Quadrangle and of the Lower Gallery. The latter fill therefore may the earlier of the two.

Outlet of Branch C of the Upper Gallery blocked by the Maussollan east terrace wall. The part of the terrace wall where the built aqueduct, UG: C, adjoins its backing (without bonding) is ruined due to various destruction. It seems clear, though, that no arrangement was made to convey the water through the wall – either by means of a spout for a fountain or to a place further east as in the previous period. Accordingly, the aqueduct fell out of use – an indication of the immense impact of the decision to construct the huge terrace.

Summary. The character of the site changed completely with the building of the Maussolleion. The older complex of chambers, corridors and aqueduct was destroyed, whereby an already partly implemented plan to incorporate the complex in the new city plan was abandoned. Despite a general similarity of plan between Cb1 and MauTb (stepped dromos, landing, chamber), there can have been no resemblance with regard to function. Cb1 existed for a long period, and its activities were closely connected with the use of water and to Cb2 and Cb3, because of their architectural unity. MauTb, on the other hand, was used only once, as shown by the fine preservation of its steps when excavated and the character of the fill and its content of offerings.

Phases 4 and 5

Partial destruction of the Maussollan east terrace wall and reopening of Branch C of the Upper Gallery. About 200 BC the propylon, Building C, in the east terrace wall was demolished as was certainly also at least partially the terrace wall to the south where the aqueduct adjoins the wall. A sloppy opening or channel was cut in top of an exposed limestone bonder and water was conducted forwards in a series of terracotta pipes one above the other. The aqueduct will have been opened again and the various repairs and the two cross walls with pipes should be dated to this period. During the 1st Century BC fill accumulated in front of the wall and the aqueduct fell out of use.

The authenticity of the adjustment phase ('2') of the pre-Maussollan structures within the new orthogonal city plan is crucial for the soundness of the above sketch of the history of the site. It moreover has important consequences for the understanding of the site: if it holds true, the Maussolleion and its terrace were not foreseen from the outset in the new city plan but were encompassed later. This is contrary to Pedersen's analysis, in which the city plan and the huge Maussolleion terrace are seen as part of the same master plan: "As no traces of urban construction have been found in the area now occupied by the terrace, the terrace area must have been laid out in direct connection with the laying out of the new town plan and kept clear until the construction of the Maussolleion started."[249]

The evidence of a building phase from before the Maussolleion in line with the new city plan therefore needs to be summed up. The 'construction' is based on the relative chronology of structures in six different places:

1. The relation between the Terrace Wall 1 where it crosses Cb3 and the East Corridor (above, p. 73). The wall crossed the corridor when this was in function. The corridor was blocked and went out of use during the period of building of the Maussolleion. Accordingly the wall can only be earlier than the Maussolleion.

2. The relation between the Terrace Wall 1 and the north peribolos wall of the Maussollan terrace (above, p. 30). The evidence is inconclusive, but a satisfactory solution of the conjunction of the coarse terrace wall and the smooth inner face of the marble peribolos wall is hard to imagine.

3. The relation between the south course of Terrace Wall 1 and the Maussollan terrace (above, p. 73). The top of the built foundation of TW1 and the bottom course of the wall proper lies about 2.5 m below the level of the Maussollan terrace and it cannot but indicate the intended

ground level. Higher up, the wall was constructed as a terrace wall, visible from the south.

4. The relation between Terrace Wall 1 and the aqueduct, Branch C (above, p. 73). The wall rests on the ceiling of the aqueduct. The Branch C, therefore, is from before or is (rather) contemporaneous with the Terrace Wall.

5. The relation between Branch B2 and the Terrace Wall 2, east of the Quadrangle. The aqueduct predates both the quarrying and the building of the terrace wall (above, p. 79).

6. The relation between the Branch C, the "Water-channel m" and the Maussollan east terrace wall (above, p. 148). The connection between the aqueduct and the water-channel was destroyed when the east terrace wall was erected. The course of water in the aqueduct was only re-established sometime around 200 BC.

Probably, the single most surprising result of this part of the investigation is the dating of Branch C to from before the cutting of the Quadrangle. Newton ascertained that it replaced Branch B as an aqueduct *either at the time of the building of the Mausoleum or on some earlier occasion.*[250] The architectural analysis resulted in the same ambiguous conclusion. The straightforward interpretation would be that Branch C replaced Branch B, when the Quadrangle destroyed the latter's course. The dating of Branch C, however, depends on the correct understanding of its relation both to the Terrace Wall 1 at one end and to the Maussollan east terrace wall and the various outlets and pipes at the other.

The 'construction' of this phase of adaptation to the new orthogonal city plan implies an intended level south and east of Terrace Wall 1 at c. 7 m a.s.l. rising towards the west and the north, as well as around its SE angle. We have no means of imagining the limit of this artificial terrace towards the east. The top-level of the built eastern part of Branch C will have been at c. 6.5 m a.s.l. Was this part visible or buried in terrace fill? If this was the case, how would the terrace have been limited towards the east?

Whereas there is strong evidence for a rebuilding phase, we have only few means to date it except the relative chronologies summarized above. The deep fill in the ravine south of the Terrace Wall

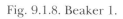
Fig. 9.1.8. Beaker 1.

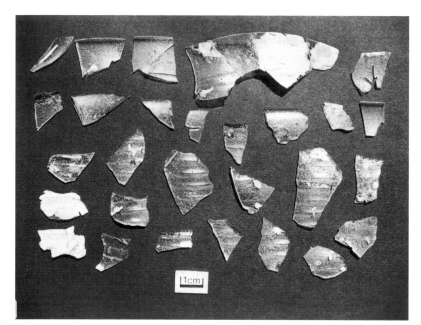

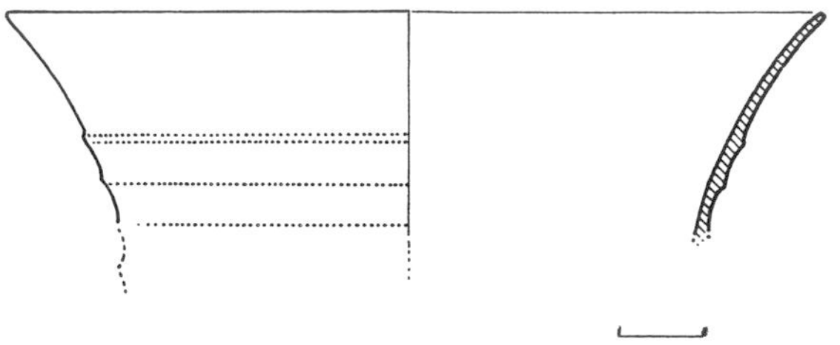

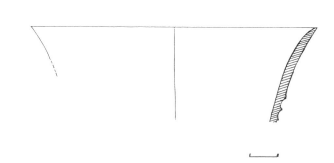

Fig. 9.1.9. Beaker 1.

Fig. 9.1.10. Beaker 2.

Fig. 9.1.11. Beaker 2.

Fig. 9.1.12. Beaker 3.

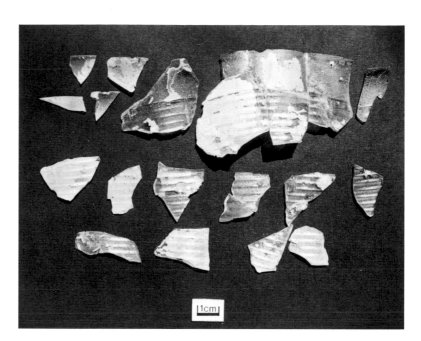

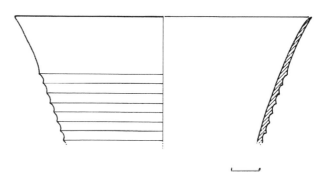

Fig. 9.1.13. Beaker 3.

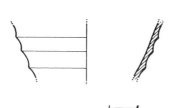

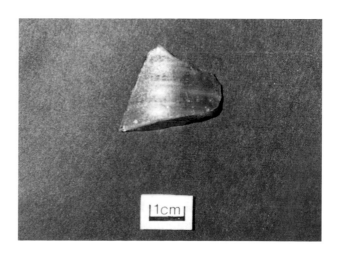

Fig. 9.1.15. Beaker 4.

Fig. 9.1.14. Beaker 4.

Fig. 9.1.16. Situla.

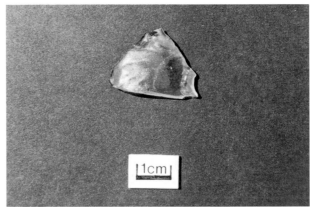

Fig. 9.1.17. Situla. Fragments a-c.

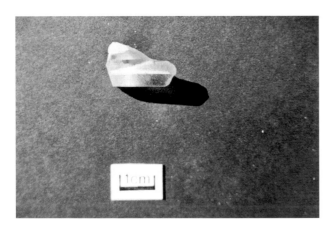

Fig. 9.1.18. Situla. Fragment d.

Fig. 9.1.19. Situla. Fragment e.

Fig. 9.1.20. Situla. Fragment g.

Fig. 9.1.21. Situla. Fragment h.

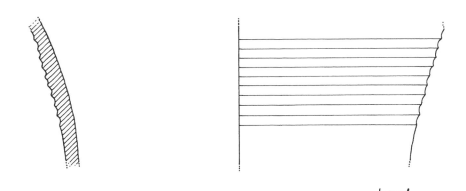

Fig. 9.1.22. Situla.

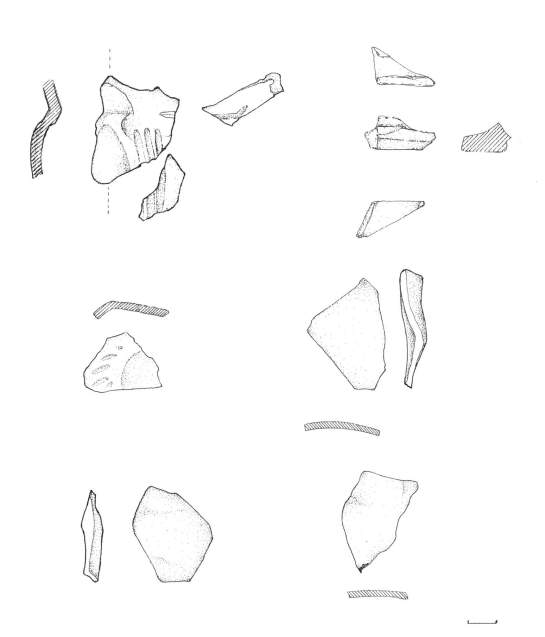

Fig. 9.1.23. Situla. Animal-head fragments.

9.3. The Attic Red-figure Pottery
by Vinnie Nørskov

The pottery catalogued in this appendix derives from a cavity cut in the bottom of the tomb chamber of the Maussolleion.[327] In his publication of the Quadrangle Kristian Jeppesen concluded on the basis of technical similarities that this was cut in connection with the cutting of the grave robbers' mine.[328] The tomb robbers thus accessed the grave chamber through the cavity. The excavation produced a number of very small fragments of pottery, glass, gold, alabaster, and ivory mixed with earth. The small size of the objects could point to the fact that they were stepped on and crashed during the looting of the tomb.[329] Part of the fill may also have been washed in through the robbers' tunnel after the emptying of the grave. None of the fragments from the cavity can be securely dated after the middle of the 4th Century BC, implying that they derive from the content of the tomb chamber. Only the rim, cat.no. 25, is possibly a rim of an unquentarium and thus the youngest of the fragments, perhaps an intruder from the tunnel. If more of the fill had been from a later date, it could perhaps have given us an idea of the date of the robbery. As this is not the case, we are left with a date of the robbery anywhere between 351 BC and 1522 AD.[330]

The grave chamber was first recognised during the Danish excavations in the early 1970s. Newton had estimated the placement, but did not recognise the cuttings in the bedrock or the few remaining blocks.[331] Maussollos' grave chamber was found totally robbed by the Danish excavators, the marble pavement having been removed by stone robbers, probably already in connection with the stripping of the monument by the Hospitallers in the 16th century.[332] However, the eyewitness account from the discovery of the tomb chamber in 1522 may give an idea of the original arrangement and embellishment, describing a room "adorned all around with columns of marble, with their bases, capitals, architraves, friezes and cornices engraved and carved in half-relief."[333] The walls were described as covered with slabs of differently coloured marble. Behind the tomb chamber the Hospitallers found a smaller room – an anteroom – with a sarcophagus of white marble. This had been opened when they came back the following day, and pieces of cloth of gold and gold appliqués were found strewn on the floor. The finds of pieces of gold appliqués in the grave robbers' tunnel and in the cavity during the Danish excavations provide a certain credibility to the 1522 account.[334] As no finds of coloured marble have been registered, it seems more probable that the walls of the tomb chamber were in fact painted in different colours.[335] The account actually reveals very little about the portable objects that must have been placed as grave gifts. The material found in the cavity is thus the only evidence of the rich furnishings of Maussollos' tomb chamber.

The finds from the cavity included tiny fragments of gold plate, glass and agate beads, red-figured pottery, ribbed glass vessels, and alabaster vessels as well as objects of bone and ivory. Comparable rich graves have not been found in the area. In 1989 the richest grave in Bodrum was excavated, belonging to the so-called Carian Princess, a woman who has been suggested to be Ada, the sister and wife of Idrieus.[336] It is clear from the large amount of gold jewellery in the tomb that the woman belonged to the nobility of Halikarnassos. On the other hand, the tomb itself was of no particular significance, a cist grave built of limestone with a sarcophagus of the local green stone, and it is striking that there were no other objects than the jewellery, apart from a black-glazed oinochoe found "between the tomb and the chamber".[337]

For parallels we have to turn to the royal Macedonian tombs. In the publication of the gold objects from the Maussolleion, parallels have been found in the Vergina material.[338] Glass vessels are found in other Macedonian graves (see p. 182). It may be suggested that the tomb of Maussollos may also have contained metal vessels of the kind found in the Vergina tombs, at least for the containers, whereas glass vessels were used as drinking-cups.[339] Only one red-figure vessel was found in the Vergina tombs, an askos, which is a shape not represented in the material found in the cavity.[340]

The pottery
There were found 933 fragments of pottery in the cavity. All the fragments are quite small, the

Bags	Black-gloss external	Black-gloss internal	Red-figure	Miscellaneous
MTB I	1		31	
MTB II	44 (1 vase)			
MTB III			36 (1 vase)	
MTB IV			26 (egg-and-dart)	
MTB V			13 (egg-and-dart)	
MTB VI			36	
MTB VII			77 (mix)	
MTB VII+IX			47 (mix)	
MTB VIII			11 (1 vase?)	
MTB IX	1		101	16 slipped (1 vase?)
MTB X 8-191	146	1		3
MTB X+XI	36 (1 vase?)			
MTB XI 14-250	132	1		3
MTB XII				85 without slip 11 coarse ware
MTB XIII	10	7		
Without number	24	2	31	1
In total	394	11	409	119
				933

Table 1: Number of pottery fragments found in the cavity.

largest being 6.6 × 7.5 cm (cat. no. 21), the smallest only a few millimetres. Table 1 summarises the total amount of fragments. In the catalogue only the most significant pieces have been described in detail, but when possible it has been remarked when a number of smaller bits were considered to belong to the same vessel.

The table shows that the number of black-gloss fragments and red-figure fragments is about the same. However, some of the black-gloss fragments probably derive from vessels with red-figure decoration. Many of the black-gloss fragments may derive from the ribbed hydria (cat. no. 23).

The number of red-figure vessels in the grave cannot be estimated with certainty. There are 22 catalogue entries, but they do not have to derive from 22 different vessels. The grouping has been made according to the style of drawing, fabric, clay colour and size of the fragments.

Differences in all these elements were of a kind that could also be found in different parts of the same vessel. All red-figure fragments were Attic clay. It is remarkable that there are nearly no open vessels. There are definitely no fragments of kraters, a shape which tends to dominate the picture of imported red-figure vessels in this particular period and is also common in the material found around the Maussolleion.[341] They may have been there, though, but removed by the tomb robbers. There are also no fragments from drinking-vessels. Here the glass vessels supplement, but it is possible that further vessels connected to the symposion were of precious metal, as seen in the royal tombs from Vergina, such as that of Philip II.[342] Only two diagnostic fragments were found: a handle that may derive from the black-gloss hydria (cat.no. 23), and a rim that may be from a hydria or pelike (cat.no.

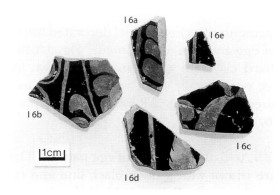

Fig. 9.3.17. Cat. no. 14: I6a-e.

15

Nine fragments of a closed vessel. Fig. 9.3.18. Hard clay with few fine light brown inclusions and rare fine voids, 5YR 6/6. Interior surface 5YR 7/4.

IX32: h. 2, w. 1.8, th. 0.25-0.28. Part of a floral decoration. Below, is a tiny part of a band, probably with egg pattern.

IX36-43: h. 0.8-2 w. 0.95-1.75, th. 0.2-0.25. Eight fragments with floral decoration consisting of wavy lines and triangles with dots.

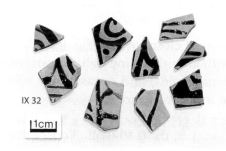

Fig. 9.3.18. Cat. no. 15: IX32, IX36-IX43.

16

Two fragments of closed vessel. Fig. 9.3.19. Hard clay with abundant fine light brown inclusions, 5YR 6/6. Interior surface 2.5YR 6/4-6/6.

VII71: H2.3, w. 2.4, th. 0.42-0.5. Volute and three leaves of a palmette.

IX5: h. 1.9, w. 1.5, th. 0.5. Volute.

Fig. 9.3.19. Cat. no. 16: VII71, IX5.

17

Two fragments of a closed vessel. Fig. 9.3.20.

Hard clay with abundant fine light brown inclusions, 5YR 6/6. Interior surface 5YR 5/6.

IX44: h. 2.6, w. 2.4, th. 0.3. One leaf of a vertical palmette and lower part of the other leaves.

IX45: h. 2.8, w. 3.2, th. 0.3. Part of palmette with five leaves separated by dark brown lines.

Fig. 9.3.20. Cat. no. 17: IX44-IX45.

18

Four fragments of closed vessel, all with thin black lines separating palmette leaves. Fig. 9.3.21. Medium-hard clay with abundant fine light brown inclusions and rare small voids, 5YR 6/6-5/6.

I8a: h. 2, w. 2.9, th. 0.48.

I8b: h. 2, w. 1.2, th. 0.4-0.45.

I8c: h. 1.6, w. 1.7, th. 0.35-0.4.

I8d: h. 0.8, w. 1, th. 0.4-0.5.

Fig. 9.3.21. Cat. no. 18: I8a-d.

Fig. 9.3.23. Cat. no. 20: IX19.

19

Four fragments of a closed vessel IX9-12.
Fig. 9.3.22.
Hard clay with frequent light brown inclusions and few small voids, 2.5YR 5/6-5/8.

IX9: Part of volute.

IX10: Part of volute and a large leaf with wavy border.

IX11: Part of volute.

IX12: Leaves separated by thin lines.

Parallels: The large leaf with wavy border is found, for instance, on a squat lekythos in Providence, Metzger 1951, Pl. 11.2; CVA USA 2, pl. 77/2.

21

Fragment of a closed vessel (two joining fragments). Fig. 9.3.24.
Hard clay with frequent fine light brown inclusions and rare voids, 5YR 6/6-5/6. Interior surface 2.5YR 6/4.

VII72+IX4: h. 3.9, w. 3.5, th. 0.41 (below), 0.32 (above). Below volute, heart of palmette and thin brown lines separating palmette leaves.

Fig. 9.3.24. Cat. no. 21: VII72+ IX4.

Fig. 9.3.22. Cat. no. 19: IX9-IX12.

20

Fragment of closed vessel. Fig. 9.3.23.
Hard clay with abundant fine light brown inclusions, 5YR 6/6. Interior surface 5YR 7/4-6/4.

IX19: h. 1.8, w. 1.6, th. 0.3. Part of volute.

22

Fragment of closed vessel. Fig. 9.3.25.
5YR 7/6.
Soft clay with abundant fine light brown inclusions and few voids, 5YR 6/6. Interior surface 5YR 7/6-6/6.

IX35: h. 5.1, w. 1.8, th. 0.3. Volute.

Fig. 9.3.25. Cat. no. 22: IX35.

Black-gloss
23
44 fragments of a large closed vessel, presumably a hydria, with ribbed body. Fig. 9.3.26.

Fine, medium-hard clay with abundant small light brown inclusions, occasional voids and few flecks of silvery mica, pale brown 10YR 6/3 towards the interior, reddish yellow 5YR 5/6 towards the exterior. Fine black-gloss on the surface. On the interior the lower part of the vessel has no slip, and there is occasionally silvery mica visible on the surface, light brown 7.5YR 6/4. Further up it is covered with a thin, brownish-black slip.

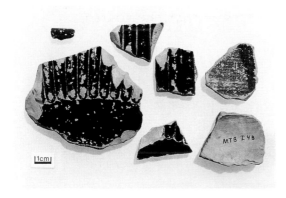

Fig. 9.3.26. Cat. no. 23: 7 fragments including a rim fragment.

One thiny rim fragment is preserved, without number: h. 0.8, w. 1.55, th. 0.6. Fig. 9.3.27.

The largest of the body fragments has a large flat area from where 10 ribs begin: h. 6.6, w. 7.5, th.

Fig. 9.3.27. Cat. no. 23: Rim fragment. 1:2.

1 cm at the bottom, 0.9 at the ribs. This fragment may derive from the shoulder.

I5: Fragment of a horizontal handle.

29 fragments from TB X, XI and XIII are of the same fabric. They are very thin, 0.2-0.4, but could perhaps belong to the upper part of the ribbed vessel?

Parallels: Attic parallels can be found in the National Museum in Athens, 2356, from 360 BC, and in the Berlin Museum, 2854, from Rhodos dated c. 350-340 BC, see Kopcke 1964, 35, 72, Beil. 23.3 and 36.77, Beil. 23.4. The oinochoe found in the grave of the Karian Princess in Bodrum (Özet 1994, 89-90, Fig. 3), dated to the last quarter of the 4th Century BC, is also ribbed and could be of the same fabric.

Coarse wares
24
Fragment of an open vessel with red slip on the interior and exterior. Fig. 9.3.28.

Soft clay with abundant fine light brown inclusions and a few dark brown ones as well. Few medium-size light brown and dark brown inclusions. 5YR 5/6. Red slip on surface 10YR 5/8.

XII3: h. 1.75, w. 1.1, th. 0.3-0.4.

Fig. 9.3.28. Cat. no. 24: XII3; Cat. no. 25: XII1, Cat. no. 26: XII4.

25

Rim of bottle or unquentarium? Fig. 9.3.28+ 9.3.29.
Hard clay with abundant small red, white, black and light brown inclusions, 5YR 5/6. Reddish yellow surface 5YR 7/6, rough with visible inclusions.

XII1: h. 0.7, w. 1.5, th. 0.3, Ø: 2.6.

Fig. 9.3.29. Cat. no. 25. 1:2.

26

Rim of bottle? Fig. 9.3.28.
Medium hard clay with abundant small light brown, white and black inclusions, translucent grits, 2.5YR 5/8. Interior surface 5YR 5/6. Surface 2.5YR 6/6.

XII4: h. 1, w. 0.8, th. 0.25, Ø 4.

9.4. Synopsis of the Finds of Alabaster

by Jan Zahle

In the cavity in the burial chamber of Maussollos 16 fragments of alabaster (aragonite) were discovered. Several could be put together, reducing the number to eight pieces. During the Danish excavation five fragments were moreover found in front of the tomb, in the Western Staircase, where Newton discovered the remains of perhaps 17 alabaster vessels. These were undoubtedly connected to the burial of Maussollos, even if they were not found in undisturbed layers.[366]

They may have been deposited in front of the tomb together with several vases[367] and not least with the deposit of sacrificed animals published by F. Højlund and K. Aaris-Sørensen in the first volume of this series.

Below, our finds shall be presented together with Newton's finds – hardly ever published. It will be tentatively argued that the finds in the area of the Western Staircase originally may have formed part of the burial gifts in the chamber proper; and that they were carried out by the robbers but then discarded. Except for only four fairly well-preserved vessels, the others were reduced to small pieces. Our findings reveal a destruction to have taken place in the chamber proper.

A. The finds in the burial chamber of Maussollos

TB XIV	Description	H	W	Thickness	Diam.	.	Remarks
1	Fragment of body (7 pieces)	13	12	0.8 / 1.4	13.3 max	Figs. 9.4.1-3	Cf. B1, 4-5
2	Fragment of lower part of body	4.0	6.6	1.3 / 0.8	9.2 c.	Figs. 9.4.1-2, 4	
3	Fragment of body (2 pieces)	7	3.9	0.6 / 0.7	6.4 c.	Figs. 9.4.3-5	
4	Fragment of body	6.8	4.1	0.55 / 0.7		Figs. 9.4.3-4	Same as A8?
5	Fragment of body	3.05	2.75	0.5		Figs. 9.4.3-4	
6	Fragment of body (2 pieces)	4.6	3.8	0.8	6.4 c.	Figs. 9.4.3-4, 6	
7	Fragment of body	2.3	1.75	0.45		Figs. 9.4.3-4	
8	Fragment of body	3.6	2.1	0.6		Figs. 9.4.3-4	Same vessel as A4

B. The finds in the landing of the Western Staircase and in the quarry area just to its south.

	No	Description	H	W	Thickness	Diam.		Find spot	Remarks
1	Co6/9 1972.26.09	Fragment of body	3.8	6.4	0.4 / 0.65		Figs. 9.4.7-8	In soil below great plug block	Colour and structure reminiscent of TB XIV.1
2	Co4/8 1972.15.06	Fragment of body	2.3	1.3	0.32				
3	Co4/9.1 1972	Fragment of body, bottom of neck	10.0	4.7	1.2 (neck)	6.7 / 8.8 max	Figs. 9.4.7-8	Lower landing. Measured drawing	
4	Co4/9.2 1972	Fragment of body	4.9	3.6	0.7		Figs. 9.4.7-8		Colour reminiscent of TB XIV.1
5	Co5/7 1972.06.29	Fragment of body	4.1	3.5	0.6 / 0.8		Figs. 9.4.7-8	South of south parapet	Colour reminiscent of TB XIV.1

Fig. 9.4.7.

Fig. 9.4.8.

C. In the stairwell of the Western Staircase Newton found the remains of 17 alabaster vessels, three of which were complete or nearly complete.[368] Of these vessels the famous Xerxes Vase was shown in *HD*, pl. VII.

In the British Museum the alabaster vessels were numbered G&R 1857.12-20.1-17, and nos. 1-3 are illustrated in Højlund 1981: 41 Fig. 37-39. In his discussion of Newton's find spot(s), Højlund tends to conclude that the alabaster was found between the plug-block in the stomion of the tomb and the stone packing across the stairwell and in a secondary, post-antique position and may have been moved from elsewhere. Remarkable is the state of preservation, two are complete, two nearly complete; the rest are very fragmentary, reminding one of the general state of the finds in the burial chamber.

G&R 1857.12-20.1-17

No.	Description	H	W	Diam.		Reference
1328	Jar with ears, well preserved except for breaks in side. With cuneiform and Egyptian inscription	29.2		18.1	Fig. 9.4.9	Smith Cat. no. 1099. R. Kent, *Old Persian*, 1950: XVf. Højlund, *MH 1*: 42 Fig. 38
2	Jar with ears, intact	10.1		12.7		Højlund, *MH 1*: 42 Fig. 39
3	Alabastron with ears, intact with Greek letters	27.9		8.7	Fig. 9.4.10	Højlund, *MH 1*: 42 Fig. 37
4	Upper part. With Greek letters	17.78	0.7 1.3	10.6	Fig. 9.4.11	
5	Lower part. With Greek letters	20.0	0.55-1.1	11	Fig. 9.4.12	
6	Fragment of neck and lip	3.5	0.4	2.4-6	Fig. 9.4.13	
7	Fragment of lip			7.94	Fig. 9.4.13	
8	Fragment of body	7.37	0.4-0.8		Fig. 9.4.14	
9	Fragment of body, bottom of neck	8.26	0.8-1.1		Fig. 9.4.13	
10	Fragment of body with ear	6.67	0.7-1.1			
11	Fragment of body, lower part	7.62	0.6-1.0		Fig. 9.4.13	
12	Fragment of body	9.53	0.7-1.1		Fig. 9.4.12	
13	Fragment of body	5.72				
14	Fragment of body	7.62	0.9-1.1			
15	Fragment of body, in two pieces	6.1	0.4-0.7			
16	Fragment of body	4.45	0.6-0.7		Fig. 9.4.14	
17	Fragment of body	4.83	0.7-0.8		Fig. 9.4.14	

The Danish excavation produced clear evidence for the looting of the burial chamber, and some of the treasures were found in the robber's mine west of the tomb chamber.[370] The finding of alabaster fragments in the chamber and also in the front of the tomb together with gold wire[371] connects to Newton's finds in the latter place. Both Newton and D. Williams have suggested that other precious small finds from elsewhere in the area may be left-overs from the looting of the tomb-chamber.[372] Could all the alabasters originally have been deposited in the chamber, and been discarded during the escape with the booty? In order to check this possibility, the finds in Bodrum were photographed and partly copied in plaster and a comparison was made in the British Museum. There were, however, no joints.

Fig. 9.4.9.

Fig. 9.4.10.

Fig. 9.4.11.

Fig. 9.4.12.

Fig. 9.4.13.

Fig. 9.4.14.

BIBLIOGRAPHY in three parts

1. Jan Zahle and Kjeld Kjeldsen, The site

Abbreviations:

FP Newton 1859

HD Newton 1862.

MH ed. K. Jeppesen 1981-2003, *The Maussolleion at Halikarnassos 1-7, Jutland Archaeology Society Publications* XV: 1-7, Aarhus.

1, 1981 Højlund F. & K. Aaris-Sørensen, The Sacrificial Deposit

2, 1986 Jeppesen, K. & A. Luttrell 1986, The Written Sources and their Archaeological Background

3,1-2 1991 Pedersen, P., The Maussolleion Terrace and Accessory Structures

4, 2000 Jeppesen, K., The Quadrangle. The Foundations of the Maussolleion and its Sepulchral Compartments

5, 2002 Jeppesen, K., The Superstructure. A Comparative Analysis of the Architectural, Sepulchral, and Literary Evidence

7, 2002 Vaag, L.E., V. Nørskov & J. Lund, The Pottery. Ceramic Material and other Finds from Selected Contexts

P Newton 1858

TD Newton 1865

Bibliography:

Ashmole, B. 1950, An archaic fragment from Halicarnassus, *Festschrift Andreas Rumpf*: 5-9.

Bean, G.E. & J.M. Cook 1955, The Halicarnassus peninsula, *BSA* 50: 85-171.

Biliotti, G.M.A. 1865, Diary of the excavations on the site of the Mausoleum, published by Pedersen, *MH* 3.1 1991: 117-173.

Bundgaard Rasmussen, B. 1998, Gold ornaments from the Mausoleum at Halikarnassus, in Williams (ed.) 1998a: 66-71.

Burn, L. 1997, Sculpture in terracotta from Cnidus and Halikarnassus, Jenkins & Waywell (eds.) 1997: 84-90.

Burn, L. & R. Higgins 2001, *Catalogue of Greek Terracottas in the British Museum* III, London: 187-203.

Carstens, A.M. 1999, *Death Matters. Funerary Architecture on the Halicarnassus Peninsula*, unpublished PhD. thesis, University of Copenhagen.

Cook, B.F. 1997, Sir Charles Newton, KCB (1816-1894), in Jenkins & Waywell (eds.) 1997: 10-23.

Dickson, W.K. 1901, *The Life of Major-General Sir Robert Murdoch Smith*, Edinburgh & London.

Dinsmoor, W.B. 1908, The Mausoleum at Halicarnassus, *AJA* 12: 141-171.

Fabricius 1884, Die Wasserleitung des Eupalinos, *AM*: 165-192, Tf. VIII.

Ferguson, J. 1862, *The Mausoleum at Halicarnassus Restored in Conformity with the Recently Discovered Remains*, London.

Feyler, G. 1987, Contribution à l'histoire des origines de la photographie archéologique, *MEFRA* 99.2: 1019-1047.

Gifford, J.A. 2000, Geological aspects of the construction of the Mausoleum at Halicarnassus, in *MH* 4: 144-149.

Grewe, Kl. 1998, *Licht am Ende des Tunnels: Planung und Trassierung im antiken Tunnelbau*, Mainz.

Higgins, R.A. 1954, *Catalogue of the Terracottas in the British Museum* I, London: 102-141.

Hornblower, S. 1982, *Mausolus*, Oxford.

Højlund, Fl. & K. Aaris-Sørensen 1981, The Sacrificial Deposit, *MH* 1.

Işik, C. 1994, Das Brunnenhaus an der Hafenagora, *Kaunische Forschungen / Kaunos Araştırmaları* II,2, Ankara.

found in the area of LG in front of the entrance to MauTb. Its original position and purpose are enigmatic.

63. Jeppesen 2000: Fig. 1.19, 21, 34-36, 1.58; p. 34 Fig. 2.2, p. 88. Sections E10, E13, E15.
64. *HD*: 142-145.
65. Jeppesen 2000: 34-36.
66. Gifford 2000: 146-147.
67. I am grateful to Dr. Jørgen Hansen for this information.
68. Pedersen 1991,1: 18, Pedersen 1991,2: 57-58 figs. 243-249, and above, p. 30.
69. *P*10: 23, *P*13: 30, *P*15: 47, *FP*16: 92, and *HD*: 118-119, 130-134, and 149.
70. Pedersen 1991,1: 122-129.
71. *HD*: 118.
72. *Diary* 1865.04.28-29, Pedersen 1991,1: 129.
73. Pedersen 1991,1: 122-123.
74. Pedersen 1991,1: 124.
75. Pedersen 1991,1: 124.
76. Pedersen 1991,1: 126.
77. Pedersen 1991,1: 129.
78. *HD*: 134.
79. *Diary* 1865.04.01 + 7-8 + 17-19, 21 and 28-29; Pedersen 1991,1: 124-129.
80. Pedersen 1991,1: 82.
81. *Diary* 1865.04.01; Pedersen 1991,1: 124.
82. Jeppesen 2000: 56-60.
83. Pedersen 1991,1: 121.
84. *Diary* 1865.03.18; Pedersen 1991,1: 121.
85. Pedersen 1991,1: 42-44, and 1991,2: 63-66.
86. *Diary* 1865.03.16-17; Pedersen 1991,1: 121.
87. Pedersen 1991,1 1991: 18, 83-85, 86, 93, 95 with Figs. 89 and 92.
88. Pedersen 1991,1: 83.
89. Pedersen 1991,2: 72-74, in Trench *K*2.
90. Pedersen 1991,2: 67, Trench *P*4.
91. Pedersen 1991,1: 96; idem 1994: 22.
92. The precise measures in *P*13: 30 "in length 2 feet by 18 inches, by 15 inches thick."
93. *FP*16: 93.
94. Pedersen 1991,1: 54-55.
95. *P*13: 31.
96. *HD*: 154.
97. Pedersen 1991,1: 12.
98. 1922: 88-91.
99. Vaag, Nørskov & Lund 2002, Context A.
100. Jeppesen 2000: 41, 48.
101. *Letter* 46: 1857.03.03, Dickson 1901: 47.
102. *HD*: 149.
103. *P*16: 51, 1857.12.10, full quote below, p. 101.
104. Cf. *HD*: 141.
105. *HD*: 325-332 pl. 45 (the finds of terracottas pl. 46-48); Pedersen 1991,1: 97 Fig. 95;

Higgins 1954: 106ff. Burn & Higgins 2001: 188 note 1 list the finds.
106. *P*2, 1857.01.12; Murdoch Smith, Diary 1857.01.10, and 1857.01.17.
107. *Letter* 45, 1857.02.03.
108. Waywell 1978: 117 cat. 47, see below, p. 159.
109. *HD*: 150-151, 264.
110. *P*15, 1857.09.30: 47-48. *P*16, 1857.12.10: 49 with Inclosure 1-2. *FP*2, 1858.02.10: 7-8. *FP*16, 1859.04.12: 90-91.
111. *HD*: 145-154, pl. II-III, V, XII-XIII.
112. *Diary* 1865.03.22; 1865.04.12, 20 (with a section); 1865.06.07-09, 15, Pedersen 1991,1: 121, 125, 127, 142-143.
113. 193´ as it is stated in FP2: 8; in HD: 150-151, however, is stated only 48.5 m = 160´.
114. *Letter* 61, 1857.10.02.
115. *HD*: 150, note m.
116. *Diary* 1865.06.08-09, Pedersen 1991,1: 142.
117. Pedersen 1991,1: 61 and 1991,2: 14-19.
118. *Letter* 45, 1857.02.03.
119. A mutilated pyramid step and column drum from the Maussolleion remains in situ.
120. Also noted by Newton, *HD*: 152.
121. I am grateful to Jørgen Hansen, MA, and Prof. Dr. Klaus Grewe, Köln, for this information.
122. *Letter* 45, Feb. 3rd 1857.
123. Jeppesen 2000: 142 states that water could still flow as before, but this is not the case.
124. Gifford 2000: 147.
125. *HD*: 154.
126. Jeppesen 2000: 9 and in the text to his section E2.
127. Newton, *FP*2: 7; *HD*: 124, 154.
128. Pedersen 1991,1: 57; 3.2: 34 and plan p. 31.
129. *HD*: 151, 195´.
130. *Diary* 1865.06.09; Pedersen 1991,1: 142.
131. *Diary* 1865.04.13; Pedersen 1991,1: 125.
132. *Diary* 1865.04.28-29, Pedersen 1991,1: 129.
133. *P*16: 50, cf. Pedersen 1991,2: 73-74 on possible mistakes by Newton in his description of the search for the east and south terrace walls.
134. *FP*16: 91.
135. *HD*: 151-152.
136. *Diary* 1865.06.08-09, Pedersen 1991,1: 142.
137. Pedersen 1991,2: 16 Fig. 151, 154.
138. Pedersen 1991,1: 61-62 with Pl. IV-V; 1991,2, 14-19 with Fig. 154.
139. Pedersen 1991,1: 12.
140. Pedersen 1991,1, Pl. IV-V, 1991,2: 18 Fig. 159 upper left corner.

141. Pedersen 1991,1: 70; Vaag, Nørskov & Lund 2002: 183, Context J.

142. Pedersen 1991,1: 61-63 with Pl. IV-V, and 1991,2: 14-19, 21.

143. Vaag, Nørskov & Lund 2002: 191, Context K.

144. Pedersen 1991,1: 62 states the length to be 2.6-2.8 m and in 1991,2: 14 to be 2.5-3.0 m. The correct length, however, appears from his figures 150 and 153 on plates V and VI.

145. Cf. "Waterworks in the Athenian Agora", *Agora Picture Book* 11, 1968: Figs. 21, 24: 2nd Century BC.

146. Pedersen 1991,1 pl. VI Fig. 152, 1991,2: 16.

147. In the Maussolleion site museum, box unnumbered "BE Balk 1 B".

148. In the Maussolleion site museum, box 143 "Balk AF 1966".

149. In the Maussolleion site museum, box 149 "Balk AF 1966".

150. Vaag, in Vaag, Nørskov & Lund 2002: 191 Context K.

151. Fabricius 1884: 175, 183, 185 Taf. VIII. His typology and chronology is accepted by H. Fahlbusch, *Geschichte der Wasserversorgung 2. Die Wasserversorgung Antiker Städte* 1987: 140-141. Also the pipes in the Hellenistic well-house in Kaunos, published by C. Işik 1994: 40 Abb. 43, 45 Beilage 19e, are of this type, except for a pair of shallow grooves in both ends. Işik very usefully lists several dated pipes of the late Classical and Hellenistic periods.

152. Pedersen 1991,1, pl. V Fig. 150.

153. Other pipes in the area shall be noted: in Trench R2 "Pipe q" was encountered running N-S 1.6 m from the terrace wall at level 4.9 m a.s.l. (Pedersen 1991,1, pl. V Fig. 150; 3.2, Fig. 165). Above, in Ch. 2 p. 43, several pipes are noted in 'Building D'. All these must have been fed from another source.

154. Pedersen 1991,1: 62-63; 1991,2: 7-8; 15-18; 21-22.

155. Vaag, Nørskov & Lund 2002: 72-75, 130-182, Contexts G, H and I.

156. Pedersen 1991,1 Fig 152 / Plate VI; 1991,2: 16 layer 9.

157. Pedersen 1991,1: 63, Vaag, Nørskov & Lund 2002: 73.

158. Vaag, Nørskov & Lund 2002: 74.

159. Cf. the ashlar built well-house in Kaunos, 5.36 x 8.02 m in plan and with an elaborate system for the induction and the outflow of the water, Işik 1994. He dates it to the first half or perhaps quarter of the 3rd Cent. BC.

160. Pedersen 1991,1: 70, 1991,2: 36 trench R_{13}; Vaag, in Vaag, Nørskov & Lund 2002: 183 Context J.

161. 'Drain 2', 0.14 m × 0.38 m. H.A. Thompson, "The Tholos of Athens and its predecessors", *Hesperia Suppl.* IV, 1940: 88 Fig. 66.

162. H.A. Thompson & R.E. Wycherley, "The Agora of Athens", *The Athenian Agora* XIV, 1972: 200; "Waterworks", Agora Picture Book 11, 1966, Fig. 32.

163. Pedersen 1991,1: 62-63; 1991,2: 15.

164. Pedersen 1991,1 Fig 152 / Plate VI; 1991,2: 16 layer 9.

165. Newton, FP 16: 85; *HD*: 101-02, Jeppesen 2000: 9, with note 3, Section E1.

166. Jeppesen 2000, Fig. 1.1; 1.7-8 and Sections E1 and E4.

167. Op.cit. Fig. 1.1.

168. Op.cit. Fig. 1.14, Section E1; Pedersen 1991,2: 60-61 Fig. 251.

169. Jeppesen 2000, Section E3, hardly discernible on his Fig. 1.40.

170. *HD*: 101-102, 123, 154-156, *TD*: 203-205.

171. February 1858, *FP2*: 7, repeated *HD*: 123.

172. *HD*: 123, 154-155.

173. *P15*: 48; *P16*: 51.

174. *FP2*: 7.

175. *FP2*: 7; *FP16*: 91; *HD*: 123-124.

176. *HD*: 334.

177. Özet 1994: 89-90 Fig. 3.

178. Jeppesen 2000: 169; Carstens 2002: 399.

179. Carstens 1999: 94 with figs. 116-123.

180. Trenches R_{12} and R_8, Pedersen 1991,2: 34, 51.

181. Pedersen 1991,1: 127.

182. Pedersen 1991,1: 12.

183. B. Poulsen, "The new Excavations in Halikarnassos", *Halicarnassian Studies I*, 1994: 115.

184. Cf. Waywell 1978: 1-13.

185. Pedersen 1991,1: 145.

186. Pryce 1928, Cat. B 283, E. Akurgal, *Die Kunst Anatoliens* 1961: Fig. 214-15.

187. F. Brommer, AA 67, 1952: 56 Fig. 7, Akurgal, op.cit. Fig. 229-232.

188. Pryce 1928, Cat. B 323.

189. I.N. 2817, Poulsen 1951, Cat. 4a, Johansen, Catalogue 1994: 44 No. 7.

190. BMC 1051, Waywell 1978: 106 no. 30. Jeppesen 2000: 114 Fig. 11.5

191. Listed and discussed by Waywell 1978: 71-72.

192. Pryce 1928, Cat. B 102.

193. Blümel 1964, Kat. 19 Abb. 48-51.

194. A. Stewart, *Greek Sculpture* 1990, pl. 245,247.
195. Pryce 1928, No. B 475.
196. Blümel 1964, Kat. 31 Abb. 85-86.
197. Pedersen 1991,1: 153.
198. H. Cassimatis, "Statuette appartenant à une collection particulaire parisienne", F. Vandenabeele & R. Laffineur (eds.), *Cypriote Stone Sculpture*, Brussels-Liège 1994: 133-144 pl. XLI-XLII. I am grateful to Dr. Lone Wriedt Sørensen for this reference.
199. Pedersen 1991,1: 137. In the same place are also mentioned several fragments of drapery and a heel with sandal strings. The following day a few fragments from marble statues requiring no special mention were also found. These finds could (or could not) derive from the Maussolleion. The stratigraphic context appears to be post-Antique.
200. Cf. Schmidt, *Samos* VII, 1968: 65, Taf. 116-117. C. Blinkenberg, *Lindos* I, 1931: No. 1825-, pl. 77-.
201. During the current Danish excavations in Halikarnassos one specimen was discovered in the Hellenistic house (frg. of horse's neck with mane, reg. RUF II 2820), one in the Crusaders' castle in the excavation of the Palace of Maussollos, reg. POM 02 II 26-2012. I am grateful to cand.mag. Sanne Lind Hansen and cand.mag. Mette Hvelplund for this information.
202. Cf. for this fabric Nørskov, in Vaag, Nørskov & Lund 2002: 45.
203. Higgins 1954 No. 320 and 323.
204. Higgins 1954 No. 320.
205. *HD*: 147. Higgins 1954, nos. 302 & 321 pl. 51, Reg. 1950.11-16.1 + 2.
206. Pedersen 1991,1: 126, 136, 144.
207. Higgins 1954: 103, note 1.
208. Schmidt, *Samos* VII, 1968: 44, Taf. 4, 83
209. Højlund 1981: 28.
210. In Maussollan fill, above Ch. 3.2, and Vaag, Nørskov & Lund 2002, Cat. C22.
211. Radt 1970: 265-272 with Taf. 44.
212. Radt 1970: 268 n. 13.
213. See V. Karageorghis, *The Coroplastic Art of Ancient Cyprus* IV, 1995: 61-97. K.F. Kinch, *Fouilles de Vroulia*, Copenhagen 1914: 12 ff. C. Blinkenberg, *Lindos* I, Copenhagen 1931: col. 475 nos. 1941-1945, Pl. 86. Schmidt, loc.cit. in note 208. P.N. Ure, *Aryballoi and Figurines from Rhitsona in Boeotia*, 1934.
214. Higgins 1954, no. 351, pl. 53, (G&R Reg. 68.4-5.63).
215. Higgins 1954, no. 371, pl. 56 (G&R Reg. 68.4-5.69).
216. Higgins 1954, no. 373 pl. 56 (G&R Reg. 57.12-20.134)
217. In Trench Q_6, Vaag, *MH* 7, cat. D56-D61, and in Trench Q7, op.cit. cat. E24.
218. Burn & Higgins 2001: 187-203. The finds of Newton are nos. 2546-55, 2557-58, 2561, 2565-66, 2568, 2571-74, 2578-79, 2581-82, 2584, 2586-89, 2591, 2594, 2597, 2606-10, 2615, 2619-23, 2625-27. The finds of Biliotti are nos. 2631-39. Also among our finds, not selected for publication, are several more terracottas of the late Classical or Hellenistic periods.
219. Also noted in Burn 1997: 85 with Fig. 111.
220. For example "strata of broken pottery" FP16: 51.
221. We are grateful to V. Nørskov for the following treatment based on photographs made by J. Zahle at the British Museum.
222. Vaag, Nørskov & Lund 2002: 75.
223. Op.cit.: 75, cf. also p. 22.
224. Op.cit.: 20-22, 68.
225. Op.cit.: 74.
226. Op.cit.: 56, 105, cat. B56 ("Levantine"), discussed in Højlund 1981: 51 with Fig. 57 ("Cypriote").
227. Vaag, Nørskov & Lund 2002: 69-71, contexts E, G and H.
228. Pedersen 1991,1: 141, 125.
229. Walters 1903, Cat. C 912. W. 13.9 cm, h. 7 cm.
230. Cf. above, Ch. 4.
231. Bean & Cook 1955: 94 "and fragments of archaic stone statuettes and terracotta animals and a decayed clay sarcophagus were found along the edges of the peribolos; ··· ".
232. A.M. Snodgrass, *Arms and Armour of the Greeks*, 1967: 73 Fig. 42.
233. Newton *P*l5: 48. *FP*9: 37 nos. 296.4 and 296.6. *HD*: 150-151, 264.
234. Perhaps = *FP* 9: 296 no. 14.
235. Jeppesen 2000: 129 nos. 102-104.
236. Vaag, Nørskov & Lund 2002, Context A, nos. 105-108.
237. Vaag, Nørskov & Lund 2002: 74, Vaag, p. 82-97, Context A.
238. Quoted above, p. 21.
239. *P*10: 23; *P*l6: 51; *FP*16: 89; *HD*: 123, 147, 154.
240. *HD*: 139-141.
241. Pedersen 1991.1: 18, 83-85 with Figs. 88, 89, p. 93 with Fig. 92. See the discussion, above p. 76.

242. A. Westholm, *OpArch 2*, 1941: 29-58; E. Gjerstad, *SCE* IV:2, 1948: 29-47, 421-424.

243. "Tomb Cult on the Halikarnassos Peninsula", *AJA* 106, 2002: 391-409.

244. Jantzen 1973, 1974.

245. S. Kasper 1976-77, "Der Tumulus von Belevi (Grabungsbericht)", *JbAÖ* 51, Beiblatt: 142.

246. Hellström & Thieme 1981.

247. Radt 1982; Carstens 1999 and 2002.

248. Contrary to Jeppesen & Zahle 1975.

249. Pedersen 1991,1: 95.

250. *HD*: 152.

251. Hornblower 1982: 188; Pedersen, 1991,1: 95 c. 367/66 BC at the latest.

252. Cf. Hornblower 1982: 81-82.

253. Hornblower 1982: 188.

254. H. Ingvaldsen, *Cos – Coinage and Society The chronology and function of a city-state coinage in the Classical and Hellenistic period c. 390 – c.170 BC*, Oslo 2002.

255. Jeppesen 1968: 50; Pedersen 1991,1: 88.

256. Jeppesen 2000: 112-118.

257. Op.cit.: 119-140.

258. The fragments had been sorted out, in a few cases also mended in small groups, basically described, and attributed to individual vessels by Dr. Jan Zahle and architect Kjeld Kjeldsen before the material was allocated to me for study in July 2002. The shapes had been reconstructed in drawing and the most recognizable fragments photographed. It was most useful to me that all this preparatory work had been done before I actually saw the finds in Bodrum in September 2002. For this, I am most grateful to the Director of the Bodrum Museum of Underwater Archaeology, Dr Oğuz Alpözen, to the Director of the Danish Expedition in Halikarnassos, Dr Poul Pedersen, and to Dr Vinnie Nørskov for her constant help. During my stay in Bodrum I was able to verify some of the already recognized shapes, as well as recognize new ones, and attribute more fragments to shapes. Consequently, I had to correct some of the prepared drawings, and make new photographs of the re-assembled groups.

259. Jeppesen 2000, 167-168

260. Jeppesen 2000, chapter 23.

261. Lierke 1993, 324, Fig. 2. Wedepohl 2003, 47, Abb. 16.

262. Vickers & Bazama 1971. In the tomb there was space for a second burial, but only one sarcophagus. Dr. m. Vickers informed me that there is a surplus of wood that cannot be associated with the main sarcophagus. He kindly agreed to consider my suggestion that there was a second, later, burial in the tomb, from which came the glass vessel. I thank him for this.

263. Triantaffyllidis 2000, I.1: 128-129, I.4: 134, I.5: 135, I.9: 142-143. The excavation report for the omphalus calyx-cup (vessel I:1) appears in Yakoumaki 1997, 1087-1089, pl. 411 (published in 2003). Two more vessels (nos. I.8 and I.10) are dated to the same period but come from burials that cannot be dated with certainty.

264. Mallwitz & Schiering 1964. Schiering 1991. Schilbach 1995, 12-14. The find is problematic for many reasons in regard to its chronology, typology, and technology, so its interpretation remains open.

265. Melikian-Chirvani 1993.

266. Schmidt 1957, 91-93. Fukai 1977, 18-20. Oliver 1970. Grose 1989, 80-81. Byvanck-Quarles van Ufford 1970. Byvanck-Quarles van Ufford 1991.

267. Walser 1966. Calmeyer 1993. Tourovets 2001, esp. 241.

268. Goldstein 1979, 119-120, no. 250, pl. 37. Goldstein 1980, 50, fig.10-11.

269. Similar, but not identical to the calyx-cup is the skyphos (essentially a small deep bowl); it has a vertical neck, convex body, and rounded bottom. R. Lierke suggests that the elongated shape of the tall calyx-cup is the outcome of an actual "elongation" during the manufacturing process by rotary pressing. We cannot be sure that the Corning vessel was made by this method, but it is highly possible, also on account of the irregular rim. It is inconceivable that any artisan would mould or wheel-cut a rim with such a visible flaw; it can be explained only as an inevitable "side-effect" of rotary pressing; see Lierke 1999, 35-36, Abb. 69-71, 162. For the shape of the tall calyx-cup, see also Pfrommer 1987, 68-74.

270. For the Macedonian finds, see Ignatiadou 2002. The others are discussed below.

271. For the Macedonian finds, see Bessios 1991, 41, 43a; the gilt one also in Tsigarida & Ignatiadou 2000, Fig. 17. For the Aegina vessel, also called a beaker, see Von Saldern 1959 a, 42-43, no. 23, Fig. 30.

272. Amandry 1959, 38-65. Walser 1966, 78-80, Taf. 46. Calmeyer 1993, 152-153. See also note10.

273. Kuban 1987, 48-49, 106 – no. 104, Fig. XIX-XX.

274. The objects were smuggled out of Turkey in the 1960s. After a legal battle, they were returned by the Metropolitan Museum of Art in 1993. Özgen & Özturk 1996, nos. 65 and 66. Von Bothmer 1984, 110-111.

275. Unfortunately the colours of the vessels are not described and the only published pictures are in black-and-white. Vani I, 1972, 282-283 nos. 215, 216. Lordkipanidzé 1995, 59-76, esp. 64. Gagošidze & Saginašvili 2000, esp. 72, Abb. 2,3. An antecedent to the Vani vessels is the light blue to turquoise glass vessel unearthed in the tomb of Amenhotep II (1428-1397 BC); see Nolte 1968, 55, pl. II.6. Since its shape is not Egyptian it can be considered a product of glass workers from abroad. I thank Dr B. Schlick-Nolte for providing the reference and other information on the find.

276. Oates 2001, 245, Fig. 155. Curtis & Reade 1995, 143, no. 107.

277. Oates 2001, 46-47, 133-134, 251-252, figs 23, 84, 158 (158d depicted here as Table I.3A), and 155 (silver beaker). Mallowan 1966, vol. I, 51, 178-180, figs. 14-17, 110-115. Curtis & Reade 1995, 154-155, nos. 129 and 134 (Nimrud), 130 (Nineveh).

278. Melikian-Chirvani 1993, 119-120, Fig. 13.

279. Alessandro Magno, 254, no. 43.

280. It was found in Level II, Palace, Court m 100. Barag 1970, 140, no. 15, figs 14A-B.

281. Barag 1970, 140, no. 15, figs 14A-B. Ars vitraria 2001, 12, "button-based goblet"

282. Macalister 1911, 292-293, fig.154, 156. Grave no. 4 belonged to a group of graves which the excavator S. Macalister and J. L. Myres attributed to the Philistines. This attribution is no longer accepted, and B. Shefton discussed the contents and dating of the tomb, calling it n "élite grave." Shefton 1993, esp. 182. Shefton 2000, esp. 277-278. The vessel perhaps follows the style of the earlier artistic tradition of Luristan; a similar two-handled vase of the 11th-9th Century BC from that area is part of the Houshang Mahboubian Family Collection; see Mahboubian 1997, no. 45.

283. Mallowan 1966, Fig. 113.

284. Taylor 2001, 190-192, fig.134.

285. Oates 2001, Fig. 137.

286. It is depicted by Newton, upside down, together with a colourless-glass acorn pendant. Newton 1862, 264: "In the soil of the platform were found two pendants from glass necklaces represented in the accompanying cuts. One of these is in the form of an acorn. These may have been part of the spoils of the tomb. ... It is, however more probable that those objects lodged at this place after having been brought down by the rush of water from higher ground." The acorn pendant is also depicted in Williams & Ogden 1994, Fig. 2. For early Greek gold vase-pendants see Sindos 1984, figs. 148, 285, 325, 350, 429, 483, 511 (the two middle beads are depicted here as Table I.2F). For glass vase-pendants, see Popovi 2000, with relevant bibliography.

287. Von Saldern 1959 a, esp. 25-27, fig.1. Von Saldern 1970, 217-218, figs. 14-16.

288. Von Saldern 1970, 222-223, figs. 30-32.

289. Schmidt 1957, 92, pl. 67: 9-10.

290. Gordion skyphos: Von Saldern 1959 a, 36, figs.16 and 19 middle right. Caunus skyphos: Roos 1972, 1974, vol. I, pl. 62: 1, 10, vol. II, 17-18 no. 40, pls. 3, 14. Pydna skyphos: Ignatiadou 1993, esp. Fig. 8). Aenea skyphos: Vokotopoulou 1990, 61, Fig. 28, pl. 35a. Argilos calyx-cup: unpublished. Vergina calyx-cup: unpublished. Aslaia skyphos: Vickers & Bazama, 78-79, pl. XXXI. Corning Museum of Glass: tall calyx-cup (fluted beaker): Goldstein 1979, 119-120, no. 250, pl. 37, omphalos bowl: 118, no. 248, pl. 37. Jerusalem calyx-cup: Barag 1968, esp. 18, Fig. 5. Munich calyx-cup: Stern & Schlick-Nolte 1994, 53, Fig. 67, also Oliver 1970, esp. 15, fig.14. Löffler Collection: omphalos calyx-cup: La Baume 1976, 24 no. 6, Taf. 2.1.

291. Wilson 2001, 169-171. Halaf bowl from Arpachiyah, see Wilson 2001, 167, Fig. 8:6. Hajji Muhammad plate, see Mellaart 1965, 65, Fig. 40m.

292. Markoe 1985.

293. Toker 1992, no. 24 (Alacahöyük), nos. 65-73 (Gordion). Marinatos 1959, Fig. 191b (Mycenae). Mahboubian 1997, no. 312 (Luristan). Oates 2001, 81-84, Fig. 46, pls. 2b, 6-8.

294. Wilson 2001, 105, Fig. 3:15. A cavetto with long petals decorates the Outer Shrine and the Golden Shrine, and the Royal Sceptre

(with a similar decoration) appears as a papyrus flower in Tutankhamun's tomb; see Tutankhamun 1976, 120-121, nos. 13, 52. Twentieth Dynasty metal vessels are decorated with long petals; see Rotroff 1982, 34, note 79. Other plants, like the lotus bud, or the palm tree, are also depicted with curved tipped petals, and we must take into account the possibility that the long petals occur also as a combination of different plants.

295. Miller 1993. A production of undecorated pottery beakers is encountered in Olynthus, at the end of 5th- early 4th Century BC; Robinson 1950, 424, nos. 1075, 1076, 1076A, pls. 232, 255, and Robinson 1933, 47, no. P 85-P87, pl. 43.

296. Sadberk Hanım Museum 1995, 26-27, no. 6 (Urartu). Mahboubian 1997, no. 318 (Luristan), Alizadeh 1985, Fig. 5C (Elam).

297. Erzerum: Earlier in the H. Weissmann Collection. Oliver 1970, 13, fig. 10. Pfrommer 1987, 174, Anm. 1203. Vickers 2000, fig.1. Vani: Vickers 2000, Fig. 2. Panderma: Antikenmuseum Berlin 1988, 344-345, no. 4. Boukyovtsi: Thracian Treasures 1976, no. 266. Thracian Gold 1987, no. 275. British Museum: Miller 1993, see note 21, Taf. 29.2. For a discussion of these and other beakers, see Ignatiadou 1997a. Vickers 2000.

298. Walser 1966, Taf. 59 and 65. For the interpretation of the reliefs see note, 10.

299. Discussed mainly in Ignatiadou 1997a and Themelis & Touratsoglou 1997, 79-80, pl. 93. Vickers 2000. Also in Oliver 1970, 13. Grose 1979, 81. Pfrommer 1987, 174, Anm. 1203. Von Saldern 2001, 214. Ignatiadou 2002.

300. Von Saldern 1959 a, 35, Fig. 15. Von Saldern 1959 b, VIII/5, Bild 13. Oliver 1970, 13. Pfrommer 1987, 174, Anm. 1203. Ignatiadou 1997a. Vickers 2000, 264, Fig. 3.

301 National Archaeological Museum, Athens; Troy – Mycene 1990, 291, no. 239.

302. Toker 1992, nos. 61-64.

303. Özgen & Özturk 1996, 55 and cat. nos. 11, 12, 22, 63, 71.

304. See note 10.

305. Schmidt 1957, 92, pl. 67, no. 11.

306. For animal-head beakers and situlae, see Calmeyer 1979, Muscarella 1988, and Miller 1993, 115ff, all with bibliography.

307. Young 1981, 122-123, notes 49-50. Calmeyer 1979, 197-198 (S2-18), Abb. 7.

308. The beaker was allegedly found in Iran. Miho 1997, 97, no. 44. Von Saldern 2001. For permission to study the beaker I thank the curators of the Miho Museum, Y. Azuma and H. Inagaki.

309. Schmidt 1957, 92, pl. 67:9.

310. Von Saldern 2001, note 1. Von Saldern 1991, 119, pl. XXXd. Von Saldern 1976, Taf. 32. Fukai 1977, 20 Fig. 8.

311. Alessandro Magno, 253, no. 41.

312. Young 1981, 121-123, pls III, IV, 62-63 (Gordion). Oates 2001, 253, Fig. 158b (Nimrud). Alpözen, 92 (Bodrum).

313. Von Saldern 1966, 629-630, figs 588-590. Von Saldern 1970, 219-221, figs 21-26.

314. Observation was done with a simple hand-lens, so the remarks that follow are by no means a proper technological study.

315. For the lost wax (chip-casting) and sagging techniques, see Stern & Schlick-Nolte 1994, 50-55 and 68-71. For the glass-pottery technique, see Lierke 1999.

316. See note 269.

317. Vickers 2000.

318. The fragments were sorted out, mended, drawn, and also basically described by Dr. Jan Zahle and architect Kjeld Kjeldsen before the material was allocated to me for study in July 2002. During my stay in Bodrum, in September 2002, I verified the accuracy of the drawings and made slight improvements to the existing descriptions. I also photographed the main fragments. For facilitating my visit on the site I thank the Director of the Bodrum Museum of Underwater Archaeology, Dr Oğuz Alpözen, the Director of the Danish Expedition in Halikarnassos, Dr. Poul Pedersen, and Dr. Vinnie Nørskov.

319. Gill 1992. Lapatin 1997. Vickers 1984.

320. No. 11863, now in Berlin. See Richter 1966, 76, fig. 402.

321. Vaulina & Wąsowicz 1974, 135-137, no. 58, pl. CXVIII. Other similar finds are mentioned.

322. Vaulina & Wąsowicz 1974, 137-144, nos. 58-66, pls. CXIX-CXXV.

323. On couches see Kyrieleis 1969. Richter 1966. Sismanidis 1997. On the ivory, amber, and glass decoration of the Macedonian finds, see Ignatiadou 2001. Ignatiadou 2002a. Ignatiadou 2002b. On couches and sarcophagi from the North Pontus, see Vaulina & Wąsowicz 1974, Pinelli & Wąsowicz 1986. Richter 1966. Sokol'skij

1969. Watzinger 1905. On the dating and interpretation of the North Pontic finds in comparison with the numerous Macedonian ones, see Ignatiadou 2003.

324. Andronikos 1984, 132, fig 88.

325. The tomb is dated to 315-300 BC. Sismanidis 1997, 61-67, pls 4, 6b, 10-11, 14-15, 17-19, 26-28.

326. On the Kul Oba ivories, see Peredolskaja 1945. On the interpretation of the find as a couch and for a discussion of the Kul Oba and other North Pontic ivories, amber and glass, see Ignatiadou 2003.

327. This appendix and catalogue is based on a registration made by Jan Zahle in 1986 and adjustments made by Bodil Bundgaard Rasmussen in 1994. I studied the fragments during three days in September 2002.

328. Jeppesen 2000, 115-118.

329. Jeppesen 2002, 118. Rasmussen 1997, 68.

330. Jeppesen 2000, 116-118.

331. Jeppesen 1976, 48-58.

332. Jeppesen 1976, 52-53

333. Jeppesen 2000, 168. The account is analyzed by Jeppesen (2000, 155-168) and Anthony Luttrell in Jeppesen 1986, 170-174.

334. Rasmussen 1987. Jeppesen 2000, 119-130.

335. Kurtz & Boardman 1971, 275-276. No stucco was found in the cavity, but a small fragment has been reported found by Newton (OBS).

336. Özet 1994, 88-96. For the identification, see Prag & Neave 1994. Carstens 1999, 90-92.

337. Özet 1994, 88.

338. Rasmussen 1987, 67, 70 no. 27. Jeppesen 2000, 125 no. 13b.

339. Andronicos 1984, 146-168, 208-217.

340. Andronicos 1984, 156, 159.

341. Vaag et al. 2002, 22-23. For other cities in Asia Minor: Smyrna: Tuna-Nörling 1998, 175; Labraunda: Hellström 1971, 11-12; Kaunos: Roos 1964, 43.

342. Andronicos 1984, 146-168.

343. Winter 1887, 376-377. London E428 (Smith 1896, 262-263) and F14 (Walters 1896, 31; *ARV*[2] 1464.62, attributed to Group G). Carstens 1999, 94. Bean & Cook 1955, 94 note 57.

344. Akarca 1952, 401-403, pls. LXXXIII-LXXXIV, XCV. Akarca 1971, 22 no. 53, pl. XIII. Hellström 1971, 11.

345. Vaag et al. 2002, 22-23 and 223, note 36.

346. This is the case in Smyrna and Clazomenae, Boardman 1958/59, 152 and Tuna-Nörling 1998, 175. In Phokaia, however, there is nearly no import after 400 BC, a fact Tuna-Nörling explains through the changing political alliances during the Ionian war when Phokaia left the Delian League in 412 BC and joined the Spartans, Tuna-Nörling 2002, 164-166,

347. Robertson 1992, 280-284.

348. Fless 2002, 39-40.

349. St. Petersburg, Ermitage 15592. Fless 2002, 84, note 725.

350. Herbig 1940, 71-75. Metzger 1942-43, 234. The earliest rendering is found on a fragment from the Athenian Agora P1457, Moore 1997, 30.1677, pl. 156, attributed to the Group of Polygnotos. Attributed to Polygnotos is the hydria in Naples, 81398, *ARV*[2] 1032.61; *FR* III, 319-324, pls. 151-154; Matheson 1995, 23-25, pls. 14A-D.

351. Metzger 1942-43, 234 note 3. For instance a Paestan bell krater in the British Museum in London, *CVA British Museum* 2, IV E a, pl. 2, Fig. 3.

352. Apulian bell krater in the Victoria and Albert Museum 4803.1901, from Ruvo, *ARVp* 16. no. 57. Herbig 1940, Abb. 13.

353. Tübingen S101279/E174, *CVA Tübingen* 4, pl. 38; Schefold 1934, 37.331. Metzger 1951, 282-283, Pl. 38.3. Rasmussen 1997, 67, 71 note 18.

354. Tarent 8263, *LCS* 55, no. 280, pl. 24. Herbig 1940, Abb. 14.

355. Burkert 1985, 234-236.

356. Benda 1997, 103. Herbig 1940. The kalathiskos dance seems to have been very popular, not only in Sparta but also in regions influenced by Spartan culture, but it appears in other contexts as well, such as the fragment in Tübingen with the wedding of Menelaus and Helena, Metzger 1942-43, 236-238 (see note 27). For kalathiskos dancers as part of the Athenian wedding choir, see also Froning 1971, 23. See also Cain 1985, 135.

357. Benda 1997, 104-107, Abb. 7.

358. Metzger 1942-43, 236-237.

359. Metzger 1942-43, 242, mentions a kandelabra in Villa Albani (Galleria del Leda no. 199) on which one of the dancers carries a small portable object for incense burning. And according to Cain, kalathiskos dancers symmetrically arranged around a thymiaterion should be known in Roman art (Cain 1985, 135-136 with further references to the Roman monuments, note 817), but

I have not been able to find any examples comparable to the fragments from the Maussolleion. On fragments of Arretine pottery the kalathiskos dancers are combined with columns, pillars or tripods, Dragendorff & Watzinger 1948, 56.

360. Fuchs 1959, 91-98.
361. Guide des Delphes, 84-91.
362. Rohde o.J. 18-19, Taf. 20a.
363. Dragendorff & Watzinger 1948.
364. Benda 1996, 102-104. Metzger 1942-43, 235. Benndorf & Niemann 1884, pl. XXIX.1).
365. Eichler 1950, 10-11. Stewart 1990, 271-272.
366. Højlund 1981: 41.
367. Vaag, Nørskov & Lund 2002: 56, 98 Context B.
368. Newton, *P5*: 12-13; *P11*: 26 List of Cases shipped in her Majesty's ship "Gorgon", no. 188, *HD*: 91-93 and App. II: 667-670; *TD*: 99.
369. The vessel 1857.12-20.1 was in 1956 transferred to Western Asiatic Dept., where it received the no. 132114.
370. Jeppesen 2000: 112-114.
371. Højlund 1981: 52 Fig. 61.
372. Se above, p. 167.

PLATES

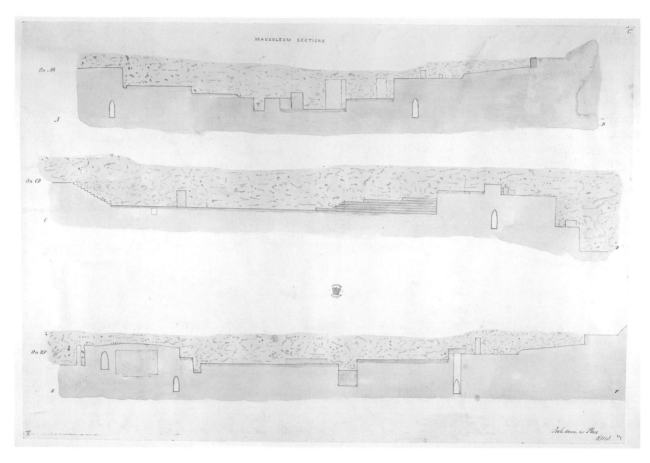

Pl. 1. Murdoch Smith's three sections of the Maussolleion site, cf. the plan Fig. 1.2.1: A-B south-north, C-D west-east, E-F south-north, probably January 1858. First published in *FP*16, 1859 and later in a shortened version in *HD* 1862, pl. V.

Pl. 2. View of the terrace wall, TW1s, on the south side of the Maussolleion from the SE. It faces south, and eight courses above a rough foundation are preserved. Watercolour by R.P. Pullan, January 1858. Published in *HD* 1862, pl. XII top left.

Pl. 3. View of the northern part of the terrace wall, TW2, and the even rock on the east side of the Maussolleion from the SE. Watercolour by R.P. Pullan, January 1858. Published in *HD* 1862, pl. XII bottom right.

Pl. 4. View of the northern part of the terrace wall, TW2, and the even rock on the east side of the Maussolleion from the NE. Watercolour by R.P. Pullan, January 1858. Published in *HD* 1862, pl. XIV bottom right.

Pl. 5. View of the terrace wall, TW2, and the level rock on the east side of the Maussolleion from the south. In the centre, the east end of UG:B2 and the sarcophagus in its opening. Watercolour by R.P. Pullan, January 1858. Published in *HD* 1862, pl. XII top right.

Pl. 6. View of the southern part of the terrace wall, TW2, and the level rock on the east side of the Maussolleion from the NE. In the centre the east end of UG:B2 and the sarcophagus in its opening. Watercolour by R.P. Pullan, January 1858. Published in *HD* 1862, pl. XII bottom left.

Pl. 7. Plan of Cb1 with details of the opening from Cb1 into UG:B1, stucco and cuttings. Plan and view. Measured drawing by R.P. Pullan, September 1857. Published in *HD* 1862, pl. XIII, centre.

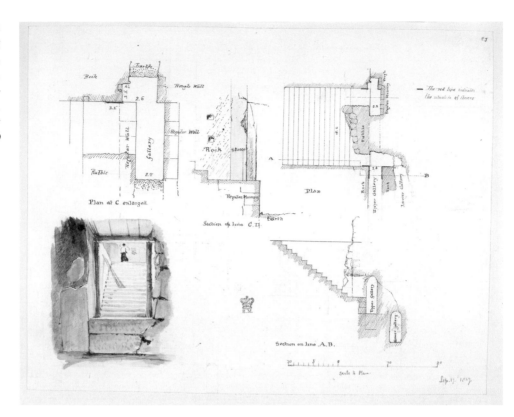

Pl. 8. Section and view of opening from the Main Corridor into Cb2. To the right a Turk standing in the Main Corridor. Measured drawing by R.P. Pullan, October 1857. Published in *HD* 1862, pl. XIII, top, right.

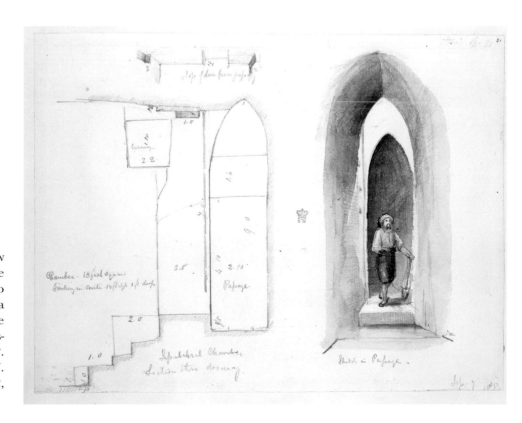

Pl. 9. View in Cb2 from the north-west with the east side with the two 'windows' into Cb3, the opening into the chamber from the Main Corridor. Also shown is the shallow ledge along the north, east and south sides. Watercolour by R.P. Pullan, January 1858. Published in *HD* 1862, pl. XIV top left.

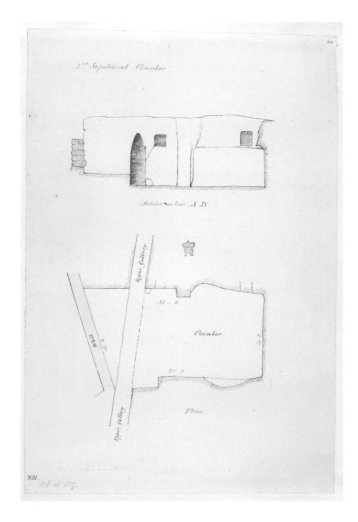

Pl. 10. View and plan of the west side of Cb3. Measured drawing by R.P. Pullan, October 1857. Published in *HD* 1862, pl. XIII top left.

Pl. 11. View NE in Newton's "broken tomb", Cb3. To the right the rear wall of TW1. The man sits on the north wall of the transverse gallery, the interior of which appears unexcavated. Watercolour by R.P. Pullan, October 1857. Published in *HD* 1862, pl. XIV bottom left.

Pl. 12. View towards the west in Newton's "broken tomb", Cb3. To the left the channel wall and the rear wall of TW1. Watercolour by R.P. Pullan, October 1857. Published in *HD* 1862, pl. XIV top right.

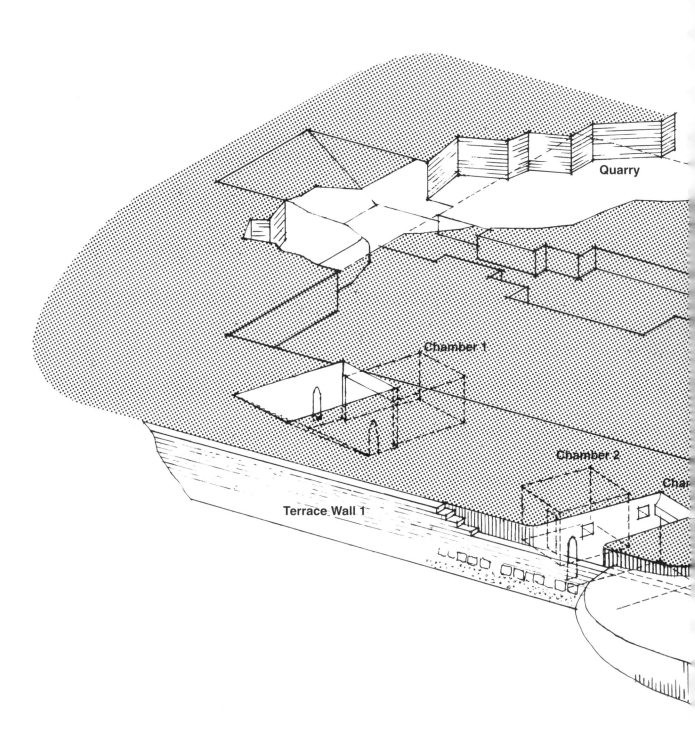

Quarry

Chamber 1

Chamber 2

Char

Terrace Wall 1